SOME NEWSPAPERS
AND NEWSPAPER-MEN

THE LIBERATOR.

VOL. I.]   WILLIAM LLOYD GARRISON AND ISAAC KNAPP, PUBLISHERS.   [NO. 17.

BOSTON, MASSACHUSETTS.]   OUR COUNTRY IS THE WORLD—OUR COUNTRYMEN ARE MANKIND.   [SATURDAY, APRIL 23, 1831.

THE LIBERATOR.

IS PUBLISHED WEEKLY
AT NO. 11, MERCHANTS' HALL.

WM. LLOYD GARRISON, EDITOR.

THE LIBERATOR.

CHRISTIAN SECRETARY—COLONIZATION SOCIETY.

PRODUCTS OF SLAVERY.

William Lloyd Garrison's *Liberator:* Its Seventeenth Issue, April 23, 1831

SOME NEWSPAPERS AND NEWSPAPER-MEN

by
OSWALD GARRISON VILLARD

New and Revised Edition

Essay Index Reprint Series

 BOOKS FOR LIBRARIES PRESS
FREEPORT, NEW YORK

INTERNATIONAL STANDARD BOOK NUMBER:
0-8369-2206-9

LIBRARY OF CONGRESS CATALOG CARD NUMBER:
79-134148

PRINTED IN THE UNITED STATES OF AMERICA

To

WENDELL PHILLIPS GARRISON

Co-Editor and Editor of *The Nation* 1865-1906

Devoted Upholder of a Noble Journalistic Tradition

PREFACE TO SECOND EDITION

The three years that have elapsed since the first publication of this volume have merely emphasized many of the tendencies set forth in its several chapters. Thus in New York City the mortality due to consolidations has been extremely heavy, the *Globe*, the *Mail*, and the *Herald* all disappearing, as well as the Socialist *Call*. The latter's successor, the *Leader*, lived only a few weeks. Meanwhile the rise of the tabloid picture daily, with its incessant harping on sex and crime, constitutes an ever growing menace both to the old-line dailies and to democracy itself, and this is true whether, as is believed by some, the tabloids are finding a new group of readers which formerly never bought any daily, or whether they are limiting the field of the old type journals. It is surely of extreme significance that the tabloid *Daily News* has reached a million circulation by gaining 203,000 readers daily between April 1, 1925, and April 1, 1926, that the *Times* gained during the same period only 10,000, and the greatly improved *Herald-Tribune* but 11,000, while the *World* lost 51,000, largely because of its raising its price from two to three cents.

If there are those who can see in these figures a basis for the optimistic statements as to the health of the press which regularly emanate from press gatherings and from some schools of journalism, they are welcome to do so. Meanwhile, the decadence of the labor press, the failure of the *Call*, and the *Minnesota Daily Star*, prove that some of the counter, irritants are also disappointing to those who see no present hope in the endowed daily or in the corrective force of public opinion. These symptoms, like the recent control of all the dailies in Springfield, Mass. by a single ownership, only hasten the day when the question of news distribution will have to be earnestly considered by all who believe in the necessity of an enlightened electorate if the United States is to remain a democracy.

OSWALD GARRISON VILLARD.

May, 1926.

PREFACE

These studies in current daily journalism, most of which have appeared in *The Nation,* are less haphazard than may seem at first sight. The various journals selected were chosen less for geographical reasons than to illustrate the prevailing tendencies in the rake's progress of our press, due to the commercialization of what should be the noblest of professions. Fortunately it has not been necessary to record only retrogression; notably in the non-profit-making *Forward* of New York is there the promise of a way of avoiding what to many seems the inevitable subordination of journalistic public service to sordid money-making. In the *Minnesota Star* we also have an experiment worth watching. That a way of escape will be found the author has no doubt. It is inconceivable that so great a Republic should find itself unable to secure for its voters that stream of unbiased and truthful news without which an electorate can be neither informed nor intelligent.

Several studies of bygone editors and journals have been added to illustrate the change, in newspapers, methods, and men, which has come over the trade.

ix

The sketch of Mr. Garrison appears not because of the author's relationship to that militant reformer, but solely to recall to the public mind the hour when "a poor, unlearned young man," as Lowell called him, could create without a single cent of capital a medium to expound his burning views.

While nothing has been set down in malice, the author must admit a bias. It is the bias of one who has belonged to the profession for twenty-six years, when many another fruitful and less arduous intellectual opportunity beckoned; of one who cannot witness its rapid decadence without sharp pain. It is also the bias of one who, together with three other members of his family, has had the privilege of serving journalistic ideals for one hundred and five years, as long a consecutive newspaper service as that of any other American family.

OSWALD GARRISON VILLARD.

New York, *October* 1, 1923.

CONTENTS

xi

CONTENTS

ILLUSTRATIONS

SOME NEWSPAPERS
AND NEWSPAPER-MEN

CHAPTER I

MR. OCHS AND HIS *TIMES*

THE twenty-fifth anniversary on August 18, 1921, of his control of the New York *Times* gave Adolph S. Ochs an opportunity to review the period of his ownership and to set forth the journalistic success he had achieved. The *Times* was a decrepit, losing proposition when he took hold of it, running behind $1,000 a day and having a circulation of only 18,900. On this anniversary its circulation was 352,528; its advertising had increased from 2,227,-196 lines to 23,447,395 yearly. It does an annual gross business of $20,000,000 and Mr. Ochs was especially proud to set forth that of its annual gross income only three per cent had gone to the owners, the rest having been "ploughed into" the property for its betterment. For 1922 its net profits were reported to be $2,500,000. Regarded simply as a business venture it is an extraordinary achievement, comparing most favourably with similar feats in purely mercantile lines, all the more so because, on account of the lack of funds, Mr. Ochs had to carry

3

it largely with borrowed money until the property began to earn a profit. He had a clear vision of what he wanted to achieve and had the faith to stick to it against great odds. And Mr. Ochs's frankness is not limited to statistics of circulation and advertising. He has laid bare once more the details of the ownership with a view, probably, to putting an end forever to the whispered charges that there is British capital in the *Times*. There are only American owners and he and his family hold 64 per cent. of the paper's stock. Nobody in journalistic circles ever believed this gossip as to foreign control. In the first place the *Times* is naturally so pro-English that the British would never have had to pay money to it even had its owner been venal; in the second place during our late hysteria it was the fashion to charge any newspaper whose views one did not like with being in the pay of the other side. It is true that some rich Wall Street men helped Mr. Ochs at times, notably in the matter of the bonds of the Times Building. But it is false to deduce from that certain characteristics of his paper; it would have taken precisely the course it has followed had Mr. Ochs never needed to borrow a penny from anybody. No journalist has ever questioned the fact that it was Mr. Ochs's paper, or that it bore the stamp of his personality.

During these twenty-five years the *Times* has been

clean and enterprising, able and shrewd. Not that it has lived up to the suggestion in its motto of printing only the news fit for publication—witness recently its debasement in the Stillman scandal—nor has it printed all the news—far, very far, from it. It has simply purveyed all the news which especially interested its owners and editors and, as far as possible, only that which supported its editorial viewpoint. But it has rendered a genuine public service in increasing the volume of news and especially of foreign news. Mr. Ochs's greatest contribution to our journalism has been his faith in news as a sales asset. Many men in a similar position have wanted to gamble on future success by filling their columns with original news, but since the time of the younger James Gordon Bennett perhaps no one, except Mr. Ochs and the Chicago *Tribune,* has dared to do so. Others would have taken much more than three per cent of their earnings and have put back far less. Like the Chicago *Daily News,* Mr. Ochs has supplemented the Associated Press service with extremely costly special dispatches and letters. Newspaper men are like sheep; if one hits upon a rotogravure supplement, or a comic "ribbon," or a Sunday comic section, or a humorous column on the editorial page, and it is successful, everybody else strives to follow suit. Hearst's financial success had by 1898 debased a good part of the American press; Mr.

Ochs's increase of the volume of his news and the number of his news departments (notably in the commercial field) has had a beneficial influence upon the entire press of the country. It has led many thousands to read the *Times* to whom its opinions were anathema. Particularly worth while and public-spirited has been the cabling of important speeches and documents in full, notably the utterances of Lloyd George, even when extensive summaries were carried by the Associated Press.

Full credit must also be given to Mr. Ochs for keeping his advertising columns clean and for the excellence of his auxiliary publications. His rotogravure supplements are still the best, while his Sunday magazine is in a class by itself as to its technical make-up and its half-tone illustrations. His *Midweek Pictorial* and his *Current History Magazine* deserve their success. His *Annalist* though dull, and apparently unsuccessful, has at least been dignified. Moreover, Mr. Ochs's refusal to stoop to a comic supplement when it would indubitably have largely increased his circulation during his critical days ought long to be remembered to his credit. If all journalists are to be measured simply by the superficial outward aspects of a daily and by the yardstick of business success, there can be no question that Mr. Ochs has earned a place in any journalistic Hall of Fame.

But as men cannot live by bread alone, so no news-

The New York *Semi-Weekly Times'* First Page Just after
the Assassination of Abraham Lincoln

paper can or should be finally judged by the amount either of its revenues or of the number of its advertising lines or of the yards of news it prints a day or by the multitude of its readers. If these were the sole tests Hearst would rank high on at least two counts. There are fortunately other tests, above all the ethical one. True, the facile historians of journalism, notably two recent ones, James Melvin Lee and George Henry Payne, have preferred not to use the ethical measuring stick. Yet any definite worthwhile survey of the rise and fall of American journalism must apply that test above all others. It must ask last of all what were the returns of the counting room but must first inquire what ideals a given journal upheld, what moral aims it pursued, what national and international policies it championed, what was the spirit of fair play and justice which actuated it, and above all on whose side and under whose banner it fought. The minute one begins to measure and to value Mr. Ochs's *Times* from these points of view the whole picture he has drawn of his own achievement changes profoundly for the worse.

Mr. Ochs, I have no doubt whatever, sincerely believes that when he says his is an "independent newspaper" that "tolerates no tampering with the news, no colouring, no deception," and that it has attained a high reputation "for the fulness, trustworthiness, and impartiality of its news service," he paints a just picture of his daily.   It would be pleasant to be able to agree with him, but the truth lies elsewhere.   It is an entirely false statement.   The *Times* is no more independent than it is swayed by a desire to be just. It is a class paper, pure and simple, as much so as the *Call,* or any labour journal.   Its news can pass only the quantitative and no qualitative test.   No journal has exceeded it in disseminating falsehoods, misrepresentations, and half truths during the unparalleled era of wholesale lying in which the whole world has lived since 1914.   Just how shameless, for instance, it has been in its treatment of Russian news has been repeatedly set forth both by *The Nation* and the *New Republic* without any refutation. To excuse it, as some try to do, by placing the responsibility upon the Associated Press is ridiculous. In the first place many of the worst fabrications have come from special correspondents; in the second place no newspaper is compelled to print the Associated Press news it receives; in the third place Mr. Ochs is, with one exception, probably the most influential director in the Associated Press and could, if he tried to, stop the kind of reporting which made his newspaper relate within a comparatively brief period that Petrograd had fallen six times, been on the verge of capture three times more, been burned to the ground twice, been in absolute panic twice and in revolt against the Bolsheviks on six different occa-

8

sions—all without the slightest foundation in fact. Only in the columns of Hearst could one find a record to equal this.

As for the careers of Messrs. Yudenitch and Kolchak in the columns of the *Times*, they must ever stand as the high-water mark of false propaganda, lying, and misrepresentation intended to confuse or mislead the American public. This record alone should have prevented Mr. Ochs—unless he fails to understand it and appreciate it—from even referring to the "trustworthiness and impartiality" of the news service he gives to his readers.

Surely, if any rulers were ever justified in excluding correspondents from their country, Lenin and Trotzky were in shutting out those of the *Times*. For Mr. Ochs's *Times* is read in Moscow and these two men know well that the *Times*'s special correspondents are primarily propagandists and not only in so far as Russia is concerned. These writers, to judge them by their work, exist primarily to defend a point of view and that interpretation of society for which the *Times* exists. Again, Lenin and Trotzky, if they are like other students of the times, know that the *Times* rarely if ever apologizes when it has committed a wrong or done an injury. Take the case of Jane Addams for one. With what abuse did not the *Times* cover her, one of the noblest of our women, because she told the simple truth that the Allied

9

troops were often given liquor or drugs before charging across No Man's Land?   Yet when the facts came out at the hands of Sir Philip Gibbs and others not one word of apology was ever forthcoming.   Not even the dead are safe at its hands—as witness the recent case of Robert G. Ingersoll whose memory the *Times* would not clear even after the truth was presented to its heads.   Endless are the letters of correction and reproof which go to the *Times,* never to appear in print—for "lack of space" doubtless—and so justice is denied again and again.   Certainly the protestant has no standing whatever, in the *Times's* court, unless he is of the elect and the powerful and on the popular side.   Before the god of wealth the *Times* ever bows down.   It has even said, with almost incredible callousness and heartlessness, that "a certain degree of unemployment is curative of many social disorders.   It is the argument to the stomach which becomes necessary when the appeal to reason and industrial morality fails"—let the dogs of workers eat cake if they have no bread!   But how it bleats if Congress or the tax-gatherer squeezes the rich to whom it toadies day by day, year in, year out, every reader of it knows.   At the feet of the rich—chiefly the vulgar rich—and the powerful it fawns day in, day out.   That is Mr. Ochs's chief philosophy, a great secret of his business success—that and his unending devotion to the God of things as they are.

At his doors have knocked in vain for help those who seek fundamentally to better the world, woman suffragists, land reformers, tax reformers, the toiling masses, all who strive internationally for peace and good will on earth, anybody who could ever be remotely suspected of endangering the existing order or of threatening capitalism. For not even the Jews, Mr. Ochs's race, has it pleaded as ardently as have others, apparently for fear lest it be further decried and criticized as a Jew paper; how else can one explain its refusal to print the British report on the Polish pogroms save as paid advertising? Mr. Ochs cannot deny that his newspaper printed a false Associated Press summary of Sir Stuart Samuel's report, making it acquit the Polish Government when Sir Stuart actually held that Government guilty, or that his trustworthy and impartial journal refused to print either the Associated Press's correction of its error or the full text of the report when it arrived— save as an advertisement paid for at the hands of some of his coreligionists. Nor has the *Times* ever commented on the *Tribune's* editorial proof of the *Times's* textual alteration for its own purposes of an editorial reprinted from the Boston *Transcript*.

As a teacher of race hatred the New York *Times* is unsurpassed; it leaves no stone unturned to make clear its belief that there are two kinds of American citizens—the privileged and the disadvantaged—the

11

blacks and the whites. What has the *Times* left undone since 1917 to spread bitter hatred of great classes of our foreign-born citizens? No, no; it may count its successes in dollars and cents, but never in moral values. It may praise itself as the defender of the *status quo* as much as it pleases, but if Mr. Ochs or anybody else should declare that it is a great champion of popular rights, a journalistic John Bright, an incessant pleader for the lowly and the oppressed, an invariable and ardent defender of all who seek to rise, a never-failing protagonist of the true spirit of American liberty, his tongue should cleave to the roof of his mouth forever. On the East Side, where live lowly masses of the Jewish people, the race of Jesus, the *Times* is not worshipped. They admire Mr. Ochs's unusual modesty, his business sagacity, his total lack of all notoriety seeking, his aloofness from politics and personal aggrandizement, his skill, his courage, but it is not to him that they turn when their skies are overcast and the God of his fathers seems to have veiled His face to His wanderers of the earth.

What the New York *Times* should be, perhaps what Mr. Ochs means it to be, is an American *Manchester Guardian*. The difference is the difference between Chattanooga, Mr. Ochs's former home, and Manchester. The *Guardian*, too, has just had a jubilee; all over England the chorus of praise was universal;

12

there no one ever questions the responsibility and reliability of its news correspondents; there every one admires a great open-minded, noble-spirited editorial page keen to right every wrong, eager for advance and reform, champion of the workers as often as of the rich, buttressed upon inviolable principles of human liberty which *it* never abandoned, not even in the craze of the war; above all else never silent in the presence of sin by whomsoever committed. No, it is the London *Morning Post* with which the *Times* must be contrasted, but here also the *Times* fails; Toryism is better served, more ably defended in London. Both deserve well of every Gary and every Calvin Coolidge, of every Curzon and every Bonar Law. In them the existing, broken-down order has its staunchest defenders. If the world is out of sorts, it is because of them, their kith and kin. It will progress not because of but in spite of them and their fulminations. Certainly in this country, since the *Times* has kept silent or defended the persecution of the Socialists, the prostitution of the Constitution, the trampling under foot of the sacred rights of individual liberty which still goes on, it is idle to expect that as long as Mr. Ochs lives it will in any way serve or preserve the spirit of the America of Lowell and Wendell Phillips and Sumner and Emerson and Abraham Lincoln.

CHAPTER II

WILLIAM RANDOLPH HEARST AND HIS MORAL PRESS

OF William Randolph Hearst it is related that when he came to New York to enter journalism he debated as to whether he should found the best or the worst newspaper. The story may be apocryphal, but there is no doubt as to which kind of newspaper he has fathered. Nor can there be any question that he has as many journalistic lives as a cat has feline existences. How else could he have survived the waves of intense popular dislike, yes, bitter hatred of him, that have repeatedly swept over this country, which would surely have driven any one else into retirement? When McKinley was assassinated it was widely whispered that Czolgosz had a copy of the *Evening Journal* in his pocket when he was arrested. Out of clubs, reading-rooms, and libraries went the *Journal* and *American*. Again, during the World War, his equivocal position drew fire from many sides; thousands upon thousands of our returning soldiers felt themselves utterly outraged when they

14

were greeted at New York by a Hearst reception committee.

Undoubtedly it is the shortness of the American public's memory that is Hearst's best ally. People simply do not remember. Every journalist knows that; every journalist knows that he must begin a "story" of past events with a recital of facts which every thoughtful person ought to recall. Who remembers today the wicked and dastardly part which Hearst played in bringing on the war with Spain? Who remembers his strident appeals then to the basest of passions? Who remembers the bitter outcry against him? Only a few, and it is a question not of years but of months before even the members of our university clubs will have only a vague idea as to what Hearst did or did not do during the World War. Time is thus the chief ally of Hearst and of his type of journalist. But even time cannot wholly efface certain facts. Hearst the man has recently been correctly called "one of the most melancholy figures of our time." He has done more to degrade the entire American press than any one else in its history—more than Pulitzer and both the Bennetts combined. He has achieved enormous material success—it is said that his net profit in 1922 amounted to $12,000,000—but he is without popular respect or regard. He is a man dreaded and feared, much sought after by a type of politician, but he has never

15

been personally beloved, never even by those deluded fellow-citizens of his who at times made the
welkin ring with their cheers for him during campaigns which have almost invariably resulted in his
defeat. A man of mystery, he will never be anything
else than anathema to great masses of citizens. If
at times he is the champion of the poor and oppressed,
he has no personal following of the kind that worshipped Roosevelt. Millions will read him, but following him is a different matter.

Men have not stuck to Hearst in great numbers and
with enthusiasm always at white heat, because of just
doubts as to his sincerity and intellectual honesty.
Let it be set down at once that Hearst is as unstable
as the winds; like them he can blow hot in Chicago
and cold in Atlanta or Boston at the same time.
Thus, when his newspapers published an appeal to
the Governor of Georgia that the life of the unfortunate Frank be spared it was carefully omitted
from Hearst's Atlanta newspaper where its publication would have made him unpopular. So it constantly happens that his newspapers advocate different policies in different cities. Similar examples
of this yielding to expediency, of this moral and
political instability, could be multiplied indefinitely.
The man is infirm of purpose, at times lazy, at times
paralyzingly indifferent. That he has become an extremely able and successful business man since the

16

reckless days of his first appearance in New York journalism, when it was the hope and belief that he would quickly dissipate his patrimony, is none the less true. Especially in the magazine field has he demonstrated his ability to make money.

What Hearst's actual material achievements are can be set forth by some few figures. There are (April, 1923) no less than 38,000 persons upon his pay roll in this country and in London, where two of his magazines are published, exclusive of those who work in paper-mills whose entire output goes to Hearst publications. Hearst began with the San Francisco *Examiner* which his father turned over to him in 1887: he is now the sole owner of the following dailies (9 morning, 15 evening) and Sunday newspapers (14), with the circulations claimed:

THE PROGRESS OF GROUP OWNERSHIP
WILLIAM RANDOLPH HEARST NEWSPAPERS

Morning

Chicago *Herald and Examiner*	383,936
New York *American*	225,081
San Francisco *Examiner*	167,025
Los Angeles *Examiner*	171,606
Boston *Advertiser* (Tabloid)	137,226
Seattle *Post-Intelligencer*	84,368
Washington *Herald*	54,029
Baltimore *American*	56,764
New York *Daily Mirror*	310,333

SOME NEWSPAPERS AND NEWSPAPER-MEN
Evening

Albany *Times-Union*	39,689
New York *Evening Journal*	696,447
Chicago *Evening American*	488,492
Boston *American*	243,721
Detroit *Times*	241,481
Washington *Times*	54,289
Wisconsin *News*	94,308
Atlanta *Georgian*	58,070
Oakland *Post-Enquirer*	47,507
* Syracuse *Journal*	65,326
Rochester *Journal*	43,188
Baltimore *News*	115,647
San Francisco *Call*	101,098
Los Angeles *Herald*	182,313
San Antonio *Light*	34,454

Sunday

New York *American*	1,083,911
Chicago *Herald and Examiner*	1,151,978
Boston *Sunday Advertiser*	502,565
San Francisco *Examiner*	346,510
Los Angeles *Examiner*	393,168
Detroit *Times*	304,779
Washington *Herald*	121,978
Seattle *Post-Intelligencer*	148,841
Milwaukee *Sunday Sentinel*	172,206
Atlanta *American*	131,606
Syracuse *Sunday American*	78,873
Rochester *Sunday American*	67,581
Baltimore *American*	154,945
San Antonio *Light*	55,671
Total	8,811,010

* Syracuse Journal and Telegram consolidated Nov. 4, 1925.

18

Even this does not tell the whole story because besides these he owns an interest sufficient to give him practical control of the San Francisco *Call-Post,* and the Los Angeles *Evening Herald.* In the magazine field, he and his wife are the proprietors of the following publications:

* *Cosmopolitan* [1]	1,519,642
Good Housekeeping	1,233,765
Nash's Magazine (London)	166,166
Good Housekeeping (London)	180,000
Harper's Bazaar	86,071
Motor	36,176
Motor Boating	20,259
International Studio	18,500
Smart Set	506,200
Town and Country	22,500
McClure's Magazine [2]	
Total	3,789,279

It takes over $90,000,000 a year to produce these Hearst publications. Today so many copies of them are printed that a single page in each of the papers calls for more than thirty-two tons of paper. With genuine business daring Hearst has raised the price of his Sunday papers everywhere to ten cents. Instead of losing by that the circulation of the Sunday *American* went over one million copies. One of his Washington papers had 28,000 readers at one cent when the Hearst managers took it over; it was self-supporting within eight weeks and now has nearly three times as

* All footnotes for the revised edition will be found at the end of each chapter.

many readers at two cents. In Milwaukee the Wisconsin *News* has grown under Hearst's ownership from 18,000 at one cent to 69,000 [3] at three cents. In Detroit the *Times* under Hearst has shot up from 16,000 copies at one cent to 160,000 [4] copies at two cents; its revenues have increased from $300,000 a year to $3,000,000. Of the $87,034,539 spent in one year for advertising in the 35 leading morning newspapers in the United States, 31.87 per cent. or $27,733,754 went into six Hearst newspapers. There is no doubt that there are talent and ability in the Hearst forces; nor are they hampered by conscientious scruples as to taste, decency, or good morals.

The possession of these properties enables Hearst to claim that 6,972,512 families, or one out of every four families in the entire United States, regularly read a Hearst publication. Probably the figure is utterly exaggerated since there must be great duplication of circulations, but if it is even approximately true the fact is both alarming and reassuring—alarming in the total number of readers, reassuring in the thought of how comparatively little the owner of these publications has really been able to affect the political or social life of the country, particularly when it is remembered that Mr. Hearst also controls a widely distributed motion-picture service, which, however, has not by any means been always financially

20

The *Tribune's* First Page before Hearst Invaded the New
York Field

successful. More than that, it must not be forgotten that Hearst has not only his own press service but that his special features, which cost more than $2,000,-000 a year, are marketed through the King Features Syndicate, which also sells his special news and wire services. Finally more than 2000 papers stamp the Hearst style of journalism with their approval by taking these features. These newspapers together print 26,277,227 copies daily.

It is being said in Fleet Street that already almost all trace of Northcliffe, the man, has disappeared; that his influence is today nearly dissipated. There is probably an omen in this of what will happen when Hearst disappears from the American scene. But, leaving the future to take care of itself, it is certainly a ground for encouragement that with all the power of the Hearst press, with all its ability to speak to millions, as its touts are so endlessly boasting, it has not yet achieved any of the greater causes for which his newspapers have stood. The railroads are still privately owned and the water powers, as well. The cities are only just beginning to own and operate their traction lines and so on down the list. It is thus perfectly plain that Hearst has not begun to exercise, even with his own readers, the influence which he could have had. Fortunately for America there are some inhibitions strongly upon him. The man has failed from every point of view save money-mak-

21

ing, because of lack of moral purpose, of sound and consistent political principle, of enthusiastic and unselfish devotion to such causes as he has espoused. Without these shortcomings he would have overcome the handicap of his cold, unattractive, and, from the public point of view, rather mysterious personality. These faults have saved America from the disgrace of having him in high office.

A study of his political career only confirms this view of him, for, especially of late years, he has in this field displayed an amateurishness and bungling quite out of keeping with his business sagacity. Thus, in the 1922 campaign for nomination for Governor of New York he was easily defeated by Alfred E. Smith. He was playing for high stakes, for had he been nominated and elected in the Democratic tidal wave he must have been a dangerous candidate for the next Democratic Presidential nomination in view of the existing dearth of available material. He could easily have controlled many more delegates and won over some more local bosses had he really set himself to the task. Again there was that fatal vacillation; he and Mayor Hylan bowed low and each begged the other to take the nomination—with which Governor Smith then easily walked off. It would not be safe to say today that this has ended Hearst's political career, but it has certainly been a severe blow to the chances of his winning high office in the future. In Congress, where he sat from a safely Democratic district by grace of Tammany, he had an excellent opportunity to show what political talents he possessed; he was an indifferent, colourless Congressman who impressed nobody, neglected his duties, and left absolutely no mark behind him. He has been dubbed a "monster of publicity" and a specialist in the psychology of crowds; but when it comes to going before the people, even in the rôle of a St. George, to rescue them from the sinister dragons of the business controllers of our wealth and our government, his talents fail. Behind the editorial page he can accomplish much. In the open he can fool no one. His personal stature shrinks as his newspapers and magazines grow in number and in readers. The ghosts of his evil deeds, all the incalculable things he has done to degrade and debase the press of the country and to pervert the public taste, rise up to confront him as the ghosts of Macbeth's victims confronted and finally helped to overcome him.

Thus true leadership is not and cannot be his. Indubitably he has fought and is fighting many a good battle—no one can advocate so many things over a long period of years as he has and not be right sometimes. In opposing and exposing the evils of our big business in politics, which Woodrow Wilson used to say called for a revolution in America, he has served the public well. He has been a pioneer in advocating municipal ownership of public utilities, government ownership of railroads, and of natural resources, and State and municipal development and sale of electric light and power. He has stood for home rule for cities, for the initiative, referendum, and recall, for direct primaries, an eight-hour day, a minimum wage; but it is all tarnished by self-interest, by self-seeking, and arouses the never-failing and justified suspicion of his sincerity. For at the very moment when he has been crying out most loudly for the people's rights, he has never hesitated to strike hands with the worst of the politicians who rob the people of their rights at the behest of big business, their real masters. What better illustration of that could there be than Hearst's picturing Murphy, the boss of Tammany Hall, in prison stripes in searing cartoons in one year and soon after making a bargain with him to turn over New York to Tammany at its worst—all for selfish personal reasons? Short-lived as the public memory is, that went a little too far, was just a little too hypocritical to be wholly overlooked or forgotten. He is always virtuously against "Newberryism"—the use of great sums of money to obtain office—but he spent half a million nonchalantly in his own campaign against Charles E. Hughes for the governorship of New York.

Some hitherto unpublished telegrams which passed

between Hearst, Arthur Brisbane, and S. S. Carvalho during the New York mayoralty campaign of 1917 throw equally interesting light upon the methods and morals of these gentlemen in their conduct of the Hearst press and their treatment of public affairs.* In that contest there were four candidates, Mitchel, Bennett, Hillquit, and Hylan. The Hearst papers were backing Hylan, a hand-picked, small-calibre Tammany politician. It therefore occurred to Mr. Brisbane that by praising Hillquit he and his beloved corporation-baiting boss could scare the corporations into working for the Tammany Hall from which Hearst gets favours in return for support. Hearst did not fear Hillquit enough, so the scheme fell to the ground. But the telegrams give a delightful picture of the inside of the Hearst machine:

Western Union Telegram

J   New York NY 325P   Oct. 21 1917

W. R. Hearst,
    Examiner Los Angeles Calif

There is actual possibility of Hillquits election in four cornered fight Conditions ought to disturb the corpora-

---

* Those interested will find in the Report of the Senate Judiciary Committee on The Brewing and Liquor Interests and German and Bolshevik Propaganda, 3 volumes (66th Congress, 1st. Session. Senate Document 62. 1919), most illuminating matter regarding the relation of Mr. Hearst and his editors and their conduct of their papers during the war. This material must not be overlooked by any student of the subject. The hearings contain many telegrams exchanged by Mr. Hearst and his editors.

25

tions working for Mitchel   They will sweat and pay taxes
on their personal property if Hillquit elected   Shall I
write editorial warning corporations that their effort to get
everything from Mitchel may cost them dear through Hillquits victory   If they understood situation and danger they
would drop Mitchel and vote for Hylan   Editorial would
describe Hillquit's ability and sincerity   Remarkably able
lawyer Rosenwald who asks me introduce him Hillquit
says latter one of ablest men in country   Can write editorial in such way as to transfer many votes from Mitchel
to Hillquit   Please reply

A. Brisbane
339 PM

To this Hearst replied:

San Francisco California 1256AM Oct 23 1917
Carvalho   American New York
Brisbane wants to write editorial praising Hillquit   Brisbane thinks Hillquit may be elected   Of course Hillquit
will not be elected although governments policy will make
socialists very strong   Editorial of kind Brisbane suggests
would be construed as disloyalty to Hylan and upset all
our plans   Please prevent it.

Hearst
453AM

The reader will notice the reference to "all *our*
plans."   It reveals the close co-operation of the newspaper owner and Tammany Hall in 1917, and
Hearst's hope of future favours.

Hearst belongs to no political fold or category.

26

He is neither a Socialist, nor a liberal, nor a conservative liberal, nor a radical liberal, nor even a consistent imperialist liberal.   The latter rôle seems to
fit him most nearly, for he gleefully twists the British
lion's tail and baits the Japanese.   He favours a huge
fleet and a large army.   He is not wholly averse to
the exploitation of weak and backward countries, but
every now and then he comes out against American
imperialism and murder in Haiti and Santo Domingo, which he ought consistently to be defending
since he demands that we hold the Philippines.   So
it is surprising to find him urging the recognition of
the Soviet Government.   That may, however, be only
for today; tomorrow his editorial hired men may
make him say the opposite or say it at his behest.
Why not?   On May 3, 1916, over his own name his
dailies bellowed as follows: "Our flag should wave
over Mexico as the symbol of the rehabilitation of
that unhappy country and its redemption to 'humanity' and civilization.   Our right in Mexico is the right
of humanity.   If we have no right in Mexico then we
have no right in California or in Texas, which we re-
deemed from Mexico. . . ."   More recently somebody got hold of Hearst, whose views as to Mexico
cannot be wholly uncoloured by the fact that he is the
alien and absentee owner of hundreds of thousands
of Mexican acres which he is holding for future exploitation and is also the credited holder of mining

27

interests in that country. Apparently it was made clear to this tribune of the people that he should change his tune and he did so. As a result he is now working hard for the recognition of the Obregon Government and has forgotten all about our "right" to intervene. Thus, on February 7, 1922, he asked plaintively: "Every human interest that appeals to a nation calls on us to do justice to Mexico—politics, diplomacy, business, national defence. . . . Why inflict conspiracies and injuries on a government that is trying to be friendly and from whose friendship we can derive only benefit?"

His attitude toward the World War is further proof that he is not only without statesman-like vision but that he handles a given situation with a maximum of ineptitude. There can be no doubt that he saw the folly of the war and realized America's fatal blunder in going into it; this he rightly harps upon today. But he did not say so clearly and candidly at the time and then state that he would uphold the government during the war while reserving the proper rights of criticism. Had he done so and then compelled his editorial writers to wisdom and moderation, he could have rendered enormous service to his country by influencing the Administration in the direction of justice and sanity. But his writers were, as usual, careless and inconsistent and so there arose a terrific outcry against him, with the result that our war-mad

The *Tribune* as It Is Today, Showing the Hearst Influence
upon Its Headlines and Make-up

local officials began to suspend the Constitution on their own account and to ban or to burn his paper. One of his editors was so stupid as to omit from a proclamation of the President that part praying for victory for the American arms. Then the storm broke. He pluckily kept up his anti-war propaganda and his just criticism of our Allies for a while, but finally the fire got too hot and he had to resort to all sorts of means of defence, including page advertisements testifying to his great services to the country during the war.* After that he, too, went with the mob. As has been said, Time the Healer has helped him; he has suffered no permanent financial or circulation losses because of the bitter attacks upon him in 1917 and 1918.

There is something particularly despicable in the man, whether he be President or editor, who arouses

---

* It was during the war that he introduced the use of many flags on his papers. How and why they were removed is shown in the following telegram which was introduced at the hearing of the Senate Committee investigating German and Bolshevik propaganda:

Western Union Telegram
March 3, 1917

S. S. Carvalho N. Y. American N. Y. City

If situation quiets down please remove color flags from first page and little flags from inside pages, reserving these for special occasions of a warlike or patriotic kind. I think they have been good for this week, giving us a very American character and probably helping sell papers, but to continue effective they should be reserved for occasions. HEARST the hopes of great masses of people by pointing out their wrongs and then leaves them in the lurch for selfish reasons, or because of a weak surrender to powerful enemies. But when one considers the technical journalistic side of Hearst's career the condemnation which he merits can only be intensified. Let any student of the American press turn back to the files of the metropolitan dailies as they were before Hearst came into the field and then compare them with the editions of today and he will see for himself how lasting has been the injury done to the profession by Hearst in the lowering of journalistic tastes and standards. If he had only published the worst papers in America that would have been bad enough. But almost every other newspaper has followed in his trail and adopted something of his features. While he has grown with time more conservative both as to headlines and sensations, the others have adopted the comic strips and other Hearst features. Even the smug, stupid, and frequently intellectually dishonest *Tribune*, once the pride of the country, has imitated the journalist it assails most. At least it *does* assail him; the bulk of the fraternity keeps silent because of a certain professional fellowship, or in frank worship of his success, or because of simple cowardice. The indictment of the press because of Hearst does not stop with the charge of servile imitation or the bowing down before his millions. The majority of our papers do not attempt to combat his influence or to show up the absolute lack of honesty and decency in his news columns, though they know what his influence has done to degrade their profession. Yet our journalists wonder why it is that the standing of the daily press with the American people has suffered so tremendously during the very years of Hearst's career in our journalism!

But, the reader may ask, what could the profession have done to set standards of conduct and to punish derelictions, since there is no institute of journalists, no body as yet comparable to the bar associations in the legal and the professional associations in the medical professions? To this the answer is that the profession does meet in conventions * or is otherwise so organized as to make it quite possible for it to have expressed its opinion emphatically. The clearest and most flagrant case in this connection is that of the Associated Press, whose refusal to expel Hearst from its membership is proof positive how dulled some editors are to offences which in any other profession would certainly send the guilty man to Coventry—to say the least. The Associated Press found that the Hearst International News Service was systematically stealing its news; that in violation of

---

* Since these lines were written the American Society of Newspaper Editors has held its second annual session at Washington and adopted a code of ethics.

its by-laws the Hearst publications which were members of the Associated Press were allowing its news to filter out to the non-member Hearst newspapers. The Hearst service bribed employés of the Cleveland *News,* an Associated Press newspaper, to furnish it with Associated Press news as soon as it came over the wire. This was then wired back to New York and was sent out as an International News item. It systematically copied dispatches from early editions and bulletin boards of Associated Press newspapers, particularly after the British, Canadian, French, Portuguese, and Japanese governments had barred the Hearst service from their countries and prohibited the use of their cables for any Hearst messages.

The difficulty of running down dishonesty of this kind was obviously not slight, especially since the ownership of news had not been judicially or legally defined in the United States. To this task Mr. Melville E. Stone devoted himself, inspired by the desire to wind up a long journalistic career by obtaining a judicial ruling on the rascalities of Hearst and establishing a needed principle of enormous value to all who originate news. He was completely successful. Hearst's agents were convicted on every count of cheating and stealing from the Associated Press, which Hearst as a member was in duty bound to protect. When the case was won the Associated Press was duly jubilant, but its then board of directors comprising such men as Adolph S. Ochs of the *Times,* Victor Lawson of the Chicago *Daily News,* Charles A. Rook of the Pittsburgh *Dispatch,* Clark Howell of the Atlanta *Constitution,* Elbert H. Baker of the Cleveland *Plain Dealer,* Frank B. Noyes of the Washington *Star,* and others did nothing to relieve the Associated Press of the odium of Hearst's presence in the association which he had not only betrayed but deliberately sought to wreck, or, if expulsion was not possible, to make clear their moral condemnation of his acts by a resolution of censure and reprobation.* So far as the public is aware the question of Hearst's disciplining was never brought up in the Board of Directors or in the annual meetings of the members. What more striking illustration could there be of the depths to which the leaders of the profession have lowered it? These men were not willing to purge themselves of Hearst's presence in what is avowedly not a money-making corporation, but a membership organization chartered under the same law of the State of New York as are its social clubs. Is any answer to this amazing riddle possible

* The author of this book was a Director of The Associated Press at the time of the suit and he has been criticized on the ground that he did not move against Hearst. This was in response to suggestions from within The Associated Press that it would be best to await a final decision in the case before acting. The decision of the Supreme Court was rendered December 23, 1918; the author's resignation as a Director had been sent in on August 8, 1918.

33

except that the directors of the Associated Press were afraid to denounce Hearst, that they bowed their knees to his success, his power, his wealth? But if this is the answer, how can the directors of the Associated Press complain if the public's opinion of the whole newspaper profession steadily falls?

This picture goes a long way to explain Hearst's power. But what shall be said of men outside the profession who take service under this confuser of ideals? I do not refer, of course, to the rank and file of Hearst's workers who see in his pay only a means to a livelihood. It is the long list of men of distinction who have accepted the shilling of this king of sensational journalism which comes to mind. What shall be said, for example, of Charles H. Parkhurst? Long a preacher of Christian morals in New York and a tower of strength in the fight against municipal misgovernment, he has used Hearst's columns to address the multitudes who scan his pages. Obviously this noted divine took Hearst's pay either because he was in need of money or because he laid the flattering unction to his soul that his ethical teachings could offset some of the evil done by those self-same publications. Ambrose Bierce once wrote: "If asked to justify my long service to journals with whose policies I was not in agreement and whose character I loathed I should confess that possibly the easy nature of the service had something to do with it. As to the point of honour (as that is understood in the profession), the editors and managers always assured me that there was commercial profit in employing my rebellious pen, and I, O well, I persuaded myself that I could do more good by addressing those who had greatest need of me—the millions of readers for whom Mr. Hearst was a misleading light." It is, of course, the old, old ethical fallacy that the end justifies the means. You abhor this man Hearst and then this Mephistopheles comes to you and says: "See, I shall turn over to you part of the garden in which I work. You shall spade it as you please and draw golden ducats for doing so," and behold Faust yields as readily as ever a Faust did. So the minister of the Gospel preaches his sermon between the sex appeals and murder "mysteries," the cheap gossip and tales of the beautiful maiden lured to her destruction, that sell the paper to multitudes.

Thus man after man has found himself called to offset the teachings of his employer while accepting the employer's base metal. "Of course, I don't believe in Hearst, but one must get some straight thinking over to the masses." "There are no strings tied to me, so I can say what I please; besides I don't have to come into contact with the man himself." "Isn't it well that somebody should give a moral viewpoint to those deluded readers?" The language

35

of compromise is always the same; there is the same jargon in the pulpits whose occupants have forgotten Christ to serve Mammon, who take the conscience-less rich man's dollar in order to help him into the kingdom of heaven. Ethically, there is no justification whatever for an alliance like that of Mr. Parkhurst with Hearst. Some pitiful excuse may perhaps be made for the petty politicians who go hat in hand to this man to ask his support when in their hearts they loathe and despise him. But for teachers of ethics to wear his uniform is to do the terrible disservice of further confusing the moral values of multitudes. Hearst cares not a snap of his fingers for their views or whether they uplift or depress the souls of his readers. These men become Hearst's veil, his camouflage, his garment of respectability, the coiners of more pennies. But the ignorant ask: "How can Hearst be so bad if so saintly a person as Dr. Parkhurst writes for him?"

The problem becomes more complex and difficult when one leaves the Hearst newspapers and considers his magazines. What of Norman Hapgood? Mr. Hearst has given him a wonderful opportunity for his exceptional editorial talents by conferring upon him the editorship of *Hearst's International Magazine*. If my information is correct Mr. Hearst has had the business wisdom to give Mr. Hapgood a free hand. What is wrong in such an arrange-

THE CIRCULATION OF THE JOURNAL YESTERDAY WAS **1,369,315** ALL FREE COPIES, EXCHANGES, SAMPLES AND WASTE DEDUCTED

WAR SECTION.

EDITION FOR GREATER NEW YORK
NEW YORK JOURNAL
AND ADVERTISER.

WAR SECTION.

NO. 5,040. NEW YORK, THURSDAY, APRIL 28, 1898.—16 PAGES. PRICE ONE CENT

BOMBARDED!

OUR FLEET ATTACKS MATANZAS.

CITY MAY BE IN RUINS

KEY WEST, Fla., April 27.----The New York, Puritan and Cincinnati bombarded the forts at Matanzas this afternoon.

The engagement began at 12:45.

It was all over at 1:15.

There were no casualities on the American side.

Great damage is known to have been done.

The Morello Fort began the action.

The Puritan was steaming in shore and came within two miles of

She was chasing a little craft.

This proved to be a small gunboat, supposed to be the Gab

A Spanish War First Page of Hearst's *Evening Journal*,
April 28, 1898

ment?   Well, primarily it was Mr. Hapgood himself
who convicted Hearst of long selling the editorial
page of the *Evening Journal* for $1000 advertise-
ments from theatrical concerns.   You agreed to take
a page of advertising and you drew an Arthur Brisbane editorial praising your play with all the unc-
tuous sophistry of this chief of editorial trumpeters.
So *Collier's Weekly* under Mr. Hapgood exposed
and ended this moral turpitude and more beside.
Hence somehow it will always be difficult to reconcile oneself to the spectacle of Mr. Hapgood in
Hearst's pay.   He doubtless is as free as air; he can
truthfully declare that his editorial soul is his own.
But this union is as confusing and as misleading and
as discouraging as any of the many similar phenom-
ena.   There is no argument to be advanced that is
not an excuse and it is the excuse that accuses, as
the French say.   All of Mr. Hapgood's friends and
admirers must hope for an early dissolution of this
alliance; that he may rejoice soon on quitting Hearst
even as did Ambrose Bierce.

An amazing and, in this case, amusing instance of
Hearst's striking hands with one who formerly bitterly fought him is afforded by the fact that no less
a person than David Lloyd George has become
Hearst's most distinguished contributor to his dailies.
What a reflection this is upon both of these distinguished humbuggers of the public!   This is the

same Lloyd George who had the Hearst representatives expelled from England during the war for what
was called their persistent pro-Germanism, lying,
and misrepresentation—offences deemed to be so
serious that the mere possession of a copy of a Hearst
paper was made a prison offence in Canada during
the hostilities. It is, of course, true that Lloyd
George sold his articles to the United Feature Syndicate and gave it the right to dispose of them in the
United States and that the Syndicate sold them to
Hearst, but the spectacle is there for gods and men
—Lloyd George writes for Hearst. As for Hearst,
he doubtless reads with entirely cynical amusement
the advertisements in which he sets forth the virtues
of his distinguished ex-ministerial contributor whom
he for years abused so roundly, and recalls the
breakfast in London given to him by David Lloyd
George at which the hatchet was apparently buried.
What would you? The war is over; business is
business. "L. G." openly declares he needs the
money—and Hearst needs features to advertise. So
the "Saviour of England" lends his prestige to white-
washing Hearst, and makes it easier for members
of the Union League or the University Club to forget just what it was that Hearst did and said that they
did not like during the war. The more men bow
down before the flattery of Hearst's offers of publicity, the lure of his money, the temptation of his

power, the stronger Hearst is, and the muddier the public thinking about him becomes. At least one or two of his nine lives he owes to this readiness of public personages to avail themselves of his money or his columns.

The circumstance that Hearst has not done more mischief than he has should not, however, blind any one to the dangers of multiple ownership of newspapers. The rise of the Hearst chain and other similar ones like the Scripps-Howard, which now numbers twenty-four dailies, is a phenomenon fraught with evil, particularly when one considers it in connection with the steady trend toward consolidation or absorption of the weaker dailies by the strong, and the large number of cities which now have only one daily apiece. Any modern democracy is peculiarly dependent upon the obtaining by its members of sound information. Should all the city dailies of the country be owned by four or five individuals or groups of owners, the situation in this country would become extremely serious. So far as Hearst is concerned, there are indications that his invasion of the smaller cities is not likely to extend very rapidly. The Hearst machine as it operates in our largest cities is not a good training-school for men who are to conduct dailies in cities in which the possible advertising and circulation are distinctly limited. In Rochester, for instance, the problem is entirely different from

39

that in Los Angeles or Seattle or Chicago; in that city, by the way, the large advertisers, under the leadership of George Eastman of Kodak fame, are opposed to Hearst's appearance in that city where he has merged the old *Post-Express* with his *Journal.* Usually Hearst overcomes such business opposition because merchants do not hold long to an attitude of civic virtue when tempted by large circulations.

In justice to Hearst it must be said that many of his heads of departments profess great admiration for him and profound faith in his mission. Mr. Brisbane asserts that "for twenty years I have seen things appearing in the New York *Evening Journal;* then I have seen them in Roosevelt's speeches; in the New York *American* and then in Wilson's speeches. The public, of course, will in time know it—they won't know it while Hearst is alive because people never do, but they will eventually." Mr. Bradford Merrill asks what the Hearst policies are and then answers himself as follows: "Are they not simply this: That the public affairs of every city, every state, and the nation as a whole, shall be controlled by the inhabitants thereof, for their own welfare, and not controlled by privilege and plutocracy for the benefit of a few already highly privileged individuals?" But these apologists for Hearst forget to mention the utterly despicable methods through which Hearst preaches his doctrine of war upon privilege—the lying, chicanery, dishonesty, yes, at times the venality (as in his relations to the Southern Pacific Railroad in his early California days), and the consequent measureless degradation of the public taste. Were it some one else than Mr. Hearst, Mr. Brisbane's easily moralizing pen would find in the moral failure of his employer a wealth of material for "sermonettes" to present to the Hearst millions of readers.

As one considers these men and the injury they have done one is reminded of Lowell's question: "Why should a man by choice go down to live in his cellar instead of mounting to those fair upper chambers which look toward the sunrise . . .?"

[1] Hearst's International has been combined with the Cosmopolitan.
[2] McClure's Magazine has only recently been acquired by the Hearst Corporation, and no circulation figures are available as yet.
[3] On March 31, 1926, the circulation of the Wisconsin *News* was 94,308.
[4] The circulation of the Detroit *Times* on March 31, 1926, was 241,481.

CHAPTER III

THE NEW YORK *WORLD*, A LIBERAL JOURNAL

A MONUMENT to Joseph Pulitzer the New York
World unquestionably is. It is even more than
that; it is really a monument to the idealism of the
many men from Central Europe who came to America
as to the promised land, so joyous at having turned
their backs upon the falsities, the hypocrisies, the
military autocracies of the Continent that they
brought to America a devotion quite unsurpassed by
any native born. Theirs was a far keener appreciation of the true principles of a democratic society
and of the fundamentals of American idealism than
is held by nine-tenths of the college graduates of today who claim admittance to the Sons of the Revolution. True, Mr. Pulitzer was not like three others
who left their mark upon American journalism—
Carl Schurz, Oswald Ottendorfer, and Henry Villard
—a product of the Revolution of 1848. He belonged
to a later generation of immigrants and did not cross
the ocean as a result of that idealistic uprising which

42

would have liberalized Germany and spared the world its greatest agony had it succeeded. But the fact is nevertheless that New York owes what is to-day its most liberal English-language daily to a simple Jewish-Hungarian immigrant of humblest origin, who came to this country friendless and unknown with so little money it is a question whether he would not have been excluded had the laws been what they are today. If men like Congressman Johnson, who are now so bent on excluding all aliens from America in pursuit of the narrow, selfish, nationalistic dogma of "America for those who are already here," could ever be brought to measure the contributions of some of the thousands who came penniless to these shores in foul-smelling steerage quarters, they would surely be shamed into something different. They would at least have to concede that the morning *World* is to-day one of the few remaining assets in the field of journalism in which Americans with ideals can take pride.

Yet it does not begin to approximate what it ought to and so easily could be. The fact that the *World* is and always has been a creature of compromise is responsible for this. Nothing could be finer than the vision of its purpose, which Joseph Pulitzer published when he purchased it in 1883, and which it now daily carries under its "mast-head" on the editorial page:

43

An institution that should always fight for progress and reform, never tolerate injustice or corruption, always fight demagogues of all parties, never belong to any party, always oppose privileged classes and public plunderers, never lack sympathy with the poor, always remain devoted to the public welfare, never be satisfied with merely printing news, always be drastically independent, never be afraid to attack wrong, whether by predatory plutocracy or predatory poverty.

His platform, dubbed radical, demagogic, socialistic, and altogether upsetting (in the lack then of the easy epithet of "bolshevist"), called for the taxation of luxuries, inheritances, large incomes, monopolies, all the special privileges of corporations, as well as a tariff for revenue only, and the reform of the civil service—most of the taxation proposals are now law.

At the beginning of Mr. Pulitzer's ownership the *World* (which was originally founded as a one-cent religious daily!) proceeded to touch even lower depths of journalism than had the *Herald* under the elder James Gordon Bennett. Mr. Pulitzer played far more directly to the base passions of the multitude than Mr. Bennett, yet his was a moving vision of a great daily of the working masses among which he had himself toiled, suffered, and almost starved, until his feet reached the road to renown and to riches. It was by this appeal to the basest passions of the crowd that Mr. Pulitzer succeeded; like many an-

44

other he deliberately stooped for success, and then, having achieved it, slowly put on garments of righteousness. I am old enough to remember that forty years ago in New York it was impossible to find the *World* in any refined home; it was regarded much as Hearst's *Evening Journal* is today. It was the *World* as well as the *Journal* which Mr. Godkin had in mind when he wrote in the *Evening Post* some twenty-four years ago that "a yellow journal office is probably the nearest approach, in atmosphere, to hell existing in any Christian state, for in gambling houses, brothels, and even in brigands' caves there is a constant exhibition of fear of the police, which is in itself a sort of homage to morality or acknowledgment of its existence." If this language seems preposterously strong today it was pretty well justified at the time by the devilish work done both by the *World* and the Hearst press in bringing on the war with Spain. Then Mr. Pulitzer was willing to outdo Hearst in shameless and unwarranted sensationalism lest Hearst inflict on his papers irrevocable injury. That chapter in the *World's* history is not one to be read with satisfaction today by any one connected with it. To the eldest generation of intellectual New Yorkers the *World* is still anathema; to them it connotes only sensationalism and a journalism utterly without principle.

But like Mr. Bennett's *Herald*, the *World* grew

more conservative with time, because its permanence was established, because Mr. Pulitzer himself grew older, and because he and his family came to a social prominence in which a more sober appearance and less sensationalism in their chief newspaper had their merits. It is undoubtedly true also that the change lies in part in our own altered vision. A first page which horrified New York in 1880 would seem tame and commonplace today. As Pulitzer outdid Bennett so did Hearst's yellowness make the *World's* seem merely a sickly pallor. Nevertheless the *World* has been for decades under the spell of Mr. Pulitzer's constant admonition to his editors to hold its popular following. In modern slang, he wanted a "high-brow" editorial page embodied in a "low-brow" newspaper. This Pulitzer policy has long exerted an unfavourable influence upon the *World* and caused it to lose the great opportunity of becoming the newspaper of the thoughtful middle-classes which Mr. Ochs and his *Times* seized—to the community's loss, for the liberal editorial page of the *World* would accomplish great good in thousands of homes in which the dull reactions of the *Times's* editorial writers do harm. For decades, and long, long after the *World* was rich enough to buy the best of paper and ink, it kept to its poor ink and newsprint in craven fear apparently, lest, if it presented a front page as clear and typographically handsome as that of the *Times*

or the *Evening Post,* the toiling masses who rush
downtown on the East Side elevated railways or
surge across the bridges would abandon it. Only
within the last few years has the *World* slightly
spruced up its appearance without as yet, however,
so improving it as to become the formidable rival to
the *Times* that it ought to be in the most influential
quarters of the city. One hesitates to put one's
own opinions against those of the able business men
who builded, with Mr. Pulitzer, the newspaper's success, yet I have a very strong feeling that as the
Manchester Guardian has a large labour following,
so the *World* could years ago have improved its appearance and yet held a labour constituency had it
so desired, or had its editors and owners had the
vision and the necessary courage. I am emboldened
to believe that this is not a wholly mistaken theory
of mine by the fact that the *World* is now turning in
a new direction. It has not only improved the
quality of its ink and paper; through the addition to
its staff of Messrs. Walter Lippmann, F. P. Adams,
and Heywood Broun it is reaching out for a new
group of readers since those gentlemen, for all their
merits, will not appeal to the masses. After all,
the workers are best drawn to a daily like the *World*
by a friendly, understanding, appreciative, and just
editorial attitude toward the aspirations of labour.
Even now, I think, the *World* could cut deeply into

the *Times's* field; but something still keeps the management from bettering the paper other than slowly —too slowly for quick results. The insiders believe that they have exchanged about 90,000 new readers for a similar number of the old following lost. It is interesting to note that the circulation of the *World* was 382,087 on October 1, 1922, and 392,387 on April 1, 1923; it was 395,495 in October, 1912, when the price was, however, only one cent instead of two. It sank to 346,289 in 1918.[1]

The apparent duality of editorial aim is everywhere in evidence. Alongside excellent and worthwhile reporting there are still occasional vulgarities, often lapses of omission, and much poor recording of events, as in labour matters; alongside admirable foreign correspondence, notably in the Sunday issue, appear crude and sensational articles bent on keeping up the large Sunday sales. The *Times* sells nearly 600,000 copies on Sunday without that abomination known as the "Sunday Comic"; the *World* sticks to its distinctly inferior supplements of this type. But the most striking illustration of the dual aim is, after all, its relationship to the other daily published under the same roof and owned by the same persons, which hides behind the reputation of the morning *World*. The *Evening World* is the black sheep of the family, about whose whereabouts and mode of life one does not inquire too carefully.

48

Like others of questionable repute, this denizen of
Park Row lives for the moment and the hour. It is
of the earth earthy, although it, too, has been growing more respectable. It profits largely by its mode
of life and it has even been rumoured that the pro-
ceeds of its lack of high character have at times been
of generous reinforcement to the purse of the more
respectable member of the family.

So it is of the latter that one thinks when one talks
of the New York *World*. When Senators and Congressmen rise, as they frequently do, to speak with
admiration of the courage and outspokenness of the
World they mean, of course, the morning edition.
The *Evening World* rigidly continues the original
Pulitzer policy of playing down to the masses; the
morning edition slowly but steadily worms itself into
politest society and does so in part by calling to its
service the pens of men like Frank A. Vanderlip,
H. G. Wells, A. G. Gardiner, Joseph Caillaux, André
Tardieu, George N. Barnes, and Maximilian Harden
and many another writer of world-wide fame. Indeed, the most reliable foreign correspondence is to
be found in its columns. In the perusal of no other
New York daily does one rest so safe in the belief that
its correspondents are writing what they think, untrammelled either by editorial inhibitions or by subconscious consciousness of the paper's prejudices and
policies. No other New York paper told the truth

about the Ruhr invasion as did the *World*. Like the Baltimore *Sun,* the *World* gave great attention to the reporting of the Washington Conference on the Limitation of Armaments by many distinguished writers from all countries and all points of view— it brought over Mr. Wells. Yet it did not profit by this as much as it should have, again because of its appearance. It deliberately hides its own light under a bushel. The ordinary city reporting is probably done on the *World* as well as if not better than on any other New York daily, but its editors have been known to bewail, quite as if they could not correct it if they would, the shocking decadence of the modern reporter. Yet it is not the reporters' fault that every now and then there appear crime "stories" in the *World* which are not fit for print and help to debar it from many a breakfast-table upon which it ought to be. The freedom of the news columns from control by advertisers is admirably complete.

Independence is the *World's* stock in trade. To its honour be it said that it was among the first to become, with the New York *Evening Post* and the *Springfield Republican,* really independent politically. That, too, was Joseph Pulitzer's policy, and right nobly has the paper clung to it despite its natural leanings to the Democratic Party. Its championship of Grover Cleveland, its espousal of the cause of Woodrow Wilson were of enormous benefit to those two Democratic Presidents—Mr. Cleveland almost directly attributed his first victory to its support. Its refusal to accept the specious and superficial Bryan went a long way to insure that gentleman's defeats. In the local politics of New York City it has never faltered in well-doing; yet after years of battling for reform it pays its share of the price the whole press pays for its loss of public confidence by seeing the candidates it opposes, like every other reputable newspaper, overwhelmingly elected and re-elected. Despite Joseph Pulitzer's admonition to its editors "never to lack sympathy with the poor," despite the great hold it has had upon the labouring classes, the *World* has not escaped the wide criticism of New York's dailies that they are of the "kept press," and that they reflect primarily the views of the great capitalists.

Yet it has waged some tremendous fights for the people against those capitalists. It has at times, for instance, wanted to abate the Stock Exchange. It attacked its own hero, Grover Cleveland, in the matter of a national bond issue which he sold to the House of Morgan at a greater profit to them than was earned by all the bankers combined who floated the loans of the Civil War. It compelled him to convert the next issue into a popular one, thus giving the public a chance to subscribe and saving a high commission to the Government—there never was a secret bond issue after that. It has fought nobly against special privilege in the form of tariffs, subsidies, grabs, bonuses, and all sorts of raids upon the Treasury. It has not hesitated to oppose the Government in many of its overseas ventures such as the mad policy of Mr. Cleveland in the Venezuela matter. Nobody forgets like the American public and it forgets nothing so rapidly as a newspaper's good deeds. Indeed, the daily is usually judged every day afresh and a single stumble today will bring down a torrent of abuse no matter how white the record may have been for years before. So it is a fact that today the *World* does not stand so well as a champion of the people as it did two or three decades ago, and that it is the object of widespread suspicion among people who ought to be its friends and admirers. It has lost and not gained ground.

But blame for that is by no means wholly to be laid at the door of the public; the newspaper is itself at fault because its liberalism has had grave lapses, because it is not always consistent, and because it curiously lacks driving force in its efforts to ram home its views. The occasional inconsistency is doubtless partly due to the mechanics of the editorial page; it seems as if the editor on duty evenings were sometimes overruled the next day. Joseph Pulitzer in praising the alertness and promptness of expression of editorial opinion of the *Evening Post* once complained to me bitterly that he could not get his "editorial gentlemen" to write on events the day they occurred. In connection with its failure to win for its usually sound, wise, and admirably expressed views the attention and influence they deserve, it is to be noted that Henry Watterson did Mr. Frank I. Cobb,[2] the *World's* chief editor, the disservice to characterize him as the greatest editorial writer of this generation. Comparisons are still odious, if only because they set people to measuring and judging. Clear, cool, able, forceful in the presentation of his views, excellent user of English, Mr. Cobb has never equalled Rollo Ogden at his best before the World War gravely tarnished the latter's liberalism and he took his plunge into the dull senescence of the *Times's* editorial page. Once Mr. Ogden wrote with a passion for justice and righteousness which no one equalled after the retirement of his exemplar, Edwin L. Godkin. It was Mr. Ogden's fiery pen as much as any one's which made the McKinley Cabinet counsel one morning during the Spanish War whether it should not have the editors of the *Evening Post* and *Springfield Republican* indicted for treason; it was his pen which with a single stroke punctured the dangerous Hearst boom for the Presidency in 1904. That particular quality of passion Mr. Cobb lacks; nor does he somehow use as effectively as might be

53

the weapon of reiteration which was one of the deadliest in Mr. Godkin's arsenal. There is, in other words, often a failure to follow through the stroke.

Perhaps the point can best be illustrated by a really great editorial which Mr. Cobb published, double-leaded, in the *World* on December 5, 1920, entitled "An Antiquated Machine." To it was devoted the entire editorial page of that issue. Had it appeared in one of the weeklies which are called radical it would have been denounced as dangerously revolutionary. Had it been printed in the conservative *Tribune* or *Times* it would have created a national sensation. For it declared the truth that our Constitution is outworn, our scheme of government hopelessly antiquated and inefficient, our Congressional system as if planned to exclude the best minds of the country "except by accident." "The cold inexorable fact," Mr. Cobb wrote, is that "the Congressional system is no longer adequate to the political necessities of 105,000,000 people. The failure of government is largely the failure of that system, and until the legislative machinery is modernized the affairs of government are bound to go from bad to worse no matter what party is in power or what its policies or promises may be. An ox-cart cannot do the work of an automobile truck, and an ox-cart does not cease to be an ox-cart when it is incorporated into the Constitution of the United States." But Mr.

Cobb did not stop there. "We talk much of representative government in the United States, but we have no representative government." The political, social, and economic conditions of 1920, he pointed out, "bear little relation to the political, the social, and the economic conditions of 1787, yet the American people are trying to make a governmental machine which was constructed under the conditions of 1787 function under the complex conditions of 1920 and are bitterly complaining because they do not get better results"—a sentiment which is as if lifted bodily from the creed of the wicked *Nation*. Then behold this dangerous iconoclasm:

During the first half of the nineteenth century the United States remained the model of all nations seeking self-government. It is no longer the model. Of all the new republics that came into existence as a result of the Great War, not one of them has fashioned its machinery of government after that of the United States. All of them have adopted the British parliamentary system as adapted to the uses of a republic by the French. All of them have rejected congressional government in favour of parliamentary government. All of them have made their government directly and immediately responsible to the people whenever an issue arises about which the will of the majority is in doubt or in dispute. In consequence all these governments have become more democratic than that of the United States, more responsible to public opinion and more responsive to public opinion than that of the United States, and more closely in touch with the general political sentiment of the country than that of the United States.

Instead of remaining the leaders in the development of democratic institutions, the American people have lagged behind. They cling obstinately to most of the anachronisms of their Constitution although they are wholly indifferent to the great guaranties of human liberties embodied in the Bill of Rights. They retain a legislative system that time has made obsolete; but they have forgotten all about the principles of local self-government which was at the foundation of the republic, and they have equally forgotten all about the rights of the minority which are at the foundation of all freedom. While holding to the letter of their Constitution, they have so far perverted its spirit that the United States is now the one country among the great civilized nations in which the will of the people can never be definitely ascertained, in which it can never definitely be put into effect, and in which it can be successfully overruled whenever a political cabal is organized for that purpose.

Every intelligent American citizen knows that the machinery of government is breaking down. He knows that the public confidence in government is at the lowest ebb. He knows that government has ceased to function in harmony with either the political or economic necessities of the people, that it is rapidly becoming a thing apart from the actual life of the country and in a great degree indifferent to the life of the country. It is a huge, clumsy machine that requires a maximum of energy to produce a minimum of results, and those results are often worse than no results at all.

Surely an editorial so startling and revolutionary
—the only one in more than two years to which the
World devoted its entire editorial page in one issue
—ought to have brought down on the *World* the
wrath of 100 per cent. patriots, of every one of the
multitude of worshippers of things as they are. The
society for the preservation of the Constitution, whose
headquarters are in Washington, ought to have sol-
emnly resolved that the *World* was a traitor to its
country. The American Legion ought to have risen
in its wrath to point out the truth that if the *World*
had published such an editorial during the war Mr.
Cobb and Mr. Ralph Pulitzer would have gone to
jail—many went for saying less. Wall Street ought
to have removed all its financial advertising from the
World, and the New York State Chamber of Commerce should at least have demanded that Mr. Cobb
be finger-printed. None of these things happened;
indeed, so far as it was possible to ascertain without
having subscribed to the clipping bureaus, the editorial attracted surprisingly little attention—do not
editors read the Sunday *World*, or do they prefer
to golf? Or is it due to the absence in the editorial
of the passionate ring of the reformer who must
be heard no matter what the price? Certain it only
is that the Constitution and our legislative system did
not rock as they should have. More seriously, how

has the *World* followed up this magnificent beginning? Has it, after the manner of Joseph Pulitzer at the time of the secret bond deals, made itself known throughout the country as the ardent, flaming exponent of the growing demand that the strait-jacket of an outworn Constitution under which we live, and upon which our highest officials spit as and when they choose, shall be changed? On the contrary, I venture to assert that 98 per cent of the faithful readers of the *World* are unaware of its views on this subject; they have certainly not had it drilled into them day by day, or week by week, how grave the national emergency is which is set forth in that leader. No, the *World* is not living up to the great opportunity which here offers itself to make the public realize whither we are drifting, and to lead the country toward gradual reforms without which we shall some day have an overturn as far-reaching as the Russian.

But there is still another vital reason why the *World* does not lead as it once did. The *World's* editors were of those liberals who failed utterly to see that when liberalism strikes hands with war, liberalism withers if it does not die. The *World* supported Woodrow Wilson because he proclaimed in his "New Freedom" largely the *World's* own gospel of social and political reform. Today the progressive movement in America which looked so hopeful in the first three years of Wilson's Administra-

58

tion is flat on its back, every reform cause is checked
when it is not dead. The "New Freedom" reads like
a travesty today; or like a note out of the long dead
past. It bears no relation whatever to current political action, and no one more than the *World* be-
wails the political reaction of the hour—a reaction
which was as inevitable after the war as the following of night upon day, which the *World* itself did
its full share to create. Far-sighted editors truly
steeped in democratic liberalism would have fore-
seen this; Mr. Pulitzer would certainly never have
been taken in by such phrases as the "war to end
war" and "making the world safe for democracy"
and the rest of the war humbug whose falsity and
hypocrisy have been and are hourly being demonstrated by every event from Paris to the Ruhr. In
vain in the sight of so experienced a bird would those
nets have been spread.

But the *World* and Mr. Cobb differed but little
from the ordinary run of dailies and editors. They
were silent or mildly protested while liberalism was
done to death; while every right that American citizens were guaranteed was trampled underfoot with
the consent and approval of the great prophet of
liberalism, Woodrow Wilson. During the greater
part of the war the *World* ran with the herd and
was as rabid and poisonous as the rest. Only long
after the mischief was done and all danger to the

protestant was over, when the new chains, not yet broken, had long been welded upon us in place of the "New Freedom," did Mr. Cobb speak—bravely, eloquently, ably, persuasively, effectively. But the *World* ought to have suffered for assenting to the eclipse of political independence, the muzzling of the press, the denial of the famed historic American right to one's conscience at any and all times, and it has suffered.

Nor can it soon recover from this unpardonable lapse from the principles of its founder. How can the masses be expected to rise to a leader who falters and keeps silence when the enemy is most powerful and in control? To its blind faith, too, in its idol, Mr. Wilson, must be attributed some of the *World's* vagaries in regard to the League of Nations. It seems incredible that it really swallowed so many of the pro-League arguments because, democratic methods being its specialty, it ought to have resented most strongly the undemocratic character of the League. Last of all American newspapers should the *World* have given currency to the idea that, if we had entered the League, the whole history of the last three and a half years in Europe would have been different, that all would have gone as happily as a marriage bell. For that totally ignores European economic conditions and the fact that the infamous Treaty of Versailles is at the bottom of the present rapid collapse of Europe, and that the League is hopelessly woven into the texture of the treaty. Far more defensible is the contrary belief that if the United States were in the League, under a Harding and a Hughes, this country would have thrown its weight to the imperialists of Europe, especially to the French. Surely if Lloyd George could make no headway against the French policies there is little to make us believe that the United States could or would have done so.

A final illustration of the *World's* limping anti-imperialism is that after so bravely fighting against American conquest of the Philippines, it only recently discovered our bloody imperialism in Santo Domingo and Haiti. Yet the principle at stake and the menace to our own political and moral welfare are the same. One can only add again that the *World* limps far less than others, that it does often see some things where others are totally blind. But it was sad to see it using the alleged Kipling interview deliberately to arouse bitterness against England, and a worthless interview with the contemptible, brainless Ludendorff to increase ill-will in the United States against Germany and to play Germany and France off against each other again. This is treason to the old *World*. Can it be a deliberate policy of a recent accession to the managerial staff?

One word more: From all accounts there is much

democracy in the *World's* inner organization. With this the modesty and self-effacement of the Pulitzer brothers, Ralph and Joseph, must be duly recognized. Whether because of good taste or for other reasons, they have, thank fortune, never utilized their positions to secure political office, or to plaster their names all over their papers after the manner of Hearst, or to feather their nests. They have, if an outsider can judge aright, given free play to their editors. The shortcomings of the *World* are not due to its being controlled either by business considerations, or by any selfish dominance of the owners. It remains the nearest approach to a great liberal daily which we have in America and as such its owners and editors are deserving of high praise.

1 On March 31, 1926, the circulation of the *World* was 287,664.
2 Mr. Cobb died Dec. 21, 1923.

CHAPTER IV

FRANK A. MUNSEY, DEALER IN DAILIES [1]

"LET Munsey Kill It"—this is a slang phrase in the newspaper fraternity when report has it that some journal is nearing its end. "Good newspapers when they die go to Munsey," wrote that rare humourist, B. L. T., in the Chicago *Tribune*, while Mr. Brisbane in lamenting the recent deaths of the Pittsburg *Dispatch* and *Leader*, asked: "Where was Frank Munsey? His is the original patent on killing newspapers. You say to him as Henry IV said to the bravest man in France: 'Hang yourself, Crillon, you were not there.'" Seven years ago *Life* printed a cartoon showing a cemetery of newspapers and magazines slain by Mr. Munsey. In it were tombstones to the memory of the *Daily News, The Sun,* and the *Daily Continent,* the Philadelphia *Times* and the New York *Press;* the *Scrap Book,* the *Quaker,* and the *Puritan.* To this list *Life* should have added *Godey's* and *Peterson's,* two of the oldest American magazines, as well as the Baltimore *Star, Woman, The Live Wire, Junior Munsey,* and

63

The Cavalier, and since the cartoon appeared Mr. Munsey has merged the *All-Story Magazine* with the *Argosy,* given the *coup de grâce* to the *Railroad Man's Magazine* and the *Evening Sun,* and made the *Sun* of Charles A. Dana give forth a feeble light at night.   Just now (June, 1923) he has brutally destroyed the New York *Globe,* the oldest daily in that city and the newsiest of the metropolitan evening papers. He has also sold the Boston *Journal,* the Washington *Times,* and, quite recently, the Baltimore *American* and *News.* It has been common knowledge that he has also wanted to buy and chloroform the New York *Evening Post,* whose desperate struggle to keep alive he is presumably watching with the expectant eye of a man-eater awaiting a hapless bather whom he has cut off from the shore.

One might almost add to this mortuary record the New York *Herald,* for despite that newspaper's daily announcement that it is the "best in its history, with all that was best of the *Sun* intertwined with it and the whole revitalized," the truth is that the flavour of the *Herald* of the Bennetts has gone, as well as the strong character of the *Sun* of Dana.[2] Both newspapers had their separate, widely varying identities; both had historic traditions. The combination of them is a hybrid. It is a far better, broader, fairer and newsier daily than the narrow and mean-spirited *Tribune,*—which is a sort of decayed Henry Cabot

64

Lodge among dailies, without such abilities as he possesses—but as the *World* prophesied at the time (February 1, 1920), the amalgamation has given us neither the *Herald* nor the *Sun,* and the profession is the loser thereby. The *Sun* of today is merely the former *Evening Sun,* organ of the tired and hard-boiled business man who is satisfied with the first page of news, excellent financial departments, and the theatrical advertising, plus an editorial page one is never compelled to read for fear of missing something instructive or otherwise worth while.

The profession took the disappearance of the two most distinctive New York morning newspapers all the more to heart because most journalists were certain that both newspapers could have been restored to their old prestige even though the *Sun* had only 59,000 readers left and the *Herald* but 55,000. The truth is that Mr. Munsey is not popular in the profession—it is not hard to understand why. True, he is no more an interloper than many another merchant who has made a great success in other lines—like Cyrus H. K. Curtis, for instance. There is nothing to say against Mr. Munsey personally. Some criticism, chiefly political, has, of course, been levelled against him. But it is a fact that he is not a popular employer with his employés,[3] who change too frequently,—it used to be asked on the Philadelphia *Times,* as on the *Herald* and *Telegram* under the

65

second Bennett, "Well, who's editor today?"—and there are those who feel that his wealth is a bit new with him. The critics say, too, that he has broken every rule of journalism and that he has never created a successful daily, but only built up those which are now paying by amalgamations, by the suppressing of rivals, and by using already established newspaper reputations for his purposes. In that he reminds one of Thomas A. Edison; that great man often discovers something by trying everything which money can buy which might do the trick. Mr. Munsey frankly owns that his successes have come by trying first one style or type and then another, rather than beginning with a clear-cut mental conception of what he is after. He was the first to try a tabloid paper in New York but he failed where the "Chicago *Tribune* crowd" is now making a tremendous circulation success. He was the first to publish a Sunday afternoon paper and it succeeded —he still gives us the Sunday *Telegram* in New York. His latest experiment with the *Herald* is "a complete miniature newspaper" which is really nothing more than a summary of the news in something over a quarter of a page.

The fact remains that Mr. Munsey is today successfully merchandizing the *Sun, Herald,* and *Telegram* in New York, the Paris *Herald,* and has only just sold the Baltimore *American* and *News,* and that

66

through these enterprises and others in the commercial field Mr. Munsey has amassed great wealth. It was long believed that a good deal of this came from a fortunate placing of money in steel stocks in Wall Street, when a great many other people who had similar courage and foresight made great sums of money simply by investing in stock of the United States Steel Corporation, locking it up in their strong boxes and then selling it after a few years, when the phenomenal rise of common, in particular, gave them a tremendous profit. In his manly and straight-forward but characteristically naïve reply, on August 28, 1922, to the published charges that he made millions out of the war, that he was the worst kind of a war profiteer in munitions making, Mr. Munsey did not deny that he had been a successful investor in Wall Street prior to his entering daily journalism, but he did affirm positively that he owns no share of any Wall Street security and did not at the outbreak of the war, or during the war, and that he "had no connection, directly or indirectly, with any property or interest that lent itself to profiteering during or after the war." "I made no money whatever," he added, "directly or indirectly out of the war or anything associated with the war. On the contrary, my interests, due to the high cost of magazine and newspaper-making and the generally disturbed condition of affairs, suffered a very

67

heavy shrinkage during the war and in the inflation period after the war."

There is no reason to doubt the correctness of his statement. The great rise in steel stocks took place between 1903 and 1910 and he could easily have made a huge pile and put it away before the war came on. But the truth is that if he had never gone into Wall Street, Mr. Munsey would still be a very rich man. Thus, he has published his net earnings from his magazine ventures from 1894 to 1907 inclusive.* They aggregated for these fourteen years $8,780,905.70,—a sufficient reward to compensate most mortals for the labour put into them, tremendous as that was. True, Mr. Munsey did not state in this extremely interesting and self-revealing address how much money went into his private cemetery of unsuccessful publications, but a man who made more than a million a year from his magazines alone in 1905, 1906, and 1907, before we had the income tax, who has no expensive tastes and no wife or family, can afford a good deal of costly experimentation. More than that, not all the publications which Mr. Munsey has killed or sold were losing money. He is reported to have said more than once: "That paper is making only —— a year. That's not

* The Story of the Founding and Development of the Munsey Publishing House; a Quarter of a Century Old. By Frank A. Munsey. December, 1907.

worth while. I can't bother with it any longer. Kill it." This is all the more plausible because Mr. Munsey is an autocrat in his business affairs. He has never had a partner nor an all-dominant legal adviser nor a real board of directors to hamper him. He has never even found himself in the trying position of having to consider minority stockholders and only those who have been placed in that position can realize the freedom which the Munsey way of doing business brings with it. He has no one but himself to blame if money is lost and no one else to congratulate if the money pours in. The drawback is, however, that this fortunate position tends to make one domineering, arbitrary, and trying to work with in one's shop and that is one of the charges made against Mr. Munsey.

Curiously enough, very few of the many people who have busied themselves with Mr. Munsey's money-making have learned where a large portion of his revenue comes from. He is one of the most successful grocery men in the country for he owns the chain of Mohican Stores which are to be found in certain New York and New England cities. Some years ago a governor of New York appointed a commission to investigate the ever pressing question as to why the public is mulcted of such large sums by the middleman who operates between the producer and consumer of foodstuffs. A member of that commission informed me that they found in Frank A. Munsey the ablest merchandizer of all those whom they investigated. That is, his Mohican Stores were run with a maximum of ability and a minimum of waste; in them was the most skilful handling of goods and the greatest marketing efficiency. In every case the stores are exceptionally well placed, both as to trade opportunities and the receipt of freight, and being on the "cash and carry" principle, they are freed from the endless bookkeeping and bad debts which go with the system of charge accounts. No one can really take the measure of Munsey, the journalist, without knowing of Munsey, the merchant, for merchandizing is the key to his journalism as it is an explanation of part of his honestly earned wealth.

Then before evaluating Munsey, the journalist, one must also study Munsey, the magazine proprietor. If he takes a most ingenuous view of his own success and discusses it freely in public—he explained, in his statement already cited, that he owed his success to two things, "the forty dollars I brought with me from Maine to New York forty years ago, and the capacity God gave me for work,"—is he not entitled to do this under all the historic American canons? Is it not the pride of all America, the very life and breath of Main Street, that here in the United States a boy may rise from log cabin or tow path to enormous wealth, or to the White House? Does not the rise of a Munsey or a Cyrus H. K. Curtis or a Charles Schwab, or a Carnegie exemplify beyond all else American social freedom, the boundless opportunity before every citizen, the perfection of our social, our political, our moral, and our intellectual order, and of our beloved Constitution— to be defended with one's life-blood against the kickers and the dissatisfied, the ne'er-do-wells who haven't made a killing? From this point of view Mr. Munsey is surely entitled to much greater applause and public good will than he has received. Certainly his story has enough romance in it to make him properly a chief hero of *Success* and the *American Magazine*. In all seriousness, no one can read his story without being profoundly impressed by it. A restless, ambitious manager of the Western Union Telegraph office of Augusta, Maine, he risked his forty dollars and all he could borrow to come to New York to start a juvenile magazine. How he toiled, how he was his own office boy, bookkeeper, clerk, advertising solicitor, manager, editor, serial-story writer and all the rest, he has set forth. He has a right to be proud that in the face of incredible obstacles, his total ignorance of all publishing, his lack of training and education for the task, his scant book-knowledge, he succeeded in his aim—to publish and make money. They told me in Maine re-

71

cently that he has employed a man to look up the
family tree and to seek to deduce from it why he
alone of all the Munsey tribe should so have
achieved. That is an extravagance he can well afford. But the answer is his extraordinary pluck and
determination—and the absence of embarrassing
ideals and standards.

For the striking fact is that in his own narrative,
Mr. Munsey voices no ideal or aim save to succeed,
to publish something, juvenile or adult, weekly or
monthly, and to earn much money by so doing—he
felt he could never return to Maine unless he did.
There is not a drop of the reformer's blood in him;
there is in him nothing that cries out in pain in response to the travail of multitudes. He was never a
muck-raker. He has espoused no cause with real
fire and enthusiasm—he probably could not if he
would. He has sought power to voice no idealism,
to plead for no newer or a different day. His magazines are slight and ephemeral. No one will ever go
to library shelves for them to find out what was their
contribution to the literature, or politics, or science
of the country. They are made to entertain and to
sell and are perishable stuff. But in justice it must
also be added that Mr. Munsey seems to be without
personal ambitions. At least, in a position to demand an ambassadorship—("I suppose," said Theodore Roosevelt, of one New York editor who de-

sired the London post, "he'll knife me if I do and knife me if I don't")—Mr. Munsey has asked no political reward. He does not splurge with his wealth nor offend the conventional moralities, nor use his papers to puff himself. He has apparently no hobbies or avocations. He is usually absolutely absorbed in his business, notably in the *Herald* which is his particular pride, and he is credibly reported to feel that his position as the head of several American dailies is fully as dignified as, if not more so than that of the President of the United States. If he occasionally takes a trip to Europe he is nevertheless, it is said, the hardest working man in his offices. He personally directs all his dailies but he is not one of those unusual newspaper proprietors who are gifted with the news sense and are themselves able directors of news policies.

With this background, we come to Mr. Munsey's journalism. What else could it be but that of the contented, prosperous, *petite bourgeoisie?* It is dull, of course, because always without a spark of the divine fire. There is no editorial illumination, no vision, no passion, no real power, no quest of the millenium because, perhaps, for the erstwhile manager of the Western Union office in Augusta, Maine, the millenium is pretty well here. Just as his wealth did not go to his head, so it has not betrayed him into tilting at established social customs. The conven-

73

tional he supports and upholds, because he knows nothing else. In the war, for instance, he wanted us to go in before the country did; all his associates did likewise—and nothing ever creeps into his dailies to prove that the war was anything else but a glorious success, a one hundred per cent achievement of all the American aims with which our men entered the struggle. True, he early saw the facts in regard to the invasion of the Ruhr, and his *Herald* has told more about the truth of that mistaken move than any other daily except the *World,* but not in any way to offend. As a whole, his papers reflect the mind of the average prosperous American and his narrow, intellectual range. They are clean and respectable, both in their news-columns and in their advertising. No such salacious "stories," as occasionally slip into the *World* mar the columns of the Munsey papers. They are eminently safe, sane, and intellectually undistinguished.

Some of the editorials Mr. Munsey writes himself and it is interesting to note that as he grows older he now and then becomes almost excited over some policy which he opposes. Thus, he bravely fought the bonus for our returned soldiers, believing correctly that it would do them no appreciable good and the country much harm. A handsome pamphlet tells us that this is "Militant American Journalism" and announces that the fight of the *Herald* was "personally

74

directed by Frank A. Munsey." Another pamphlet
recites the *Herald's* most creditable fight against the
Fordney tariff and reprints a number of excellent
editorials. Its owner manfully says that he "cannot
stand for damn fool protectionism and the New York
Herald will not stand for it"—which illustrates Mr.
Munsey's willingness to part company now and then
with the Republican party—he is not supporting
Mr. Harding in the President's appeal for our support of the new world court.

In the main, however, Mr. Munsey is a regular;
he will not go back upon his own order sufficiently
to disturb seriously his business friends. He desires
plenty of foreign labour because "the wage of labour will never come down until the supply exceeds
the demand." What we need in Washington is
machinery which will "give service." America, he
surprisingly finds, "has cut loose from the conservatism of our fathers and penetrated deep into
the wilderness of radicalism!" Ere we recover from
our amazement, he adds: "This is true in our politics, in our statesmanship, in our social life, in our
business life, in our point of view in all things." In
this same address (before the American Bankers Association) Mr. Munsey declared: "America is worth
saving. If it is saved, it will be saved by you and by
men like you. . . . Nothing succeeds without ownership interest in the management." His own phil-

osophy is further apparent from this message: "Public service does not consist solely in holding public office. The organization back of public office is the public service quite the same as the Congress-man, or the Governor, or the President, for it is the organization that puts him in office. Service in the organization is fundamental and imperative in the life of a democracy."

If this seems the apotheosis of the mechanistic, re-form-your-organization-from-within creed of life, it must not be forgotten 'that Mr. Munsey and Mr. George W. Perkins were the two men who made it possible for Theodore Roosevelt to bolt from the Republican Party in 1912. He did not do so until they urged him to. To their largesse, to their busi-ness acumen and skill in organization, the extraor-dinary "Bull Moose" achievements in the summer of 1912 are considerably due. Mr. Munsey was quite ready then to go "off the reservation" and to seek to reform the Republican Party from without. Lately he has seen very clearly that the two old parties have had their day and he has been urging a union of them in order that the country should have the political line-up it desires and deserves—a liberal or radical party and a conservative. His growing interest in Senator Borah, as evidenced by the friendly attitude of his dailies towards the Senator from Idaho, (though the Baltimore *American* before he sold it called Mr. Borah "an idealist without ideals") is another sign that Mr. Munsey is still unafraid of a man who threatens to kick over the party traces. Mr. Munsey also favours one reform, direct election of the President and Vice-President, which is not popular with the group of which he sees most. Finally, no one can study the several positions he takes without wishing that Mr. Munsey could put in a couple of profitable years studying European political conditions, in reading deeply certain books which he has doubtless never touched, and in meeting all kinds and conditions of men at home and abroad. For there is so much that his press wots not of and so much going on right here at home which his reporters never see, and his editors apparently never hear! Some day a Cook's Tour into the hearts of plain America ought surely to be organized for a few hundred of our editorial writers. Mr. Munsey has himself said: "it is clearly more important that the newspapers should study deeply and seriously the needs of the poor, rather than the needs of the rich," but his editors have obviously never taken his advice. The poor are *terra incognita* to them.

Meanwhile Mr. Munsey's dailies remain on the whole as conventional and insular in every phase of life as they are respectable. Yet when I hear them severely criticized I have to confess that if a choice were necessary I should infinitely prefer them to the

New York *Times* or *Tribune* or the Chicago *Tribune*. Despite their reactionary or stand-pat tendencies, Mr. Munsey's papers are surely far less hurtful than Mr. Hearst's. In so huge a country as this every shade of opinion ought to have its. mouthpiece. Ought we not to be thankful that Mr. Munsey's conservative press is as good as it is? It is free from hatred and from bitterness; it treats an adversary with respect and it carries on no campaigns against personalities—that is not Mr. Munsey's nature. Barring the *Telegram* it is never sensational. They usually do not straddle—that is if they have no clear opinions about an issue they keep silent about it. If they are "organs of the Steel Trust," as many declare, and the "apotheosis of Main Street," they are also home papers and they evidently are meant to be reasonably free from propaganda. If they are without the ability of the London *Morning Post*, foremost of conservative dailies, and without its "punch," they are also without its snobbishness or arrogance. They are class organs, of course, as much so as our class-conscious labour dailies; but their attitude is less a deliberate assumption of policy than a reflection of what Mr. Munsey himself is. Had his background, his struggle and its results, been different they would have been different too. There is no pretence either about him or about them.

As to the circulation of his dailies, it is undeniably

sinking slowly, the *Herald* having lost 32,000 readers in the last two years (1921–23) and the *Sun* 28,000 in the last three years. The *Herald* had on April 1, 1923, 167,620 readers daily and 186,075 on Sunday, while the *Sun* averaged 177,934 in the evening. That scarlet trollop, the *Telegram,* for some utterly mysterious reason sells 111,000, or about the same number as when Mr. Munsey purchased it.[4] There is a curious fact about the *Telegram.* When Mr. Munsey bought it, it had been losing money chiefly because of its association with the *Herald* in their joint enterprise in the Herald Building at Broadway and 35th Street. It was supposed that the new owner would electrocute it. Mr. Munsey promptly divorced it from the *Herald,* moved it downtown to inconspicuous quarters and presto! it began making plenty of money. Why it should do so no one knows. During the war it was the most unblushing and rascally of the press liars about what went on abroad, being nothing else than an unprincipled French propaganda sheet. It is supposed to hold its circulation largely through suburban sales, the pulling power of its situations-wanted, exchange advertisements, and racing news. At any rate, it is doing so well that Mr. Munsey long ago gave up his idea of killing it to obtain its Associated Press membership for the *Sun;* hence his ruthless destruction of the *Globe.* Just who reads the *Telegram* and

79

why it should fill any special want, aside from those catered to by the *Post, Mail, Journal,* and *World,* is one of the mysteries of journalism. In Baltimore his dailies held their own in the face of the intense competition of the excellent Baltimore *Sun* and *Evening Sun* and gained slightly. They were of the same type and had the same policies as his New York papers, opposing graft and corruption and high taxes in the local field. But they made no deep impression upon the public.

Such an extraordinary success as Mr. Munsey has made in the magazine field will never be his in newspaperdom. He was able to claim in 1907 that *Munsey's Magazine* was then the first magazine in the world in point of circulation and earning power. His newspapers are far, far from the front rank in circulation or income. For instance, the *Herald* carried in 1922, 11,947,256 agate lines of advertising as compared to the *World's* 17,244,090 and the *Times's* 24,142,222. The *Sun* ranks better; it printed in 1922, 9,620,816 lines as compared with the *Evening World's* 8,673,406, the *Journal's* 11,789,500 and the *Globe's* 7,306,734. Mr. Munsey has various opportunities to expand largely the influence of the *Herald,* but it is doubtful whether he will see the need or the opportunity—by way of example, for a factual newspaper. The liberal field, too, calls loudly for the viewpoint of one who not

80

only endorsed but really believed in the planks of the Progressive platform. Mr. Munsey will hardly respond. The inhibitions of his early training, and of his financial success, rest upon him and block an unquestionably warm and honest desire to serve his country effectively. More than that, the fatal defect of Mr. Munsey as a journalist was admirably illustrated by his public declaration of his reasons for destroying the *Globe*. That was a purely commercial and materialistic statement such as might have been made about the consolidation of two boot and shoe stores. It was without the slightest recognition that there are such things as journalistic ideals, or public service, or the nobility of a great profession, or that *noblesse oblige*—and wealth as well. Mr. Munsey is a dealer in dailies—little else and little more.

[1] Mr. Munsey died Dec. 22, 1925.

[2] Mr. Munsey sold the *Herald* to Mr. Ogden Reid who merged it with the *Tribune*, March 17, 1924.

[3] He turned adrift ruthlessly the veterans of the dailies he killed, sometimes without even a week's salary.

[4] The circulation of the *Telegram* on March 31, 1926, was 182,489.

CHAPTER V

THE *FORWARD*, A NON-PROFIT-MAKING DAILY

WHICH is the most interesting, the most challenging, of New York's daily journals? If one should ask this question of one hundred New Yorkers and suggest that the answer involved the name of a foreign-language newspaper there would be indignant protests. A good many votes would be cast for the *World*, and the *Globe* would doubtless have run well. Yet in my judgment the truth is that the *Forward* in several ways outshines them all—and the vast bulk of New Yorkers does not even know that any such journal exists, much less that it has 200,000 readers, 140,000 to 145,000 in New York City. The reason is, of course, that it is a Yiddish newspaper and every one who is not familiar with that tongue must form his estimate of it by looking at it through the eyes of others. That is my plight; but the facts which have come to me for years past about this extraordinary phenomenon in American journalism make it plain that no student of newspaper conditions of today can fail to give it most careful study if only because of one feature.

82

While others have talked and speculated as to how the present crass materialism of the American press and its domination by those who profit most by our present economic organization can be offset by some such device as an endowed journal or one maintained and owned by great groups of workers, a band of men has worked out in New York a co-operative enterprise with extraordinary success. For the *Vorwärts*, to use its Yiddish name, does not represent a vision or an ideal toward which laborious and subventioned progress is being made; it is an established money-making concern with an extraordinary hold, not only upon the greater part of the Jewish groups in New York City but those in other cities as well. I doubt if the publishers of other American journals know much about it. They must have heard vaguely of the superb office building which it has erected on the East Side in the midst of its constituency and they must, most of them, gasp with envy when they hear that its circulation is now 200,000. But what must startle them most of all is the fact that all the net profits of this unique newspaper go not to the owners or the editors but are, under the by-laws of the Forward Association, distributed among the exponents of the causes to which the *Forward* is devoted.

That, we fancy, must cause uneasy comment on Park Row. "What can you expect of a bunch of foreign Socialists?" is doubtless the usual response.

83

But that hardly covers the case, especially in view of the fact that the editors belong to a race charged with acquisitiveness. Is it possible that when men of the faith of Shylock have the opportunity to line their pockets with huge profits honestly earned, they deliberately deny themselves anything beyond extremely modest salaries? It *is* possible. During the last ten years the *Forward* has earned one and a half million dollars, of which it has, after providing for its splendid up-to-date plant, donated $350,000 to union labour and to other causes for which it battles.[1] Its assets today are worth more than one million dollars. Often in enterprises like this the profit is distributed in large salaries and expenses; yet the editor-in-chief of this amazing publication, who is seventy-five per cent responsible for its success, recently strenuously resisted his colleagues' efforts to advance his salary to a figure which would be scorned by any city editor of one of our English-language morning dailies. But its lower-placed workers are well remunerated. Its scrub women receive $37 a week and where the reporters of English dailies are underpaid the average wage of the *Forward's* lesser employés is $62 a week (two dollars more than the minimum demanded and received by the members of the Jewish Newswriters' Union).

That tells only half the story, for the *Forward* is often a most generous benefactor to struggling talent.

84

There have been cases of foreigners of great parts
coming to this country without means who were not
only at once placed on the salary-roll but were told
that there was no compulsion upon them to write.
Genius, in their cases, did not have to labour at all
seasons; its product came when the spirit moved.
And it produced much because genius is warmed and
touched when in its hour of transplanting and of
need the hand of fellowship is held forth and the
fear of actual want banished by one wave of a golden
wand.   So the dollar motive cannot be attributed to
its conductors.   I have heard them bitterly criticized
and sometimes with justice, as in their unwarranted
and utterly unjust attack upon the Friends of Soviet
Russia, but not on the ground of their being swayed
by the personal profit motive.   In an inquiry during
the war into our foreign press an official investigator
rightly or wrongly testified that the *Forward* was
the only foreign-language daily in America which
could not be bought.   Yet it is attacked upon the
East Side as an enemy to Jewish culture and to racial
advancement.   Why?   Well, first because of the
colloquial style in which it is written and what is
called its vulgarizing of Yiddish, as well as the fact
that it is avowedly a sensational journal after the
manner of Hearst.   Its editor-in-chief frankly admits that it *writes down* to its public.

Here I must introduce this powerful American

journalist. He is Abraham Cahan, long a writer of brilliant humorous and pathetic sketches of the Jewish East Side for the old *Sun*, the *Evening Post*, and the magazines; sometime a remarkable reporter on the *Commercial Advertiser* (later the *Globe*); a novelist; a man of rare understanding of his race and of all human nature; finally, an American. He was the only one of the group which founded the *Forward* in 1897 who was able to speak English. They decided on a daily to combat the views of Daniel De Leon, whose dream of the coming of socialism envisioned only a beneficent Messiah imposing it from above, whereas they put their faith in a democratic mass movement. A couple of years of competition forced De Leon's *Arbeiterzeitung* to the wall, although the *Forward* itself progressed slowly enough until the idea of a purely Socialist propaganda organ was abandoned. Then Mr. Cahan came to the front and made it a newspaper first and only secondarily a political propagandist, though he is always a partisan and his daily, like many another, does colour its news and ignore what it does not like. Fortunately for him and his daily, his accession to the editorship was followed in 1903 by a vast increase in the Russian immigration to the United States in consequence of the Kishinev pogroms, by which immigration the *Forward* greatly profited.

Mr. Cahan has been governed by a double

standard in dealing with his public. He struck first for popularity; hence he decided to make the writing in his journal so simple that the least intelligent on the East Side could understand it. He not only adopted the colloquialisms of the Yiddish of New York, showing no hostility whatever to the introduction of English words, but employed editors to substitute in the news manuscripts the shortest words possible for the more learned ones. In his editorials he dealt with topics of the widest appeal, whenever possible a direct *argumentum ad hominem.* A famous editorial of his, urging every mother who read the *Forward* to see that her child took a clean handkerchief to school with him or her, illustrates his policy. Over this editorial there raged a storm; East Side intellectuals denounced it as insulting to their people, who, they insist, not only need no counsel as to handkerchiefs but are quite capable of understanding and appreciating the best language, the purest form of Yiddish. But Mr. Cahan felt that the learning of the learned orthodox Jews is of the narrowest. Often great Talmudic scholars are grossly ignorant of things of general knowledge and daily life which every child ought to know and his staff insists that there were and are many thousands of people, of the younger generation particularly, who need precisely the rudimentary education which the *Forward* gives. Wherever the whole truth lies, Mr. Cahan claims that

87

his success has demonstrated the correctness of his policy of stooping to the average man; his paper can swing, it is said, at least 65,000 votes at every election and he has satisfied many thousands of the aspiring who were not happy with the old type of Jewish newspaper run for private profit. His success has moreover been achieved despite his opposition to Zionism.

But Mr. Cahan's stooping to conquer did not stop with his simplifying of the language of his paper. He has imitated some of the worst of our English-language journals in his appeal for popular support, and his rivals and critics accuse him of printing the "most vulgar and the most sensational of the East Side journals" and of going to the very edge of the salacious in some of his news-matter and fiction. Such lapses as these are not to be defended in either the Yiddish or the English-language press; as already stated, Mr. Cahan admits that he sought to attract the man in the street and to do so he freely follows in the footsteps of those of his American contemporaries who have won the largest circulations. It is naturally not that which makes the *Forward* to me the most challenging American newspaper experiment, but the fact that its editors are unable to profit by the financial results of their efforts, that we have here a daily with the profit-motive eliminated. If it is true that it has opposed and vulgarized every spiritual attempt at readjustment of the Jew in America, then its critics, who include many of the East Side intellectuals, are justified in raising the question whether its rise has helped or hindered its Jewish clientele, which extends far beyond New York City. Unfortunately some of the best of our existing newspapers have begun as has Mr. Cahan, notably the New York *World* and the Scripps newspapers; the ethics of this policy are not to be approved, whether they result in a great liberal daily like the *World* or a newspaper like the *Forward* or the *Minnesota Star*. The point is that, if the cooperative, non-profit-making enterprise of the *Forward* succeeds over a term of years, it may be the most valuable contribution to the solution of the American newspaper problem made since the present era of intense commercialization of the press began.

To return to the *Forward*, Mr. Cahan has seen the circulation value of making his daily of personal service to its readers. In a recent week the *Forward* printed fourteen columns of the names of Jews in America who are being sought by their kin abroad. There is no more striking feature than its letters from readers regarding their personal problems, which letters it answers with advice and sympathy and often with financial aid—it is charged that these letters are sometimes suggestive in character and are often a lure rather than inspired by the desire for aid.

89

But aid these letters often do. Thus a girl suffering from tuberculosis of the throat received $3000 in quarters, half-dollars, and dollars from sympathetic readers of her letter to the *Forward* asking where she should go for a cure and how she could live during the treatment. Again, there have appeared from time to time extraordinary symposia bearing upon some of the vital problems of the East Side, such as the tragedy of the growing apart of immigrant parents and their rapidly Americanized children. When there is suffering on the East Side, or there are strikes which affect masses of the population such as are included in the needle trades, it is the *Forward* to which multitudes look for guidance and leadership together with financial aid out of its profits. All of this gives its critics the chance to say that it is purely materialistic and that it lowers and vulgarizes Jewish ideals even when it aids Jewish solidarity.

What is the organization behind Mr. Cahan? There is a Forward Association of two hundred members, which any member of a trades union or of the Socialist Party may join, the dues being one dollar a year. There is no stock and there are no bonds, but there is a board of management of nine of which the editor and the manager are members; the editor and the manager are elected yearly by this association. Usually the editor's complete control is never questioned; matters of policy may, however, and do occasionally come before the association. Thus there have been two recent meetings of the association to discuss the paper's attitude toward Russia and its policy toward the Jewish labour movement. In both cases Mr. Cahan and Mr. Vladeck, the manager, were sustained—they would have resigned had they not been. There is no question that there is true parliamentary government of this newspaper which is thus conducted cooperatively and democratically as well as without a profit motive, even though Mr. Cahan wields a controlling, his enemies say a despotic, influence. Surely it is not only New York's most interesting newspaper experiment, but America's, for it now has a large office in Chicago and appears daily in eleven cities for each of which there is provided a couple of pages of local news.

What pabulum does this unusual newspaper supply to its followers? Its eight pages of eight columns each (28 and 32 pages on Sundays) offer a variegated bill of fare. Pictures, of course; occasional cartoons; little of crime (about two columns a day) because space forbids more; often sensational matter said to be of questionable taste; extraordinarily valuable letters and correspondence from abroad together with a great deal of Jewish and labour news, all with Hearst-like headlines. In one week in July it carried 42 columns of exclusive letters and cablegrams from its own correspondents in Russia, Germany, Poland, Palestine, Austria, Hungary, and Rumania—throughout the war it printed much news not to be found anywhere else, among its foreign correspondents being such men as Longuet in Paris, Breitscheid, Eduard Bernstein, and Kautsky in Germany, and the leading British labour men like Arthur Henderson.   In that same week the *Forward* carried 154 columns of serious reading matter and 137 columns of what may be termed "light matter," though this does not adequately describe it, for the extraordinary fact is that while the *Forward* writes down to its readers it is said to be printing today by far the best fiction and *belles lettres* of any newspaper in America.   This is Mr. Cahan's second striking conception for his journal.   He has employed an amazing array of remarkable writers whose names are totally unknown to the English-reading public, yet they are printing real literature in the columns of this East Side newspaper.

When I visited Poland in June, 1922, I travelled from Warsaw to Vilna in the company of a staff writer of the *Forward* and felt as if I were motoring with royalty.   For whenever we stopped in a town, if only for a few minutes to get a cup of coffee, some one recognized the man who sat on the front seat with the chauffeur and in no time at all a crowd had gathered to gaze upon him whom I soon dubbed the uncrowned king of Poland. Sholom Asch, the novelist and playwright, has a following wherever Yiddish is spoken, not, of course, because of his connection with the *Forward* but on account of the renown of his pen; in several of the towns we passed through his plays were being given; he is known from one end of Germany to the other. And yet our literary world in America has only just begun to learn of the existence of this great writer who is an American citizen. But Sholom Asch is only one of a group of poets and writers who, like Jonah Rosenfeld, Solomon Levine, and Z. Libin, contribute their sketches and studies of human life, their psychological stories, or their humour to the *Forward* and add to its lustre. Best of all, the whole spirit of the paper, though printed in a foreign language, is imbued by a true spirit of Americanism. By that, of course, I don't mean the base metal which goes by the name of one hundred per cent patriotism. It is really actuated by the old American ideals of liberty and justice. Hence it was hounded by the Government during the war and harassed at every possible opportunity by the secret service. Naturally, it was not fooled by the war for a single second or by the lying propaganda and the false cries of democracy which accompanied our participation in the struggle.

Mr. Cahan's paper is not working to keep alive a foreign language in America or to delay the assimila-

93

tion into our body politic of those who support it. Its editors and backers are not worried by the thought that some day they may have to publish their journal in English for lack of Yiddish readers; indeed, they are doing everything in their power to make their readers acquire the English language. Recently the *Forward* printed fifty articles on learning English and bound them into a book for general sale. It has awarded prizes for the best essay in English by any one between the ages of fifteen and sixteen years. Indeed, I am told that it is even contemplating an English page and it has now added an excellent rotogravure supplement, the captions under the pictures being both in English and Yiddish. In short, it is a striking American newspaper in the Yiddish language. The men who write it are members of no Rotary Club and no Chamber of Commerce, and they belong to no social organization on Fifth Avenue. But they are Americans to the core; they have taught great masses of our working men how to stay organized and to lift themselves up and thereby to lift up the whole standard of American living. To multitudes they have brought hope and inspiration. And these men are Jews!

[1] 1913–1923.

94

CHAPTER VI

BOSTON, A JOURNALISTIC POOR-FARM

IF, as it has been so wittily said, Boston is the abandoned farm of American literature, journalistically it is the country's poor-farm. Nothing in Boston astonishes foreigners more than its press; nothing more clearly illustrates the passing of what was once the Athens of America. To understand in full the degradation of its dailies one must know not only the city's history, but also the extraordinary transformation which has come over the stronghold of the Puritans; one must realize that the Boston of today has comparatively little in common with that of forty years ago. A thin blue line of descendants of the colonials, who learn nothing and forget nothing, is intrenched on the Back Bay and in State Street and does its best to confront and hold back the multitudes of Irish, Jews, and Italians who today comprise the bulk of the city's population. The Puritan is yielding to the Catholic; the Catholic in turn may yield to some one else.

Now the decay of the press has naturally not been

95

due merely to the city's changed character; it has followed the press of the whole country downward. The surprising thing is that the ultra-conservatism of Boston did not retard the change, but, I am inclined to think, rather accelerated it. Perhaps the explanation is this: One of the worst faults of the Boston press is its parochial character. No other large American city has such localized newspapers. That trait comes from the Back Bay itself. Even when literary Boston was in fullest flower, its attention was riveted chiefly upon itself. It knew nothing of the rest of the country and did not wish to know anything about it. Some years ago a charming young bride from Albany, descendant of the most patrician of Dutch settlers, was taken to visit on Back Bay two of her husband's maiden aunts, then nearing their seventies. They looked upon her with mingled trepidation and wonder. "So you come from the West," said they. "Well, from Albany," faltered the guilty bride. "Well, *we've* never been further West than Worcester!" The bride felt properly crushed. To-day one reads the Boston papers and is convinced that some of its editors have never been further West than Worcester. At least they seem convinced that the more provincial they are the better for their bank accounts.

This parochial character is unquestionably at the bottom of the success of more than one Boston newspaper. About thirty years ago the Hub rejoiced in some excellent and most intelligent journals. There was the old *Post*, a fine Mugwumpian morning paper of the type of the old New York *Evening Post* and the *Springfield Republican*. Under John Holmes the *Herald* was independent, honest, and above board. The *Advertiser* personified Republican dignity, respectability, and conservatism, with the *Record* not far behind. The *Traveler* too, once had its day. But the *Post* failed, was bought up, and became, under E. A. Grozier, a particularly low but successful scarlet woman of journalism. The *Herald* fell upon hard times and bartered its virtue like any drab, actually taking the dollar-a-line bogus reports of the famous insurance inquiry in New York—a fact exposed during the inquiry by Charles E. Hughes himself. The *Record* and *Advertiser* had their ups and downs; the *Record* is honourably dead and the *Advertiser* in its old age has sunk dreadfully to being a *Hearst* tabloid picture daily after the model of the New York *News*. Others have faded out; the *American* and the *Telegram* have come in—to lower the general average still further. But of all of them it must be said that they are narrow and provincial, that from the perusal of but one or two of them can one get a clear idea of what is going on in the world of thought or follow events abroad. Aside from the *Christian Science Monitor*, which is treated

97

at length in the following chapter, they are all fatally *petit bourgeois*. They are filled with small town gossip, with the chatter of the suburbanite. Scandals, particularly of the movies, murders, defalcations— these are their long suites. They speak for a city which can endow a fine symphony orchestra, but which is theatrically merely a "one week stand" and, for all its wealth, cannot adequately support a brief season of opera. They draw their patronage from a huge, badly educated middle-class whose members are delighted with coloured supplements, are sadly devoid of true cultural ambition, but are each bent only on acquiring a house and lot, a car and a portable garage, a radio outfit, and means to go to the movies whenever the spirit desires.

It was General Charles H. Taylor of the Boston *Globe* who led the profession downward. It was also he who first understood how best to exploit the new-type residents of Boston. He built up his great journalistic success by several simple policies. He printed sensational headlines and "played up" crime. But what is a far more important explanation of his success, he issued orders that, if possible, every reader of the *Globe* must find his name in the paper at least once a year. Main Street must have its day in the journalistic court. Even today it prints long lists of "among those present" and gives pages and pages to clubs, societies, and society news, to meetings of fraternal orders—anything which makes possible the printing of names, names, and names.   In a city as self-centred as any parish, the *Globe* is as parochial as it knows how to be.   A true story of General Taylor further illumines his policy.   Being informed one day by an excited employé of the alarming news that the Boston *Herald* had engaged another London correspondent, the General exclaimed, "Then, by God, we'll have to get another in South Boston!"   Bits of European news squeeze in as best they can; one must have the American habit of superficiality to be content with its American political news.   To this must be added General Taylor's second recipe for sure success: Never say anything unfavourable of anybody in your daily if it can in any way be avoided; never give offence.   It was his desire, too, that no "story" should appear in the *Globe* whose writer could not shake hands the next day with the man about whom he had written.

That rule has long governed the *Globe*.   General Taylor adopted it not merely because it was good business, but because he was himself a simple, sweet-natured person, utterly undiscriminating, utterly conventional, utterly ignorant that there were such things as deep economic currents and terrible economic injustices.   A kindly employer, whose gentle spirit of goodwill permeated his whole printing plant and made him very popular in the Associated Press and wherever newspaper publishers or writers met, General Taylor none the less became distinctly cynical in public and professional affairs and more and more materialistic. He was typical of many an idealist who, under the spell of this extraordinary cold-blooded and materialistic period in our history, has more and more yielded to the influence thereof. He was without a vestige of a social policy or of any social understanding. With a really creative mind, he should have been a man of action instead of a publisher who owned fifty per cent of his paper—(Mr. Eben Jordan, of the Jordan Marsh drygoods store, owned the other fifty per cent)—and made money much too easily.

So this paper is the inheritance that has come to General Taylor's sons, of whom the younger, William O. Taylor, is now the head of the paper. He has inherited his father's kindly heart as well as his limited social vision. Generous and worthy, he is politically content to move on in the same old grooves. The *Globe* changes amazingly little; while it still has exactly the headlines and the cheap, splashy make-up which once made it appear the yellowest of Boston dailies, it has been so outstripped in yellowness by others that it seems almost conservative. Why should it change? It still has (April, 1923) 280,000 readers on week days and over 328,000 on Sundays,[1] and still makes considerable money. Why should it interest itself in a new and better world? Why should it be aware that the times are out of joint? Why should its owners care if it is banal and typographically cheap and ugly? Why should it do anything to make Boston journalistically little better than a Sahara?

Curiously enough, it does do something worth while; it contributes the best editorials printed in any Boston newspaper. One appears daily, over the signature "Uncle Dudley," which is always worth reading. Whether the Taylors realized at first the commercial value of editorials which give evidence of thought and brains and liberalism is questionable, but it is today true that the views of the apocryphal "Uncle Dudley" sell thousands upon thousands of copies to people who don't like the rest of the paper, but seek its editorial page as an oasis in the desert. The several men whose identity has been hidden by "Uncle Dudley," Lucien Price, the late Thaddeus C. Defriez, James Morgan, William S. Packer, and James H. Powers, form a roll of honour. In the war days, when it was dangerous to be an American loyal to his country's spiritual ideals, "Uncle Dudley" found pleasure in dwelling upon fundamentals; he wrote about the basic ideals of spiritual and moral liberty, dealing, it is true, largely in generalities, but often pointing the moral to adorn the tale, or leading up to an inevitable (sometimes almost treason-

101

able) deduction which one had, however, to make oneself. A liberal, a peace man, yes, even a mild radical, could and still can get much comfort out of "Uncle Dudley" and so I am sure, do many conservatives as well. One fancies that these writers did not have sufficient freedom to criticize any friends of the management; but when one finds the *Globe* actually printing on its first page a double-column story about a meeting on behalf of the imprisoned I. W. W., one is grateful indeed that the liberalism of "Uncle Dudley" seems to be filtering into the paper itself. Indeed, one often finds in the *Globe* the only accurate, unbiased reporting of labour troubles or of famous trials—Frank Sibley's accounts of the famous Lawrence strike were the best reporting done in New England in years and became a part of the subsequent court record.

Did the younger Taylors but realize what the public is thirsty for, the *Globe* could easily become the best journalistic influence in New England. As it is they rest on their oars and have the satisfaction of knowing that, if their ambitions are extremely limited, they have won for their paper the respect of a large section of the public which believes in the essential integrity of the *Globe*. As they are model employers, and have the merited confidence of their employés to a rare degree, so have they the confidence of their readers. Yet the *Globe* has been

sadly subservient to the great advertisers. It prints
editorial puffs of them and their doings, never crit-
icises them or allows their names to appear in any
unfavourable connection, such as shoplifting. When
Mr. Eben Jordan backed a season of opera in Boston
the *Globe's* musical critic invariably went into rap-
tures over every performance. There are many
"keep-outs" and "must-nots" in the *Globe* office!

As Hearst out-trumped Pulitzer in yellowness in
New York, so Mr. E. A. Grozier went General Taylor
one better in Boston. The *Post* can be dismissed
briefly: There are few newspapers of lower standards in America; this one has a circulation of
361,000 daily and of over 370,000 on Sundays,[2] a
great decrease from its high-water mark of 540,000.
It still pervades all New England, degrading as it
goes, destroying ideals, lowering the public taste and
familiarizing the homes of Vermont, New Hamp-
shire, Rhode Island, Massachusetts, and parts of
Maine with crimes, scandal, and the baser part of
life. It is a frankly commercialized enterprise beside which the two Hearst newspapers, the *American*
and the *Advertiser*, seem tame and respectable—
some excellent editorials creep into the former occasionally, doubtless from the pen or through the
influence of Grenville S. MacFarland,[3] an able writer
and thinker, who appears to represent Mr. Hearst in
Boston. It is, of course, beyond dispute that Mr.

103

Grozier achieved a great materialistic success in the *Post*. Those who think only of financial results have much praise for Mr. Grozier's pluck and dogged persistence in the face of tremendous obstacles. But in his news columns there has not been much effort toward that accuracy and reliability which are usually a hall-mark of the *Globe*. Indeed, the *Post's* loss in circulation is attributed by Boston newspapermen, whose judgment is worth while, to a growing public understanding of the *Post's* untrustworthiness in its news. There is but one special thing to be said in its favour: It did start out with the democratic idea of being a daily for the man in the street, upon the sound theory that "a man's a man for a' that."

As for the Hearst papers in Boston, they differ not a whit from the others of the group. That the once entirely staid and sober *Advertiser* should now be Mr. Hearst's first tabloid pictorial daily is truly the irony of fate and is in many respects a measure of the low estate which the whole Boston press has reached. For some excellent policies the Hearst papers have stood in Boston, as elsewhere; notably in the matter of the street railways. Their managers believe, moreover, that it is in their editorial liberalism or radicalism that their strength lies. They will demonstrate to you that the chief sensationalism of the Boston *American* lies in its headlines; that if

you were to eliminate those, a daily comparison would
show that there is less of the bizarre, the scandalous,
and the sensational than appears in the *Post* and the
new evening paper, the *Telegram.* This statement
is doubtless correct; but what a light it casts upon
Boston journalism that two dailies actually out-
Hearst Hearst! As for the *Telegram*, it has been
started by a Lynn newspaper owner, F. W. Enwright,
who angles for the Irish Catholic vote and fantasti-
cally claims a sale of much more than 100,000 copies.
Despite its streaks of liberalism it adds nothing of
value; scandals, crime, and sensations are its stock
in trade, and its probable early disappearance should
not be the occasion for any tears. Hearst's Boston
American has (April, 1923) a circulation of
238,592; the *Advertiser*, which has a small week-
day circulation, sells 481,029 copies on Sundays.[4]

When one turns to the Boston *Herald* and its editor, Robert Lincoln O'Brien, one comes upon the
greatest disappointment in Boston journalism. Yet
one must ask oneself whether, given the ownership
of the *Herald* as it was when Mr. O'Brien took hold,
any other outcome was possible. A Harvard graduate, private secretary to President Cleveland during
his second term, and then for years Washington correspondent of the *Transcript*, and later its editor,
he had a wonderful opportunity open before him
when asked to take over the general direction of the

105

Herald. True, the paper was then deliberately venal (as proved by Charles E. Hughes in the insurance investigation) and was losing so much money that its rich owners, who have at times included Senator W. Murray Crane, the New York, New Haven and Hartford Railroad, some of the United Shoe Machinery Company group, and Morton F. Plant, were sorely tried by its plight. These big-business men and corporations were unquestionably a barrier to the making over of the *Herald* into a free and independent daily, but it was supposed that if Mr. O'Brien accepted the task of rehabilitation he would secure for himself a charter of liberty. It speedily appeared that if the *Herald* no longer accepted one-dollar-a-line, bogus news, Mr. O'Brien, too, had sold himself to the god Success. He was determined to do all he could to make the *Herald* rich and prosperous; the efforts of the staff have succeeded. It is becoming rich. Its joint circulation with its evening edition, the *Traveler,* is now 239,000.[5] It printed in 1921 more "national" advertising (that is general announcements as opposed to advertising of local origin) than any other daily. Mr. O'Brien, who receives a percentage of the earnings, is believed to draw now about $100,000 a year for his services and he is also a stockholder.

But the *Herald,* for all that it bears a fair face and is typographically the best of the Boston papers, after the *Transcript,* is false behind its pleasing aspect. It is still a creature of the big corporations; it is subservient to the big advertisers. Nor is it always quite square in its advertising. A couple of years ago it joined in the general abuse of Joseph Pelletier, the former District Attorney of Boston, for not punishing or interfering with the perpetrators of the Emerson Motors swindle. But while properly berating Pelletier, it failed to state how many thousands of dollars had gone into its treasury for the extensive Emerson Motors advertising in its columns through which many dupes lost their savings. During the war the *Herald* refused to carry out a contract for publishing a perfectly proper advertisement urging the public to purchase only necessaries—evidently the dry-goods stores forbade it—for which breach of contract the *Herald* paid five hundred dollars. Mr. O'Brien, as editor, personally equipped with letters of introduction a gang of blackmailing advertising solicitors who sold to prominent people rotogravure pictures of themselves at $400 the half-page until these solicitors tried it upon Morton F. Plant—then a chief owner—himself. Its book reviews and its criticisms are suited to its advertisers—it even at one time ruled automobile accidents off the front page on Mondays to oblige the motor car advertisers. Once the *Herald* actually printed the headline "[Governor] McCall and Moxie at Barn-

107

stable Fair"—the Moxie Company was a big advertiser.

The *Herald* is without a soul, and is ruled by fear. Whereas General Charles H. Taylor's policy of offending nobody was in part due to his own kindly philosophy, with the *Herald* it is business, pure and simple. Not that it is without people to berate. Dear, no! It can lambaste the radicals, Sacco, Vanzetti, W. Z. Foster, Lenin, Trotzky, the pro-Germans, and the German people, yes, even Samuel Gompers, to the King's taste. Upon all unpopular ones, especially those who aim at the present economic order, its blows fall thick and fast. It is one of the institutions that State Street swears by; it gives the powers that be the comforting assurance that business will go on as usual, that all this rubbish about a new social and political order will disappear before such sound logic, effective argumentation, and true Americanism as appear in the *Herald* and *Transcript*. True, the *Herald* does relapse a bit now and then into a reminder of O'Brien's Clevelandism. But he is safe and sane, he can always be relied upon to go with the crowd in times of stress; his conventionalism is beyond overturning, and—well, what else would you in a big-town editor? If he sees to it that nothing ever appears in his columns to rile those who belong to the Chamber of Commerce crowd or those who control advertising, why that's good, sound, common sense, isn't it? You don't go out to offend those people from whom you expect to draw your income, do you? No, siree—not if you know which side your bread is buttered on.

Then Mr. O'Brien has the good sense to stick by his friends. Loyalty, loyalty, and again loyalty. Sometimes, however, this leads to amusing complications. There was Mr. X, for instance. Coming to Mr. O'Brien's sanctum one day he explained, with some embarrassment, that a publication would be made about him in the next few days and he did *so* hope that the *Herald* would deal kindly and gently with him. Mr. O'Brien assured him that it would; he could safely leave the matter in his, O'Brien's, hands. The visitor departed, plainly much relieved. Mr. O'Brien, about to go off for a few days of vacation, left orders that not one single word should appear in the *Herald* in his absence about his friend, Mr. X. Three days later, the news of Mr. X's honourable appointment to a high Federal office in Boston duly appeared in all the Boston newspapers except the *Herald!* Not until Mr. O'Brien returned could the lips of the loyal staff of the *Herald* be unpadlocked. The curious thing about it all is that Mr. O'Brien did not have to sell himself so cheaply and does not today.

If loyalties, as Mr. Galsworthy, as well as Mr. O'Brien, shows, can lead us far astray, I think the

109

Herald typifies only a bit more strongly than the other Boston papers the slavish adherence to convention and sham which distinguishes the whole of that parochial press. Take that midget statesman, Calvin Coolidge, Vice-President of the United States, for instance. Every honest Boston journalist knows the true inwardness of the police strike and how little, if any, credit Mr. Coolidge really deserves for his part in it. I happened to be sitting among the Massachusetts journalists at the Chicago convention when Mr. Coolidge was nominated as Vice-President. Their astonishment and their disgust were amusing to witness. Returning later to the Congress Hotel I found two of the most influential editors in New England in excited conversation about Mr. Coolidge's nomination. Never have I heard more vigorous profanity; each sought to outdo the other in his epithets. "Never," said the elder, "in years of political experience have I met a man in public life so despicable, so picayune, so false to his friends as 'Cal'!" I marvelled still more when I read the dispatches those two gentlemen sent to their respective dailies, for they were full of congratulations to Massachusetts upon the honour done to her and to Mr. Coolidge for this magnificent national recognition of his splendid services to his State, his admirable personal qualities, his statesmanlike vision, etc., etc. As they had kept up the fiction about

110

"Cal" during the police strike, so they have kept it up since, while rejoicing in their hearts that Mr. Coolidge is in Washington and not in the State House on Beacon Hill.

Somehow one cannot escape the feeling that this incident is characteristic of a good bit of the Boston press. It builds an unreal world for itself, peoples it with supermen of its own creation, and of its own kind, and lives with them. The Boston dailies are the deliberate slaves of convention. In all their technique they have originated nothing. They merely copy their Sunday graphics, coloured supplements, comic strips, sporting pages, and auto write-ups from the metropolitan daily press. Everything is, however adapted to the peculiarly suburban city which Boston has become. It is a curious fact in this connection that the morning edition of the *Globe* circulates chiefly beyond a radius of thirty miles from the city, while the evening edition's sales are within the city and its immediate suburbs.

Finally, there is the *Transcript,* staid, dignified, the personification of reaction and conservatism, catering to the business men whose minds are closed and to the Back Bay conservatives, male and female, whose horizons are as limited as their prejudices are unnumbered. Where the *Globe's* readers are hungry for new ideas and open-minded, the *Transcript's* are of the Brahmin caste whose broadcloth ancestors

111

mobbed Abolitionists and resented any interference with the slave trade or slavery because it might affect their dividends. For such as these the *Transcript* is beyond praise and it must, in all justice, be set forth that the *Transcript* is in many respects an excellent news-purveyor. Its criticisms of books, plays, art, music are excellent; they are free, honest, often very able; some people rate them higher than those of any other American daily. Certainly the *Transcript* gives a more comprehensive view of musical news and progress the world over than any other American newspaper. It does endeavour to keep up Boston's interest in things intellectual and it has been rewarded by a slow but sure circulation growth—it sells 34,000 [6] daily except when it jumps on Saturdays to 55,000. It knows well how to cultivate its little field intensively, for it has steadily improved its Saturday supplements and its numerous departmental features which do much to draw to it the interest of special groups and to add to its unquestionably great prosperity. It knows, too, the value of names, and no other paper makes more effective use of personal and society gossip and the great New England interest in genealogy, history, the hereditary patriotic societies, etc.

Had the *Transcript* the right kind of spiritual, intellectual, and political leadership it would have to be ranked very high in American journalism. But

112

it, too, is in its viewpoint parochial, narrow, nationalistic, extremely prejudiced, and filled with the spirit
of caste. It is a violent partisan; its defence of the
old order stops at nothing, and its editorial page and
often its news columns are poisoned by bitterness
and hate. Why should such a spirit of venom invariably distinguish our reactionaries, our defence
societies, all the self-appointed saviours of the
society of today? The reformers, schooled in defeat, usually seem happy, cheerful, without spleen.
Whether it is a consciousness in the other crowd that
in the long run they will lose their fight, as the
Northern defenders of slavery lost theirs, which so
embitters them, or whether there is some other reason for it, there is a personal bitterness in your em-
battled conservative which is not confined to the breed
in the United States—one thinks at once of the British drawing-rooms in which noble ladies drew their
skirts around them and left in haughty disdain during home rule days if Mr. Gladstone chanced to
enter. This spirit the *Transcript* personifies—is it
not the nearest approach to the London *Morning Post*,
guardian of the court calendar and adored of the
aristocracy, which we have in America? It is one
of the best little haters in this country and it increas-
ingly finds in Henry Cabot Lodge and his works the
true American ideal. As for any one who dares to
dissent—out with him!

113

There is no news conventionality which it ever violates. All the British and French propaganda during the war found its way into the *Transcript;* no lie about Russia is too stale for its retailing, for it the French politicians are still saints, pure and undefiled —and the Turks fiends in human form. Fortunately for its readers its news headlines are no longer quite so coloured as during the war when it was one of the worst adulterators of news that we had. Not content with partisan writing of headlines it began its stories with a "news-lead" badly coloured, so that when you got to your news you were bound to read it wrong. It still lies and still misrepresents, as in its recent insistence that the American Committee for the Relief of Russian Children has some intimate relationship with Communist organizations. It deliberately distorted President Harding's stinging rebuke to the railroad presidents who refused to make peace with their striking shopmen by putting these entirely false headlines over the President's statement: "Should End Shop Strike; President Harding Tells the Union Officials; Blames Strike for Prevailing Coal Shortage; Also for Unsatisfactory Railroad Conditions; Continuance on Some Roads Without Reason." Who would dream that this was else than an attack on the unions? Justice it cannot, even today, attempt to do toward any liberal or radical— it has recently printed a series of articles on the Red

114

menace to America which for misinformation and distortion outrank almost any similar feat in our journalism, and it has presented the other side only in response to protests. Naturally it is imperialistic, jingo, for a large army and navy and a big National Guard. Any labour union is anathema— if the beggars make too much trouble give them bayonets. In short, if it rested with the *Transcript* the United States would progress only if and when it had the permission of State Street to do so.

Of George S. Mandell, who has been for many years the moving spirit of the *Transcript,* it has been said that "his personal ideals are bounded by the heavens and his social sympathies by his elbows." He has the highest personal standards and is so truthful and honourable that it makes the *Transcript's* lapses all the more curious and censurable. But his standards are all conventional; one thinks of him instinctively as a Tory squire. His personal tastes have fitted in well with his journalistic rôle for he has been an excellent and a fearless horseman and good at other outdoor sports. Somehow it is hard to think of Mr. Mandell except with pity. He did his uttermost to get us into the war, himself marching in preparedness parades. When the war came it cost him a gifted and gallant son. Ill health has pursued him and, worst of all, the war has come and gone and has left the world in a far worse state

115

than it was, while he sees the social order of which he is such a valiant upholder menaced as never before. Much has turned to ashes in his hands! He sees Socialists behind every tree; for him Bolshevists people every shadow, and so he prints lurid and unfounded articles in which all who have a shade of liberalism are portrayed as enemies of their country. I have no doubt that his fears are real to him. But what curious conception of the strength of this country, of the security of its foundations and its institutions, must such as he have when they are so terrified by a mere handful of skulking Communists, by a Socialist Party almost devoid of leaders, split asunder, losing ground almost everywhere, and polling only 41,000 votes in the last Chicago mayoralty election (April, 1923)! These fears are shared by Mr. Mandell's editor, James T. Williams, who has out-Mandelled his chief in making the *Transcript* the most hateful, viperish, and reactionary paper in the United States.[7]

The trouble with the Mandells and their editors is that they know no history or have forgotten what they knew. Forgotten are the witch-hangings at Salem; forgotten the fact that no charge (save, perhaps, the lie as to the nationalization of women) has been brought against the Russians which was not brought against the French Revolutionists. They have forgotten in their fury over the judicial killing

116

of Vicar-General Butchkavich and the expropriation of church property that it is only seventeen years ago that the French Republic, whose decoration Mr. Mandell wears, expelled the French nuns and monks from France, deliberately stealing millions of dollars of property of the Catholic Church without a cent of reimbursement therefor. They forget that all revolutions have their period of bloody excesses and that they inevitably slough off their extreme doctrines and leave a residue of gain for humanity. They even forget the chronicle of Evangeline and it is needless to say that they would turn upon the French people with fury similar to that with which they treat Russia if a radical revolution should come to pass on French soil. The French would then also become fiends in human form.

Then our reactionaries of the *Transcript* type are utterly devoid of humour. How else could they denounce American Socialists and clasp to their bosoms the Briands and Vivianis, Millerands and Barthous, Socialists all? And Clemenceau! That artful dodger's pure anarchist doctrines, long spread all over France, would set the *Transcript* to howling for twenty years in prison if they were to be printed over the name of a dweller in America. Instead, it adores a man who is now a double-dyed Socialist, who would perforce be an ally of Eugene Debs were he a resident in America—unless his socialist views

117

are to go the way of his vermilion anarchist ones. Well, every country must, we suppose, have its intellectual cave-dwellers and so the *Transcript* has a reason for being—and those that like that kind of paper have every reason for being content with it.

This then is the daily newspaper menu of Boston, chief city of New England, foremost inheritor of the Puritan tradition, and, in the eyes of many, predestined conservator of the ideals of the Revolutionary Fathers. Worshippers of the Revolution of 147 years ago, the foremost concern of the Boston editors of to-day is the prevention of any further revolution. The mould of 1776 to 1789 is perfect; it must never be either smashed or modified. And hand in hand with this fiat goes the incessant truckling—for pennies— to the baser passions. To the credit of the Boston press—excepting the *Transcript*—it must be recalled that in war-time, of all the large city dailies, they were the most reasonable and the most tolerant, and did less to arouse war hate than any similar group. None the less, here is no triumphant journalistic democracy, but the most perfect abnegation by the press as a whole of sound, liberal leadership. Boston is a journalistic poor-farm whereas it ought to be the abode of editors to winnow the choicest fruits of the rich, scarcely touched, soil of our American democracy.

118

BOSTON, A JOURNALISTIC POOR-FARM

[1] On March 31, 1926, these figures were approximately the same.

[2] On March 31, 1926, the circulation of the *Post* was 377,443 for the daily, and 349,596 for the Sunday.

[3] Mr. MacFarland died Feb. 28, 1924.

[4] On March 31, 1926, Hearst's Boston *American* had a circulation of 243,721; the Sunday circulation of the *Advertiser* was 502,565.

[5] On March 31, 1926, these figures were 250,463.

[6] The circulation for the daily on March 31, 1926, was 35,391, and for the Sunday edition 55,885.

[7] Mr. Williams has now become editor of Hearst's Boston *American*—to the *Transcript's* gain.

CHAPTER VII

THE *MONITOR*, A CHRISTIAN DAILY

FOUNDED in 1908 "to injure no man but to bless all mankind," the *Christian Science Monitor* appears to the average "live-wire" journalist to be a daily, but not a newspaper. Why not? When the *Titanic's* sinking furnished the press with the greatest "story" that ever came from land or sea prior to the World War, the *Monitor* never mentioned the name of a single one of the 1500 men and women who died. All this evening newspaper could do was to publish the names of those who were saved. Record the dying of poor man or millionaire, wife or widow, it could not. Death must go unrecorded. In the *Monitor's* code it was not fit to print.

So you find in that daily no story of a train wreck, no mention of an automobile accident, no record of the sinking of an ordinary steamer. You may lose your best friends in the Knickerbocker Theatre collapse in Washington, or have a vital stake in the Argonaut mine disaster, so long drawn out, but you will learn little of either from the *Monitor*. So terrible and tragic a happening as the massacre in Herrin is reduced to a mere record, though the "passing" of Rathenau, because of its effect upon European politics, and the tragedy of Shackleton's death on his voyage into the mundane unknown, because of its scientific interest, may have a column on the front page. During the war the *Monitor* spoke of "terrific casualties" and "colossal human sacrifices"; and sometimes one learned that in war there are killed and wounded—chiefly by act of the wicked enemy. Atrocities, curiously enough, one learned of—that is, the enemy's atrocities, of course.

If you wish to advertise in the *Monitor* you will learn that there are still other inhibitions. Tea and coffee, doubtless because instruments of the Evil One, liquor, tobacco, medical or hygienic articles, life, accident, and health insurance may not be offered to its readers through its columns. You may lose your pet police dog or find some one else's gold watch, but you can not advertise either fact in the *Monitor*, not at any price. Rouge and powder, henna and peroxide are as forbidden as an offer to apply a "permanent wave." You cannot call for agents, or offer jobs to nurses (or to salesmen on a *commission* basis), or print anything in your advertisement that suggests that there may be a connection between life and weather conditions—which would seem to bar the lightning rod and storm-proof Kansas cellars.

120

As for the rest, all the tests applied by the most conservative dailies are also in force in the *Monitor* office. No "blue sky" advertising is possible, no suggestion of "sacrifice" or "fire" sales and no "catch-line" sensationalism; its columns are the cleanest of the clean and its business announcements about as strictly limited to the bare facts as those of the New York dailies in 1805. You cannot even advertise a camp or school until it has been established for two years, and you can't slip it in under any pretext if you suggest that special emphasis is laid in your camp upon hygiene or religious training. Of such is the kingdom—of the *Monitor*.

So this journal *is* a Christian daily, if avoiding all mention of crime, scandal, death, misery, and vice constitutes one. But its claim to that title rests on securer foundations. It carries into its columns and into its editorials a truly Christian spirit, a desire to help, to benefit, and to improve. It aims with much success to be sweetly reasonable with wrongdoers, to give offence as rarely as possible. It tries to give full credit to the other man's motives. In its news columns it seeks to present accurately and fairly the things it is permitted to report. It is proud of its staff of correspondents and its correspondents are proud of it. Dr. Herbert Adams Gibbons, one of its numerous non-Scientist correspondents abroad, has said of it that he was happy to write "for the one

great newspaper in America that had a world vision,
whose policy is to cover the entire world and to present the news of the world. . . . I mention the *Monitor* because it is this conception of journalism that
is the hope of the world." Upon none of these correspondents has the *Monitor* laid any restrictions.
Much of its correspondence is of great value—the
editors of *The Nation* are happy to acknowledge their
indebtedness to it for much that has been significant
and illuminating, for news that has sometimes appeared in the *Monitor* exclusively, or far ahead of
its appearance elsewhere. Not, of course, that all
this material has been of fine quality and distinction; there have been considerable padding and
rewriting long after the event. The salient and striking fact is that the *Monitor*, unlike so many of its
contemporaries, seeks to place its foreign correspondence on the level of that of the best English
newspapers, and to give an intelligent survey of what
is happening in all parts of the world. It keeps its
news standards up and calls upon its readers to rise
to them.

Nor does it cast a Christian Science hue over all
that it writes. Indeed, I think it must be said that
it attempts to proselytize extraordinarily little.
Every day it carries on an inside magazine page
called the Home Forum a column of Christian Science
propaganda, which also appears about once a week in

German and in French. For the *Monitor* has a remarkable international circulation in which as "an international daily newspaper" it delights—its international aim is quite as significant as the fact that the *Monitor* is the organ of Christian Science. Not more than one or two newspapers, if any, print so much foreign news; it prints more than any other newspaper if we leave out those like the Philadelphia *Public Ledger* which have their own syndicates, and it claims that it prints more cable news than either the New York *Times* or the *Public Ledger*. It never buys or sells syndicate matter, because of its widespread circulation; it feels that it would be a drawback to have a subscriber in Los Angeles read dispatches of a news service that had already appeared in a Los Angeles daily. Indeed, the *Monitor* has to conceive of itself as almost more of a daily magazine than a newspaper—that is, its editors have to consider how their editions will read from six to twelve or eighteen days after publication. Its managers are proud of the fact that they have between twelve and fifteen thousand readers in California and ten thousand in Great Britain, that they sell more papers in Chicago than in Boston, and that 10 per cent of their readers are non-Scientists.

The *Monitor* is read by clergymen of various denominations because of the cleanness of its columns and the extent of its news. To some people it seems as if it did not cover domestic news so well as foreign. But if it has correspondents all over the world —a "space" correspondent, for instance in every German town—a bureau in London with twelve on the editorial staff, and special representation in Berlin, Tokio, and other capitals, it has also a well-manned New York office with a dramatic, an art, and a musical critic attached to it—few American dailies take the stage, the concert hall, and the art museum so seriously. It is only an accident in a sense that brought about the *Monitor's* publication in Boston. It might just as well be printed anywhere else; indeed it is the hope of the Christian Science Church that some day there may be other *Monitors* in this country and abroad. This one appears in Boston because it is the property of the trustees of the Christian Science publishing committee, and is directed by the directors of the First Church of Christ Scientist in Boston, which is the "mother church." These directors have decreed that the *Monitor* shall be independent in politics; the editor meets with this board once a week to discuss with them general policies, but I am assured that, within the limits of the general conception of what the *Monitor* ought to be and the restrictions placed upon it by the Christian Science creed, the editor has full liberty of expression. Certainly no director has protested because in politics the *Monitor* often believes

124

that discretion is the better part of valour, or because in the Massachusetts campaign of 1922 the *Monitor* was entirely silent upon the candidacy of Henry Cabot Lodge.

While its typographical make-up is well constituted and handsome, there is a sameness about the *Monitor* and, perhaps, a lack of virility in its type. At least it does not make so favourable an impression on the average reader as does, for instance, the Baltimore *Sun*. It is not possible to agree with Sir Charles Frederick Higham, who declares that it is the best-printed newspaper in the world. But the *Monitor* is never sloppy, is abundantly and often handsomely illustrated, and it gives excellent business and sporting news. It has wisely refrained from being lured into a Sunday issue and the abomination of pages and pages of special Sunday articles with picture supplements.

The best known of the editors of the *Monitor* was Frederick Dixon,[1] who took charge in 1914. He is English born and bred and a journalist of distinction. I know it is said that any one could make a success of a journal which had behind it the approval and support of so great a power as Christian Science. But the reading of the *Monitor* has never been made obligatory by the Church, it has not been used as an official journal, its circulation has never yet gone above 140,000, and it sells poorly upon the news-

125

stands, the bulk of its support coming from annual subscriptions. Mr. Dixon's achievement in building up the *Monitor* must therefore not be underestimated; it was a noteworthy journalistic feat. But it must also be said that it was unfortunate for the *Monitor* to have been in his hands during the early years of the World War, for he could not overcome his pro-British proclivities. During that period he did not hold the scales even, nor did the *Monitor* live up either to the ideals which it set for itself or to what seem to be the principles of Mrs. Eddy's church. True, that organization itself failed when it was subjected to the test of fire.

How a church with its doctrines can take any other attitude than one of absolute opposition to all war I cannot understand. What is the use of ignoring the existence of such a thing as death, of withholding support from health campaigns, and from the great movements to apply science to clean up and sanitate great areas of the world, on the ground that sickness is a state of mind and can be overcome by the individual will, if you then give yourself over to wholesale support of a war in which ten millions are killed and heaven knows how many more are tortured by suffering which no amount of will power or ignoring of physical fact can overcome? To read the war-time editorials that appeared in the *Monitor*, which was intended to injure no one and "bless all mankind," makes one wonder how it was that the bottom did not drop out of the church when its authorities laid down the doctrine that opposition to the war as war was "merely an academic objection to the use of the sword." Think of it! The church which objects to advertising lightning rods, rouge and face powder, tea and coffee, sees nothing else than an "academic objection" to the greatest evil on earth, to that combination of murder, rape, and pillage which kills and maims in a couple of days more human beings than Christian Science can aid in decades! In swinging the *Monitor* to support of our entry into the war, Mr. Dixon was only keeping step with his church. But when the war was over, and people looked back upon his course, it was surely wiser to supplant this able, yes, brilliant, journalist who had achieved so much with a more old-fashioned American.

In fairness it must, however, be added that Mr. Dixon's retirement was chiefly involved in the schism which came from the quarrel between the directors of the church and the trustees of the publishing society as to the control of the latter. Mr. Dixon strongly sympathized with the trustees and refused to come out in his paper on the side of the directors; on this as on so many issues the *Monitor* took no position. The quarrel was, however, almost a death blow to the *Monitor,* for its splendid circulation of

140,000 fell away to less than twenty thousand. On February 1, 1922, there were only 17,500 readers; since that time the circulation has grown by leaps and bounds, and it is now over ninety thousand.[2] It is fully expected that within two years it will reach 250,000, in which case it will become an enormously profitable newspaper. The changed aspect of things is due to the settlement in the courts of the dispute within the church and the loyal acceptance of the decision by the defeated element. Credit must, however, also be given to the new editor, Mr. Willis J. Abbot, an old-time liberal of many associations in former years with men of the type of Henry D. Lloyd of Chicago and Governor Altgeld of Illinois. There is great difference of opinion, however, as to whether the *Monitor* is as interesting and able today as when Mr. Dixon conducted it, and there does not seem to be even a consensus of opinion as to whether it is more or less "plutocratic" than it was.

As for its editorial policy, it is making a superb fight for prohibition with almost daily articles of great value; it opposed the Daugherty strike injunction, criticized the new tariff, Newberryism, the bonus, and, very mildly, the ship subsidy proposal; it supports naval disarmament. It writes of "feudalism in the coal fields" but shows little sympathy for either railroad or mine strikers. It is quite friendly to the Negro and urges the immediate passage of the Dyer Anti-Lynching Bill. It is excited over the alleged atrocities and the aggressions of the Turks. It opposes child labour and favours the public control of transit lines. Its love of free speech is a bit dubious, for it approved the interruption of Scott Nearing's lecture at Clark University by President Atwood, just as during the war it was bitter in its denunciation of Eugene Debs. It must be added, however, that it favours the granting of amnesty to political prisoners.

On the whole, a survey of the editorial page shows a well-meaning, rather enlightened, but, as I have pointed out above, not an aggressive editorial vein, and one not intended to hurt people's feelings—which ought to conduce to satisfaction on the part of that portion of its readership which likes mild meat. Whether this "pussy-footing" is inseparable from all group control or not is a question. As it is, the *Monitor* today offers the best example of a journal owned by a group which we have yet seen in this country. But for all its high technical standards and its ideals it is far from being the perfect newspaper. Nor can it become that while it is so hopelessly enmeshed in its Christian Science inhibitions which prevent it from giving all the news and make it colour a good deal of that which it prints. But because it is the organ of a society established upon an ethical basis; because it has such ready-made bases

129

of support; because it is entirely without the profit-motive and beyond the lure of dividends; and because it has conceived its mission to be international, it is one of the most interesting and vital of contemporary journalistic experiments. It cannot be overlooked by any one who seeks an answer to the riddle which reads: What is to be the newspaper of the future and how can it be kept free from that commercial control which has so degraded the press of today? Even with the disadvantages of its church ownership, the *Monitor* stands far above the usual American daily in both manners and morals. In the hide-bound conservatism, sensationalism, and general rottenness of Boston's press, it shines as the one bright star and is in great degree commensurate with the Hub's reputation for knowledge and intellectual tastes.

Finally, the *Monitor's* editorial policy has grave drawbacks if one aims to improve conditions in the world. At least observers may well question whether this theory of speaking softly about one's opponents, about policies with which one does not agree, achieves as much as that of the man who writes with a flaming pen, who strikes hard and swiftly and repeatedly at his opponents, who cries out with emotion and passion against human injustice, wrongdoing, and wickedness. As to which is the more effective method of bettering the world there will

130

be, I suppose, a difference of opinion as long as
mankind exists. The debate waxes strongest, perhaps, over the influence of the anti-slavery agitators,
who are usually criticized for having been too violent
in their denunciations, although the fact is that they
did so sear and burn the conscience of the American
people that within their lifetime those agitators saw
the triumph of principles which no one thought could
be made the law of the land within a century. So
when I hear the *Christian Science Monitor* criticized
as having too tame an editorial page, as lacking lights
and shadows, I wonder if it is not due to its having
the defects of its qualities, or rather its policies. To
be soft-spoken is noble and generous, but it does not
thrill, nor interest, nor stir readers as does the editor
who, from time to time, gives rein to the indignation
that is within him. Certainly Christ knew how to
reach the heights of criticism and denunciation, and
the *Monitor* will probably suffer in the long run if it
does not take sides more ardently. I am hopeful
that in the future struggle between the two great
groups of thought in America, between the powers of
privilege and the masses of the people, its voice will
be heard on the side of the masses rather than of the
privileged. But admirable newspaper as it is, excellent as are its ideals, great as is the service it is
going to render in proving that an absolutely clean,
dignified, and honest newspaper can be made a tre-

mendous financial success, I fear it is long going to to be classed as "somewhat colourless," "rather dull," and "monotonous," and that it will be without the shining edge of the sword of the Apostle.

[1] Mr. Dixon died Nov. 24, 1923.
[2] On March 31, 1926, the circulation of the *Monitor* was 104,314.

132

CHAPTER VIII

THE BALTIMORE *SUNS*, A NOTABLE JOURNALISTIC RESURRECTION

THERE are two Baltimore *Suns*—the morning and the evening—and it behooves any one who writes about them to distinguish very carefully between them. Otherwise he is apt to get a letter from an Argus-eyed person, Murphy by name, and managing editor of the *Evening Sun* by profession, to remind him that they are separate entities and that of all *Suns* wherever published the Baltimore *Evening Sun* is "incomparably the greatest," like the navy that Woodrow Wilson was once determined to wish upon the United States.

But, *pace* Mr. Murphy, it is the morning *Sun* about which one thinks first. "Do you realize," said some of the British correspondents to their American friends at the Washington Conference on the Limitation of Armaments, "what a fine newspaper you have in the Baltimore *Sun?*" The question was luke-warmly answered in the affirmative—had not that paper always been respectable, dull, and ultra-con-

133

servative? But it served the purpose of making men
who had not followed the morning and evening editions of this venerable Maryland institution pay some
fresh attention to it. Forthwith they found that the
Baltimore Sun had undergone a resurrection, taken
on new life, and become a vigorous and able newspaper. Evidences of this were to be found on every
page. Its editorials showed appreciation and understanding of what was going on at the Conference and,
what was for the European correspondents still more
surprising, much editorial knowledge of the actual
forces at work abroad. Thus the criticisms of the
Conference were intelligent and reinforced by that
rarity in our American editorial writers—a background of past history. The morning Sun's readers
were treated to something else than a mere indiscrim-
inate extolling of the achievements of the Conference.

Still more striking was the way both newspapers
handled the actual news of the Conference. Here
were intelligence and thought. Where the New York
newspapers "over-played" the story, especially by
massing four or five solid pages of Conference news
and gossip, the Baltimore Sun gave some space on the
first page to the most striking news of the Conference
and then placed its special articles in different portions of the paper, notably on the editorial and opposite editorial pages. More than that, the headlines
were modest and accurate and the news in every way

134

so well handled and edited that a quick perusal for an intelligent understanding was made easy. And then it speedily appeared that this old-fashioned journal was printing so many exclusive stories that a journalist had to read it to be sure of being up to the minute on the Conference news. Particularly valuable was the *Sun's* daily dispatch from London, from one of its most trusted editors, giving a full résumé of British and French reaction to the previous day's news from Washington.

A cursory study immediately gave one the impression that all this was not accidental, and inquiry confirmed this. The management early became convinced that it would not only be a patriotic duty to "cover" the Conference well, but that it might make a real contribution to the Conference itself besides bringing to the attention of visitors from other portions of the United States and from Europe the fact that the *Sun*, like the Philadelphia *Public Ledger*, aims to be a national newspaper with a worth-while and perhaps even authoritative opinion upon international affairs. So the president and vice-president of the company went abroad months before the Conference to lay their plans for it and to orient themselves as to the possibilities of the undertaking from the European point of view. While they were not able to make a working combination as they had hoped with the *Manchester Guardian*, they took that

135

best of the world's dailies for their model and made
contracts for contributions with numerous well-known
French and English writers, always having in mind
a liberal interpretation of world issues (in connection
with which they generously acknowledged some indebtedness to *The Nation* and the *New Republic*).
Indeed, it is characteristic of the new spirit of the
Sun that its special envoys offered to the editor of the
Manchester Guardian two of its columns in which to
express himself daily by cable as to the progress of
the Conference, Mr. Scott to have complete freedom
of utterance. Unfortunately for the American public, the veteran editor of the *Guardian* was unable to
avail himself of the offer, but the *Sun* did print the
entirely unedited and quite divergent accounts and
comments of H. G. Wells, Henry W. Nevinson, H.
Wilson Harris, J. G. Hamilton, Maurice Low, Brails-
ford, Bywater—in short, the best-known liberal and
conservative journalists in England, to which it added
French writers like Millet, Le Chartier, and others.
Mr. Frank Kent, a vice-president of the company,
who stayed abroad, "scooped" even the London *Times*
and the *Daily Mail* upon Lloyd George's plans for
the Cannes Conference—a feat which naturally attracted widespread attention, just as his striking interview with M. Loucheur, the French Minister of Reconstruction, led to exchanges of opinion in public

136

utterances between Senator McCormick and various French politicians.

But the enterprise of the managers of the two *Suns* did not stop there. They undertook the entertainment of the visiting correspondents at the country residence of one of the owners near Baltimore (much marrod by a typioally Amorioan dioplay of tho oaoo with which one can dispense unlimited supplies of liquor in prohibition times), and on other occasions gave evidence of a generous hospitality to the foreign writers which cannot be too highly commended. Altogether the *Sun* made itself felt from the beginning of the Conference to the end and it is hard to see how its reporting could have been bettered unless there had been a more staccato daily résumé of happenings for the strap-hanger who will not read more.

But one fine journalistic achievement no more proves a newspaper to be awake to its duty than does a single swallow evidence a summer. Far more important than its Washington triumph and the evident plans of its managers to make it national in its interests, more important even than the fact that it continued its remarkable series of articles by many of the distinguished correspondents mentioned above and by others, is the question whether it is year in year out honest and fearless, whether it is free from any sinister control, whether it is really liberal, and

137

how far it is ready to voice the desires and feeling of all the groups in the community. For generations the *"Sun*-paper," as it has been cried on the streets, dubbed in the homes of its city, and as it has figured in stories and story books, was synonymous, under its previous ownership by the Abell family, with stodgy, ultra-conservatism; its rate of intellectual progress was that of the Maryland Club, which in turn regarded the *"Sun*-paper" much as it did the United States Treasury, or the sanctity of private property, or the Supreme Court, though the latter could not be quite so infallible as the *Sun*. Modern Baltimore is a more difficult city to serve, for besides its ultra-conservatism there is a large and powerful Catholic section to be dealt with, and the city's interests have not always run parallel with the State's, in which Republicanism has played a stronger and stronger part while the *Sun* has usually been Democratic. As the years passed the Abells themselves finally decided that the time had come for new blood and new management and sold a controlling interest to Charles H. Grasty, a Baltimore newspaper man, now connected with the New York *Times*,[1] who was in turn financed by four public-spirited Baltimore gentlemen, H. Crawford Black, Robert Garrett, R. Brent Keyser, and John Campbell White, all names to conjure with in Baltimore.

If you ask a present member of the *Sun's* staff

just when the new *Sun* was born the answer invariably is: "Under Grasty." Mr. Grasty was an
attractive and lovable personality, and it is beyond
doubt he who established the *Sun's* present independence and integrity just as it was he who gave the present staff its vision of what a big American daily ought
to be. Unfortunately his temperament and his abilities were not equal to the task he set himself. In
the pursuit of correct policies he antagonized where
Baltimoreans think that antagonism was uncalled for
and needless—this on the business side of the conduct of the paper more than on the editorial. After
several years Mr. Grasty left the paper burdened with
considerable debt, though invited to return on other
terms than those of complete responsibility. From
about that time on the *Sun* has been managed by its
own workers except that one of the owners sits in the
daily conference of editors and publishers, but as
a working member of that conference and not as a
dictator.

In brief, the heads of the departments run both
Baltimore *Suns*. Unlike many rich people who have
taken to newspaper owning, the four men who backed
Mr. Grasty (now become five by the death of Mr. H.
Crawford Black and the joining of the group by his
sons Harry C. and Van Lear Black) had the extraordinary good sense to let the practical men who were
running the papers and Mr. Paul Patterson, their

brilliant business manager and the president of the company, have complete control and absolute freedom of management and utterance. They neither sought to dominate a business in which they were untrained, nor did they, like Mr. Thomas W. Lamont when he purchased the New York *Evening Post,* turn it over to a new and for him disastrous management, wholly unversed in the newspaper business. They gave to Mr. Patterson and his associates, Frank Kent, John H. Adams, editor of the morning *Sun* ("an idealist, a hero-worshipper, a man of liberal viewpoint," who has elaborated the general editorial policy), and Mr. J. E. Murphy, managing editor of the *Evening Sun*—since reinforced by Stanley M. Reynolds, managing editor of the morning *Sun,* and Hamilton Owens, editor of the *Evening Sun,* and Henry L. Mencken—complete control of the business and the policies of the dailies.

It is pleasant to record the fact that this broad-minded and generous action of the owners has met with very handsome financial reward and still pleas-anter to add that these unusual proprietors are not mulcting the paper for heavy dividends, but are encouraging the staff in its vision of the newspapers it desires to produce and in such heavy outlays of an immediately non-productive character as the Washington Conference must have called for. But best of all is the fact that the owners *have never sought to control* the opinions of the editors. The editorial council was constituted in 1914, since when it has decided each and every position the newspapers have taken. No one man dominates; it is the majority opinion within the council which controls. Once a question of policy was submitted to the directors, not for orders or a decision, but purely to ascertain the opinions of the directors in the search for added light. Possibly this high-minded and public-spirited attitude of the owners is due in part to the fact that they themselves hold divergent views—there are Republicans and Democrats, Prohibitionists and anti-Prohibitionists, Catholics and Protestants among them—and realize that they could not themselves agree on policies. From all one can learn it is best to believe that their motives are much finer. Yet it is none the less a cause for wonder as well as rejoicing, for these are men of great wealth tied up in a hundred ways with big business, the financial world, and the entangling social alliances of the most fortunate circles of an exceptionally conservative city. The only criticism of the council which I have heard is from H. L. Mencken, himself a member of it, who writes in his usual amusing way: "The one thing it lacks is salient character, definite direction, driving personality. The way to get that personality into it is to abolish the democracy which now hobbles it, and substitute absolutism, the only feasible form of gov-

141

ernment for large enterprises. A council is quite competent, perhaps, to run a missionary society, a savings bank or a country club. But it must always be a curse and a handicap to a battleship, a city or a great newspaper. . . . But how is the absolutist to be chosen? The answer is easy: by shooting dice."

There are those who fear that this ideal condition will not survive a severe test of the pocket nerve. They doubt whether the editors would be permitted to take an extremely radical course or one diametrically opposed to the great currents of public feeling such, let us say, as opposition to a popular war with Mexico or Japan. They ask what would have happened had the editors decided to oppose the war with Germany, and they inquire whether the happiness and duration of the present arrangement is not due to the fact that the minds of editors and owners have in the main run along together. To this the only answer that can be made is that in lesser matters the *Suns'* editors *have* gone counter to the views of individual owners without trouble for themselves; they have repeatedly taken editorial positions repugnant to beliefs of one or more of the owners. So the past at least is safe, and that is something to be heartily thankful for. More than that, the proprietors have given the clearest proof that the advertising columns of their papers are not for sale. That was early settled when one of the largest Baltimore dry-goods merchants demanded the publication of a certain reading notice which 99 out of 100 American newspaper managers would have deemed perfectly proper. When the business manager of the *Sun* informed the directors of the fact that they would probably lose a $40,000 advertising contract just when the company needed it so much, because he, the business manager, would not accede to the demand, the only comment was that that was "too bad." The publisher was warmly upheld. When the advertiser was told that he could cancel his contract if he wished to but could never return to the columns of the *Sun* save on far less favourable terms, this would-be bully decided to let the editors run their own journal. It is a fact, too, that news articles which the owners would prefer not to see in the *Sun* have regularly appeared. The editors gave me their word that there is not only no censorship in their office, but no list of men to be attacked and no "sacred cows" (i. e., favourites to be spared) in their shop; that each managing editor has complete authority to say what shall and shall not be printed.

Naturally this throws a heavy responsibility upon these gentlemen and brings us squarely back to the fact that it is because of the character of the present board of directors that the *Suns* are what they are. Were these editors imbued with the philosophy and policies of the New York *Times* and the Chicago

Tribune, it is altogether probable that their papers
would be similarly distressing examples of lost opportunities to serve the public and the country. Instead this fortunately situated group of Baltimore
editors has a real social vision and independence of
thought. They have given to H. L. Mencken free
rein in the *Evening Sun*, although he is anathema to
that type of mentally sodden Americans who really
think that ours is the best, greatest, wisest, and most
perfect Government that ever was and they—though
not the public—the wisest mortals who ever lived.
They have asked the brilliant Hendrik Van Loon, one
of the comparatively few college teachers who would
not sell their souls in 1917 or bow down to the war
god, to join the morning *Sun* with complete freedom
of utterance. They do not hesitate to applaud Mrs.
Asquith when she declares that she has "never met
a single person who has been improved by the war";
that government everywhere "is more corrupt and
there is more hardness, levity, blasphemy, and materialism than I have ever seen before." A staff writer
is permitted to state in his regular department that
underneath the popular mask in America today there
is "almost universal conviction that for all its glit-
ter and assurance the old order is not only morally
and intellectually bankrupt but also doomed," and
to add that "Nemesis will overtake the institutions
which, by the war and its aftermath, proved their

utter incapacity for worthy leadership"—sentiments which in *The Nation* would of course be denounced as swirling bolshevism.

More than that, both of these journals—the *Evening Sun* always more outspoken and radical than the older paper—have stood for free speech and the release of political prisoners, and both denounced the policies of Mr. Wilson's reactionary and discredited Cabinet ministers, Palmer and Burleson, and the nation-wide persecution of Socialists and Communists because of their opinions. When the notorious W. H. Lamar, Mr. Burleson's solicitor of the Post Office Department, sought to defend his Czarist acts, the *Evening Sun* printed his letter in full only to demolish it editorially. To the *"Sun*-paper" Mr. Wilson was and is a good deal of a hero, yet it censured him for refusing to release Debs. Both are among the very few American journals to realize the gravity of the crimes daily committed against civil liberty in America. They are beginning—though only beginning—to realize the growth of militarism in America and so helped to moderate a bill in the Maryland Legislature giving the Governor the power to conscript American boys in time of peace—they had previously ignored similar legislation. On economic questions, too, these journals have a tendency to be progressive and in labour matters they shock the Baltimore Bourbons, although the editors still believe in Samuel

145

Gompers and his type of long-outworn and now hurtful leadership as a bulwark against bolshevism.
They defend his philosophy of political give-and-
take, of compromise and toadying that ought soon
to disappear.   It must also be added that the editorial
policy is strongly anti-Prohibition, though giving
endless space to the Prohibitionsts; that both papers
were bitter and unfair in their discussion of woman
suffrage and are today in equally bitter opposition to
the removal of the remaining political disabilities
of women and are also apparently defending the
race tracks against the efforts to put those gambling
games out of business.   But here as in apparently
all other matters the correspondence columns of the
Sun are open to all, save that I have heard one allega-
tion that in real-estate matters the forum does not
seem to be open to letters which would be obnoxious
to the real estate board.

As to their presentation of the news?   The columns
of both are clean; the morning *Sun* has yielded but
little to the craze for flamboyant headlines, comic
strips, and other catchpenny devices.   Somebody on
the morning *Sun* loves types and studies them to advantage; the *Evening Sun* has a much lower standard.
Indeed, the dress of the morning paper is unusually
dignified and effective; there is a distinct effort to
edit news intelligently and to guide the reader by ex-
planatory footnotes, as in the case of the recall of

146

The NEW-HAVEN GAZETTE,

AND THE

CONNECTICUT MAGAZINE.

MANY SHALL RUN TO AND FRO, AND KNOWLEDGE SHALL BE INCREASED. Dan. Chap. XII. v. 4.

(Vol. II.)　Thursday, *December* 6, M.DCC.LXXXVII. (No. 42.)

A COUNTRYMAN, No. IV.

To the People of Connecticut.

IF the propriety of trusting your government in the hands of your representatives was now a perfectly new question, the expediency of the measure might be doubted. A very great portion of the objections which we daily find made against adopting the new constitution, (and which are just as weighty objections against our present government, or against any government in existence) would doubtless have their influence, and perhaps would determine you against trusting the powers of sovereignty out of your own hands.

The best theory, the best philosophy on the subject, would be too uncertain for you to hazard your freedom upon.

But your freedom in that sense of the expression (if it could be called sense) is already totally gone. Your Legislature is not only supreme in the usual sense of the word, but they have, LITERALLY, *all the powers of society.*——Can you——can you really grant any thing new?——Have you any power which is not already granted to your General Assembly? You are indeed called on to say whether a part of the powers now exercised by the General Assembly, shall not, in future, be exercised by Con-

gress. And it is clearly much better for your interest, that Congress should exercise those powers, than that they should continue in the General Assembly, provided you can trust Congress as safely as the General Assembly.

What forms your security under the General Assembly? Nothing, save that the interest of the members is the same as yours. Will it be the same with Congress? There are essentially only two differences between the jurisdiction of Congress and of your General Assembly.—— One is,——that Congress are to govern a much larger tract of country, and a much greater number of people, consequently your proportion of the government will be much smaller than at present. The other difference is——that the members of Congress when elected, hold their places for two, four, and six years, and the members of Assembly only six and twelve months.

This first of these differences was discussed pretty fully in the last number, (when there was no idea of proceeding thus far on the subject) and has all the force as an object on against the power of Congress, that it would have if applied to a proposal to give up the sovereignty of the several towns of the state, (if such sovereigns had exisited) and unite in state government.

It would be only a repetition to enter into a consideration of this

difference between Congress and your assembly.

It has been suggested that the six or eight members which we shall send to Congress will be men of property, who can little feel any burthens they may lay on society. How far is this idea supported by experience? As the members are to pay their proportion, will they not be as careful of laying too great burthens as poorer people? Are the rich less careful of their money than the poor? This objection would be much stronger against trusting the power out of your hands at all. If the several towns were now independent, this objection would be much more forcible against uniting in state government, and sending one or two of your most wealthy men to Hartford or New-Haven, to vote away your money. But this you have tried, and have found that assemblies of representatives are less willing to vote away money than even their constituents. An individual of any tolerable œconomy, pays all his debts, and perhaps has money beforehand. A small school district, or a small parish, will see what sum they want, and usually provide sufficiently for their wants, and often have a little money at interest.

Town voters are partly representatives: i. e. many people pay town taxes who have no right to vote, but the money they vote a-

The New Haven *Gazette* Showing the Appearance of a
Powerful Provincial Newspaper Immediately
after the Revolution

Gov. Frazier in North Dakota, when the *Sun* warned its readers against accepting the early returns from opposition districts as reliable indices of what was to come. When proportional representation was adopted in Cleveland the *Sun* illuminated the dispatches by printing the principles of the system and its more important details. Yet neither of these newspapers is emancipated from the curse of unreliable or malicious reporting. They have bad reporters as well as good—men sometimes unable to comprehend the subjects they are to report or the people they are to interview and too untrained to understand the real purposes of public gatherings. This, it is to be hoped, is the explanation of the flagrant and cruel misreporting of a scientifically truthful statement made by Mrs. Donald R. Hooker in regard to racial intermarriage which critics of the *Sun* declare to have been not accidental but part of its deliberate campaign against the women's measures then pending in the Maryland Legislature. It is hard to believe this, but the fact that Mrs. Hooker's letter of denial was only partially printed by the *Sun* makes it appear again that there are exceptions to its usual rule of giving every one his or her say. When the opportunity for an absolutely clean escutcheon is apparently so unlimited one cites lapses like these with all the greater regret.

It is to be hoped, too, that in the matter of its

Sunday "comic" and its illustrated supplement, the
Sun will soon feel itself strong enough to come up to
the standard of the New York *Times,* doing away with
the former altogether and exercising a greater self-
censorship of news photographs, thus proving anew
that dignity and high journalistic ideals can still be
made to pay.   For the rest, the large volume of advertising carried by both papers has not led them to
make snippets of important news stories whether
local or national.   Every now and then they print
a bill in full even if it takes a page, or a lengthy
speech in the Maryland Legislature, and they also
find plenty of room to give admirable news of the
surrounding towns and neighbouring States, a field
wherein our metropolitan dailies no longer function.
Certainly journalistic decency and liberalism do pay
in Baltimore, for the morning issue has 118,000
readers, the Sunday 163,000, and the *Evening Sun*
114,000.[2]   And they have not yet dug deeply into
the mine of legitimate local news, which in most
cities is utterly ignored by the great dailies.

The lesson of it all for the profession is that with
the right kind of owners and broad-minded editors
realizing to the full their social and community responsibility there is still possible in some communities a free and unfettered press, dignified and worthy.
Yet there is nothing in the Baltimore *Suns'* situation
to give a definite solution to the grave problem of
our modern journalism.   Had the Blacks, Mr. Keyser, Mr. Garrett, and the other owners been so minded

we should have today a Baltimore press as low as Pittsburgh's, which a prominent railroad "persuader of public opinion" assures me is quite the most degraded in America. Nor does the admirable civic reaction of the editors of the two *Suns* to the freedom and responsibility vouchsafed to them throw any light upon the possibilities of a successful co-operative journalistic enterprise.

Curiously enough, these Baltimore editors prefer the present ownership arrangement to any ownership by themselves, feeling that they are freer and less trammelled than if they were constantly asking themselves whether any editorial position they might take might not jeopardize their all. Undoubtedly it is a resurrection and not a new development or phenomenon with which we are here dealing. Probably a Baltimore liberal is correct in writing to me that "the fair way to judge these papers is not by their imperfections but by their advanced attitude as compared with papers elsewhere." If we do this we must rate them very high. And if it is merely a happy accident, this rejuvenation and freeing of two fine old properties, Baltimore and the country benefit none the less. Whatever the augury for the future, the truth is that Baltimore has two of the best, bravest, and widest-awake newspapers in America.

[1] Mr. Grasty died Jan. 19, 1924.
[2] On March 31, 1926, these figures were 124,525 for the morning issue, 119,399 for the *Evening Sun*, and 188,221 for the Sunday edition.

CHAPTER IX

THE PHILADELPHIA *PUBLIC LEDGER,* A MUFFED OPPORTUNITY

CYRUS H. K. CURTIS, the Henry Ford of the magazine industry, has without doubt done more to mechanize and standardize the public mind of America than any other man. The London *Times* once secretly employed an ex-clergyman to go to the coffee-houses and other places of public resort to find out how the majority of those he talked with felt on a pending issue. Believing that a newspaper, as well as God, must be on the side of the larger battalions, it withheld its own views until its ex-clergyman reported. Then it thundered—and people said: "How wise the *Times* is; that is just what I think." Cyrus Curtis has also employed *agents interrogateurs* for this purpose, but he himself interpreted the mind and the hearts of what abroad would be called the "lower middle-class." With courage, skill, ability, and luck in picking executives, he achieved a result which is popularly believed to net him such part of an income of ten millions a year as the income-tax permits him to retain.

150

Then there came a day when, success having crowned his efforts with the *Saturday Evening Post* and the *Ladies' Home Journal,* Mr. Curtis felt he could leave to his Boks and Lorimers the conduct of those papers and could look for new fields to conquer. So he purchased the *Public Ledger,* for generations one of the staidest of Philadelphia's institutions, a perfect embodiment of the conservatism and propriety of Rittenhouse Square, as well as of its dullness and its sanctimoniousness. Despite its national reputation, it had gradually faded into a state of not shabby but penurious gentility toward the close of the George W. Childs proprietorship and that of George W. Ochs. Here was an event, indeed. A past-master in the magazine field, with unlimited means, had obtained control of one of the most widely known American dailies. Surely, it was thought, the world will now see a notable journalistic development, the revivifying of a great institution along original lines. The Midas-touch must bring forth millions here; all the lessons learned in piloting his twin magazines to unheard-of circulations must, in the shortest time, make over the *Public Ledger* into the most powerful of our dailies. Mr. Curtis soon let it be known that his aim was to create a national newspaper and that unlimited sums would be spent to develop the *Ledger.* Later on he founded an evening edition to round out the day.

151

It was in 1913 that Mr. Curtis bought the *Ledger*—ten years ago. He has now played with it long enough to prove that his dream of creating a national newspaper was a dream and nothing more. Millions have been lavished upon it. Endlessly has it been advertised—even as the *Manchester Guardian* of America! It is, we are told by no less an authority than David Lloyd George, more frequently quoted in England than any other American daily—but it is and remains—a muffed opportunity. True the morning edition—now beginning to go backwards—still has 93,985 readers and the *Evening Ledger* has grown from 92,022 to 183,887 in eight years, while the sales of the Sunday issue have more than doubled since 1917 and by April 1, 1923, had reached the handsome figure of 229,752.[1] It is also a fact that Mr. Curtis is building for it a home which will in all probability be the finest newspaper office in the country—unless the Chicago *Tribune's* new structure should excel it. But the newspaper which dwells alongside the *Saturday Evening Post*, for all its excellent qualities and features, is without originality or distinction, and without a soul. It has not been able to rise without the vulgar comic section or the Sunday pictorial, and the usual spread-headed Sunday features. It has what most people believe to be an admirable section devoted not merely to the news of Wall Street but to the news of trade and commerce.

152

With this section it claims to have pioneered. If so it is the only strikingly original departure of the *Ledger* under Mr. Curtis. The brain that found the brains to build his magazines along new lines which every other similar magazine today imitates, has not found the men to build up the *Ledger* as solidly, sanely, and broadly as the Baltimore *Sun*, nor win similar public friendship. This, despite the fact that the morning *Ledger* has created a remarkable foreign service which it has widely syndicated; that Colonel House has been one of its political commissioners; that William Howard Taft wrote for it for months on end many of the most short-sighted editorials that ever saw the light of day; and that many other celebrities have contributed to its columns. It has done about everything the ordinary successful newspaper resorts to, yet if my information is correct the two newspapers are only just beginning to make both ends meet in a city which is not now overburdened with dailies—Mr. Munsey chloroformed the *Times* and Mr. Curtis bought the dying *Press* to put an end to its lingering suffering and widen the field for the *Ledger*. Moreover, Philadelphia is so rigidly conventional a city and so much more impervious to new ideas than any other of the five largest cities that it should have been fertile soil for the kind of newspaper Mr. Curtis has tried to build.

What is the answer? It is probably to be found

153

in Mr. Curtis himself, in his uncertainty as to just what he has tried to achieve, and in his own philosophy of life. He has honestly wanted to make a national newspaper but he has failed, first because it never occurred to him that a national newspaper could not be published in Philadelphia, and second because he never clearly understood just what a national newspaper is and ought to be. If he really wanted the *Ledger* to be the *Manchester Guardian* of America, then he either did not know what the *Guardian* was, or he failed to find another great liberal editor like Mr. C. P. Scott and give him complete control. Mr. Curtis seems debarred from appreciating what this particular nation, as apart from the "lower middle class," would desire in a national organ, or from making his daily "popular" in the best sense of the word. He is wisely proud of his rise from lowly beginnings and so he ought to sympathize with all groups of Americans. But the change in Mr. Curtis's financial status has had the same effect upon him as it has had upon so many others—it has placed him in the society of the rich and privileged and contented. He goes daily to the Union League Club, there to meet his friends as a super-giant among giants and from this Olympian height he deigns to give his fellow-Americans the benefit of his own views, to instruct them as to what they ought to have and what they should become.

154

They should, of course, conform to his own example and achieve success as he has achieved it. There is and can be no question in his own mind that his ideas as to life, work, and social relations are the only correct ones; it indubitably troubles him that anybody can question that. His absolute sincerity is childlike beyond question and his belief has been that he was certain to accomplish his end, and to duplicate his other business successes if only he advertised this venture sufficiently and spent enough money buying "features." To this must be added that if his newspaper shows any sign of leaving the paths which the Union League Club believes in as well as Mr. Curtis, the *Public Ledger's* owner is certain to hear of it promptly. Moreover, despite his frequent trips to Europe, he is amazingly ignorant of the fundamentals of the present European entanglement; indeed, of much that is commonplace to any reasoning and reasonable reader of the *Public Ledger*.

So the wonder is that this daily has been as liberal as it occasionally has been. There is no ground for surprise that its editorial page has been vacillating and contradictory and that its character is not yet well defined. During 1917–1918, there was a period when, with men like William C. Bullitt and Lincoln Colcord writing for it, the *Ledger* made its greatest strides towards becoming a newspaper of wide influence in official, political, and journalistic circles—its circulation jumped from 59,000 to 82,000 in a year during this episode. It began to develop an interesting and, for Philadelphia, a somewhat original foreign policy—it even leaned somewhat toward the recognition of Russia and especially toward a humane treatment of that great and greatly unfortunate country. For a while it looked as if the *Ledger* were going to follow the lead of its Washington office; it would certainly have been a fine stroke of journalism if it had developed that Russian policy editorially and stuck to it. But apparently the Union League Club was too strong. The time came when the Russian tactics changed; the brilliant, farsighted Washington correspondents left its service and the liberal editorials, which the fraternity attributed to Colcord and Bullitt, disappeared.

During this time and until December 1, 1922, the editor-in-chief was John J. Spurgeon, not a commanding or dominant figure, but a liberal at heart, a clear thinker, a humane man, saddened and rendered rather cynical by his experience of life—like many another journalist. He was, moreover, greater as a news-man than as an editor and formulator of policies. As I write there is no explanation of his relief from his post. Perhaps Mr. Curtis held him responsible for the slump in the morning edition's circulation; perhaps Mr. Spurgeon slipped in one liberal editorial or article too many; perhaps, as he has been

156

known to do, he opposed one of Mr. Curtis's pet policies too forcibly, and that opposition became the last straw. At any rate Mr. Spurgeon has the respect of those who worked with him. Many of them felt that he was attempting the impossible, but they never lost faith in his sincerity. It is the old story of the newspaper editor, in need of his daily bread, coming into contact with the rich owner and compromising here and there in order to continue to be of service in a great position, until an impasse is reached. Sometimes the editorial writer is a mere cynical sycophant; for that part Mr. Spurgeon was not cast. But he was placed in an untenable position from which he now goes forth a free man; much appeared during his editorship of which he must have been or should have been ashamed.

The truth is that, especially of late, the *Ledger's* editorial page has wobbled a great deal. The criticism one hears most often from the *Ledger's* critics is the uncertainty of its policies and its lack of editorial information as to the hidden motives in the political life of its city and state. Its rival, the *North American*,[2] knows far more about what is really going on and what the political, big business, and railroad rulers of Pennsylvania are up to than does the *Ledger*, and so does the *Inquirer*. But the *Ledger* has usually stood against the political exploiters. It royally supported Mayor Blankenburg's candidacy and upheld

157

him during his reform administration. It voluntarily threw its support to Gifford Pinchot in his successful campaign for the Governorship. It is indubitably independent politically, though it would hardly be found supporting a Democrat for President or attacking a Republican tariff—instead of denouncing the proposed ship subsidy robbery, it pussy-footed by calling for more study of the problem and greater knowledge. But the *Ledger's* usual support of reform causes in the city and State and nation is weakened by the unsteadiness already referred to and the extremely uneven quality of the writing of its editorial page. Thus one day it belittled the attack upon Attorney General Daugherty as probably unjustifiable if not inspired by improper motives; a few days later it declared that Daugherty, innocent or guilty, had got to go. It attacks the liberals ("hungry," it says, "for the spoils, privileges, and powers of office") who would amend the Constitution; it is discreetly silent when it is President Harding who demands two amendments forthwith.

Most extraordinary of all, it printed on November 11, 1922, an editorial showing how completely the promises and hopes of Armistice Day, 1918, have become "ashes and dust"; how entirely the peace has failed—is it, the *Ledger* asked, "because humanity is inherently selfish, sordid, and careless?" By the time the evening edition was out it had had second thoughts which it embodied in an editorial entitled, "The War Against War Did Not Wholly Fail." In this it declared that it is worth remembering that "jingoes and jingoism, ancient afflictions of our civilization, passed forever from power and authority when the Armistice was signed"!—this just before the time that certain ultra-jingo Greeks were trying and executing ministers, a general, and an admiral for the unsuccessful jingo venture into Turkey, to say nothing of jingoism in fifty other parts of the globe. The critic finds it hard to take seriously thereafter an editorial page on which such precious nonsense, such downright fabrication, can appear, or to believe that this daily may call itself either a national journal or on a par with a second-rate English daily.

In this feeling one is reinforced by the following reference to the problem of the political prisoners in the column of a staff writer: "What we think of the so-called political prisoners and those who are leading the crusade for their release cannot be printed in a decent, self-respecting journal. It is fit only for the fireside. . . . If the friends of the so-called political prisoners will call at this desk, we'll be delighted to tell them what we think." Surely one who has so little knowledge or understanding of fundamental American principles is hardly a sound American adviser. But it must be admitted that this refined writer voices the policy of the *Ledger*. Thus,

159

one would have to search far and wide to find another editorial as full of misstatements about those same political prisoners as the one the *Ledger* printed on October 10, 1922, apropos of Senator Borah's appeal for their release. What is worse, the *Ledger* has knowingly sinned in these matters; the truth has been carried into its offices. Naturally its news columns have taken their colour from the editorial page, but the paper did at least print a letter from about twenty citizens who protested against the unfairness of its policy and statements about these prisoners whose presence in our jails gives the lie to our most sacred American claim to freedom of conscience and of belief. Curiously, its star correspondent, Mr. Lowry, by what must have been a slip of the pen, entirely misquoted a brief on these political prisoners submitted to the Attorney General by Mr. Otto Christensen by which Mr. Christensen was made to say something directly the opposite of that which he did say and thereby to strengthen the point which Mr. Lowry was making. The defenders of the political prisoners excusably did not believe that this was an accident. The *Evening Ledger* has in this respect always been more liberal and more dependable than its elder sister.

In the fight for free speech and the liberty of the American individual as made in Philadelphia, the *Ledger* has helped not at all. Yet it is again characteristic of its wobbling policy that it sent Mr. Lowry to write up sympathetically the denials of free speech in Vintondale, Pennsylvania, and elsewhere and that it has at times printed articles showing some appreciation of the aspirations of labour. When the coal strike of 1922 came on the *Ledger* insisted that the miners' demands were "indefensible and foolish," but it did admit frankly that that industrial war was inevitable because of the conditions in this "half-feudal, chaotic industry." In 1919, the *Ledger* was even more violent, declaring that "under the circumstances, a strike of the miners would be 'treasonable' and should be treated as such." In the steel strike of the same year it wanted to "Rip the Roof Off the 'Red' Mystery," and it did everything in its power to make believe that the strike was revolutionary in its purpose and bolshevik in its inspiration. Then it played the Gary game to the king's taste. But now it warns its capitalistic friends that if "capital intends to continue its fight against unionism as it has a right to do it must abide by the new rules of the game. There is a revolt within its own ranks [the Rockefeller position] that will force it to do so."

As for the rest, the *Ledger* has editorially approved the Daugherty rail injunction, the personnel of the Harding Coal Commission, and our big stick, or big business, policy toward Mexico. It has forcefully opposed the Bursum bill ("an infamous act") to deprive the Pueblo Indians of their property and rights, the Ku Klux Klan, the attempt to bar liquor on foreign ships, and the state censorship of moving pictures. It insists that "there is no present basis on which to form a third political party in the United States," and has made the interesting discovery that "no party committed to class interests can survive in a nation dedicated to no class interests"—which must not, however, be taken to predict the early death of the Republican Party.

In foreign affairs the *Ledger* has always inclined somewhat to the League of Nations and thinks that sentiment for it is now reviving in America. It feels that the Allies "have bowed their faces in the dust of the Near East," but it rejoices that Harding did not enter the Lausanne Conference. Believing that Harding was planning a general foreign economic conference it expressed itself thus: "America insists that until Europe begins to disarm, pay its debts, and reduce its budgets, until outgo falls within income, it is useless to bother us for financial help or to make a beggar's plea in avoiding just debts." To render a special service to this country abroad the *Ledger* announced (October 5, 1922) that: "In the interests of a better understanding between the peoples who make up nations and create governments and policies of those nations the *Public Ledger* has joined with certain of the great newspapers of the Old World in placing before their readers a weekly summary of the current political affairs and national happenings in America. These dispatches, will be published in England and on the Continent." As already stated, both *Ledgers* have given a remarkable amount of space to a most praiseworthy effort to give their readers accurate pictures of what is happening abroad. With all its defects the conclusion is inevitable that, editorially such as it is, the *Ledger* is perhaps the most liberal of Philadelphia's dailies and the most consistent and outspoken advocate of home rule and of political, administrative, and financial reform within the city. How much more it could accomplish were those responsible for it to dream dreams and determine to cling fast to approved journalistic ideals, each reader can judge for himself.

These papers have, for instance, of late, appreciably lowered their tone in the matter of the reporting of murders, scandals, and sensations of all kinds. The reliability of the reporting has fallen off quite as markedly as that of the New York papers; there are men prominent in the social and political life of Philadelphia who are so outraged by the *Ledger's* garbling of their words that they will no longer make any statements to the *Ledger* and prefer to have their activities ignored by it. The unusual charge is even made that the *Ledger* has frequently not respected the sanctity of statements made to it in confidence.

163

Whatever the truth as to this, the *Public Ledger* gives many evidences that there is much to be done in the way of internal reconstruction and management. Mr. Curtis is a liberal and an unusually kindly employer—though able to discharge editors at times with amazing suddenness and ruthlessness—and is reputed to pay higher wages than any other journalistic employer in Philadelphia. But there is far more to successful office management than that.

It surely goes without saying that under Mr. Curtis the advertising columns of the *Public Ledger* have been as clean as a whistle in their contents. Yet it is interesting to find that even under Crœsus the *Ledger* has not always been able to see beyond its nose when news unfavourable to a department-store advertiser was abroad. Philadelphia has been with Pittsburgh one of the worst of our cities in the domination of the press by the great department-store advertisers—some of the newspapers offering themselves for prostitution with complete harlotry, while others like the *Bulletin* have stood out well against encroachments upon their freedom of utterance. The *Ledger* ought always to have been free and unmuzzled if only because the loss of even several advertising contracts could have added but a trifle to the superb deficits which Mr. Curtis carried so nobly. But that has not been the case. It makes any one who has worked in Philadelphia journalism smile to

look over the *Ledger's* record—it is all so familiar
a story. There is the Gimbel Brothers' department
store, for instance, always a tender subject with Philadelphia dailies. In 1914–1915 an Alumnæ Committee of Bryn Mawr College called attention to the
fact that Gimbel's was one of several stores that did
not conform to the fire laws. The *Manchester
Guardian* of America could find no space for such a
trifling item of news. Even when the fire marshal
brought suit against the store the *Ledger* could not
see that there was any news value to the fact. On
February 17, 1915, the *Ledger* suddenly altered its
attitude toward the incident, then giving space to a
statement from the firm denying the charge which the
Ledger had never printed. On June 5, 1916, there
appeared a news article to the effect that the suit had
been stopped, the firm having decided to build the
fire walls demanded by the fire marshal.

On May 18, 1920, the Gimbels were indicted for
profiteering in certain articles of food. Again the
Public Ledger was mute, but it found room for a half
page of Gimbel advertising; the indictment interested the *Evening Ledger* to the extent of nearly a
half column on page two. Curiously enough, however, this story could not be found in the next edition. A month later the *Public Ledger* did report
on two occasions the indictment of the New York
Gimbel store for profiteering in clothing. Prior to

the Curtis ownership, when all the Philadelphia morning dailies were silent about the arrest of a member of the Gimbel family, the *Ledger* was among them.* During the Curtis ownership, it is needless to say, the *Ledger* index contains such interesting and vital news items as that a Gimbel was "host to waifs at circus," "host to school friends," or chosen president of this or that club. As for the Wanamaker store, it had a strike of upholstery workers during which the store was rather conspicuously picketed. Thousands who passed the store knew of the strike but not the *Ledger's* readers until October 6, 1917, when a two-inch item (all relating to the entire strike that a search of the files and the *Ledger* index reveals) announced that after four weeks the upholstery workers still refused to go back to a certain store whose name was not mentioned!

During the strike of the Amalgamated Clothing Workers in 1919 the employers, A. B. Kirschbaum and Company, ran a series of advertisements in the *Ledger*. The anti-union *Ledger* then refused to take the three carefully-worded advertisements (from the pen of a prominent Philadelphian) offered to it to present the strikers' side of the case. In 1922 the

---

* Mr. George W. Ochs Oakes, then the managing owner of the *Public Ledger,* writes me that that journal did take notice of the Gimbel crime. Renewed search of the files for the days involved fails to bear out Mr. Ochs Oakes's statement.—O. G. V.

United Gas Improvement Company, the lighting "octopus" of Philadelphia, was indicted by a Federal grand jury for violation of the criminal section of the anti-trust laws. The New York newspapers carried the news conspicuously on their first pages; so did the *North American* in Philadelphia. The *Public Ledger* gave three quarters of a column to it on the second page and when the indictment was dismissed the *Ledger* forgot to tell its readers about it, although the New York newspapers again informed their readers by means of important display articles. All of which lapses of the *Ledger* are utterly unworthy of it and are a treachery to journalism itself. They suggest neither a national newspaper nor a free one. So one wonders whether Mr. Curtis has been always entirely aware of these incidents; there is much gossip that he does not receive correct reports as to his dailies. It is beyond the power of the writer to fix the responsibility for these lapses.

Perhaps there will be a change for the better now that the facile and well-informed pen of Mr. Edward G. Lowry, the successor to Mr. Spurgeon, is to strike the editorial keynotes. An excellent political observer, the author of an entertaining volume of Washington character sketches, commanding a light and often amusing style, it will be interesting, indeed, to see if he has the needed depth of knowledge and understanding, the courage and the freedom to plumb

wisely the swift flowing economic and political currents of the day. It is by no means yet clear that
Mr. David E. Smiley has the qualities necessary for
one who is now resident executive manager of both
dailies under Mr. Lowry.[3] Will he and his editorial
associate be permitted to know that the greatest circulation builder is the one of which almost no American daily can avail itself—absolute truth telling as
to what is going on at home and abroad, stripped
of lies, hypocrisies, conventionalities, and inspired
propaganda? The muffed opportunity is still an
opportunity to be retrieved by those who have the
open sesame.

And what is the open sesame? Well, first, to
learn that business is *not* everything. Then its new
managers and its old owner must alike realize if they
would achieve a genuine success—not to be confused
with a financial one—that the way to build a truly
great paper, to say nothing of a national one, would
be to give that newspaper an intellectually honest,
consistent, and courageous public-serving personality. It would be to let it stand forth as that daily
above all others which sought the truth ardently and
earnestly, which stood four-square against error
wherever made, which was determined to sound the
depths of economic law, which held a brief for no
set of men and no class of men, and above all for no
privileged groups, but set up a journalistic standard

to which men of all faiths and all walks of life might repair certain that their views would be received with tolerance, appreciation, and sympathy. This is no unattainable idealistic vision; it is, I believe, precisely what the real *Manchester Guardian* has been aiming to accomplish and has in larger measure than any other daily achieved; but it is what its Philadelphia imitator has not even approached. Again the reason is spiritual. The vision is not there! It is not building a fine foreign service nor enlisting political lights as staff contributors which makes a national and international daily; there must be a *soul*. Having been for years a creature of many opinions but of no convictions, the soul of the *Public Ledger* is still to seek.

[1] On March 31, 1926, sales had reached 315,575 for the morning and evening editions, and 437,024 for the Sunday edition.

[2] Since this was written, Mr. Curtis has purchased and on May 17, 1925, ruthlessly destroyed the *North American*, the oldest American daily.

[3] Mr. Lowry lasted only a few months; Mr. Smiley succeeded him.

Note: In December, 1923, Mr. Curtis purchased the historic New York *Evening Post,* and undertook to run it from Philadelphia with Philadelphia standards. All the points made against the Curtis management in the above chapter have been more than borne out by his conduct of the *Evening Post.*

CHAPTER X

WASHINGTON, A CAPITAL WITHOUT A
THUNDERER

WASHINGTON is beyond doubt a difficult newspaper field. Unlike the other great capitals, it has been merely the seat of the national government and not until comparatively recently has it even taken on the outward aspects of an impressive residential city. A dozen years ago its fashionables never shopped except in New York or Baltimore; today its shopping district impresses. Only within the last twenty years has it been discovered as a delightful winter resort for retired civilians, or the idle rich who are beginning to play such a part in its social life. It is wholly without the great industrial plants usually to be found at a seat of government. The war gave it, of course, a tremendous impulse in every direction, and, despite the extra homes built in the war years, it is still building new apartments at an amazing rate. But aside from governmental activities, Washington yet bears many aspects of the small town; it is surely the only capital of a great

170

nation which does not have its own orchestra or support a permanent theatre or even an attractive resort where one may dine and hear fine music of an evening. Its huge army of departmental clerks contributes little to the intellectual or spiritual life of the town—their life is a round of deadly mediocrity and routine. If there is an increasing number of men of science and of learning, they are still comparatively few, while the higher officials are constantly changing. Moreover, most of the governmental employés have other geographical interests and ties—many of them subscribe to their old-home-town papers. There is no articulation in Washington itself of the political life of the capital to the business, or intellectual, or scientific, or art life of the country.

Under these circumstances the press of Washington has naturally been extremely provincial; it has represented not the national interests centred in the District of Columbia, but has mostly busied itself with the local small town gossip and happenings. Its intellectual level has, over a long period of time, been that of the bulk of its curiously mixed constituency. Even to get a survey of all the national news originating in Washington one has had to buy a New York, Philadelphia, or Baltimore daily. Almost never has the legislator or statesman turned to a Washington journal in eager desire to see what its

171

editorial views were about the previous day's happenings. He reads at breakfast the *Washington Post* and is duly influenced by its news articles and its headlines—its chief claim to fame is that Sousa named an excellent march after it—but he drops it just as soon as he can get his hands upon a big-city paper. For one thing, the citizens of the District are not voters, which means that the field of politics is restricted for them and that their newspapers are weakened in the eyes of the politicians because they are not the organs of a potentially trouble making electorate. Again, one-fourth the population of the District is coloured; a large part of this group does not stand high enough in the social scale to be much interested in reading newspapers, particularly as the newspapers, with one exception (the *Star*), are only in the smallest degree interested in the coloured people, or reporters of news concerning them and their doings, except that negro crime is always news.

Situated at the very fountain-head of our national government, the Washington press has thus been without a national stamp. It has not even reflected adequately the cosmopolitan character of the District's population, which comes not only from every State but, one might say, from every county in the Union. In a city full of diplomats, the editorial writers have, until recently at least, always been abysmally ignorant of foreign affairs. In the whole

172

history of the District no single editor has made his mark through a local newspaper, so there has been nothing to draw especial attention to the Washington dailies. The journalistic prizes within the District have been held by outsiders—or men originally outsiders—who were sent to Washington to represent the rich, the virile, and the influential journals of the country. The Washington correspondents, not the local newspaper men, are the journalists who have influenced the political life of the capital. They are the ones whom the politicians read eagerly, of whom they stand in awe, especially those whose duty it is to keep the folks back home informed as to what Congressman X and Senator Y are doing.

The influence of the District upon its own press has been doubly and trebly unfortunate. It is bad enough that the army of office holders is a dull and deadening clientele; the fact that there is such a preponderance of politicians or political appointees has made the papers politically timid despite the absence of local elections and candidacies. The thought has been never to offend the powers that be. Their patronage was needed and you never could tell whether an Administration would succeed itself or not, or be succeeded by one of its own kind. Moreover, since the rascals in office are no longer all turned out after every election, the army of bureaucrats is composed of men and women of both parties. If, therefore,

173

an editor criticized a Republican administration he found that he was offending the other half of his readers who were as consciously Democratic as the European workingmen are class conscious. So the District newspapers have usually, more or less unconsciously, taken on but a faint tinge of the colour of the existing Federal administration. Sometimes one could in the past read a Washington paper for months, yes, years, and not be able to guess its politics.

Still another reason for the timidity of the Washington press lies in the District's form of government. It is ruled in the last analysis by Congressional Committees composed of Congressmen and Senators temporarily in public life and drawn from all over the country. Their interest in the District is of the slightest, but from them come the appropriations and upon the appropriations depends the development of the city. Now the real estate business is the chief industry of the District. In the real estate development of the city, therefore, the newspapers have a large stake. Hence they are slow, indeed, to criticize or oppose anybody in Congress who is or may be a member of the District Committee. The papers are apt to be quite legitimately interested in civic developments whose fate rests upon their editors being on good terms with the men upon whose favour a given enterprise wholly depends. This is one of the

174

most interesting examples we have of indirect control of a press, not by any open or avowed action, but by the fear engendered lest it say something which would prevent it from obtaining a perfectly legitimate and above board revenue.

If the influence of big business is far less potent in Washington than elsewhere, the pressure to conform according to Main Street, is just as great, if not greater, not only by reason of the overweening influence of the Federal government, but because the bureaucrats do not like attacks upon the government which furnishes them their existence, and because there is no such hide-bound conservative in all the world as your retired civil official or retired army or navy officer. Of the latter Washington has long been full because of its comparative cheapness (until recently) and the fact that these unemployed lend each other company in their declining, idle years. So for generations the Washington press submerged itself absolutely in its vicinage; it played safe, originated nothing, was unquenchably conservative, and made no contributions whatever to the intellectual life of the nation, to its methods of government, or to the solution of any of its problems. I have often wondered if the World War was not more welcome to the long established Washington papers than to anybody else in the profession, for they could then at last afford themselves the luxury of being partisans,

175

of being really outspoken—about the Germans—
without hurting advertising or circulation, while at
the same time standing in more than ordinarily with
the Government. What a relief it must have been
to them to let loose some of the pent-up feelings of
decades and to do some really first class "cussing"!

Again the difficulties of the Washington newspaper
publisher have been immensely increased by the
early delivery in his territory of Baltimore, Philadelphia, and New York papers. There is no absolute
necessity for subscribing to the *Washington Post* or
Evening Star when one can have the admirably newsy
Baltimore *Sun,* or *Evening Sun,* with their far greater
recognition of the fact that there is a world outside
the District of Columbia, unless one is determined
to have the little local news items of the capital.
The government clerks rightly feel that they cannot
be without the Washington *Star* because of the departmental news it contains, the obituaries of local
worthies, the notices of entertainments and lectures.
But it is not only the clerks who read it; there are
many streets in which the *Star* is subscribed for at
practically every house. It has built its great success by being the house-organ for the District. In
other words, its proprietors recognize, as did those
of the *Brooklyn Eagle,* that the peculiarities of their
field of endeavour necessitated the paper's being absolutely identified with the interests of the District.

To be such a local mouthpiece is a legitimate and useful function; it is, of course, incompatible with the exercise of else than a local influence. Within the District, the *Star* stands high indeed, however great its obscurity beyond this government reservation. Its readers have come to believe in it thoroughly, in its honesty of purpose and its devotion to their interests and to those of their peculiar community.

The *Star* has been singularly fortunate in having as its editor Mr. Theodore W. Noyes, whose tastes and interests have happily coincided with what was the line of least resistance for the newspaper to follow. A fine character, a high type of gentleman, profoundly interested in all local enterprises, no one in the District is more beloved by the older set than Mr. Noyes. It is in the popular mouth that if you can get your case before Mr. Noyes, justice will be done you. He is believed to be kindly and fair, so kindly that the editorial page suffers from it as well as from other editorial influences which make it intellectually without distinction and politically worthless. If it goes into political matters it does so with a careful balancing of both sides, the familiar "on-the-one-hand" and "on-the-other-hand" type of editorial which impresses the thoughtless, hurts nobody's feelings, advances no cause an inch, and does not even add to the gaiety of nations. An issue in

177

the beginning of April, 1923, is characteristic in its editorial page headings: "Another Judge Needed"; "The Silver Spring Tornado"; "Flowers Blooming"; "Facilitating Traffic"; "Sugar Profiteers"; "Art Lights"; and "The Tight-Wad." One must go far, far into the rural regions to some country weekly to find editorial writings of a more kindergarten nature than these; they lack only expression in words of one syllable to be really classic. As an example, here is the philosophy of that tornado:

The tornado which struck Silver Spring is the first near-by phenomenon of this kind to happen in the Washington area in many years, and it is hoped that we may be spared another visitation for an indefinite time. The longer the time the better. That this short but severe windstorm did not do more damage is a matter to be thankful for. Some persons were injured, but none was killed, and reports indicate that the injured will get well. Most winds of this kind play strange pranks. In the news of nearly all cyclones we get narratives of one house blown to splinters and of another within a few yards escaping undamaged, not because one house was stronger than the other, but because the wind did not strike it. A big tree, survivor of a century, will be uprooted and a nearby tree will not have a twig disturbed. It is not uncommon to read that while a house was smashed its occupants escaped. Some details of a similar nature are to be read in the account of the Silver Spring storm. The people of the village and the closely settled neighbourhood about it have much to be thankful for. Though it was thrilling enough to satisfy

178

an exacting taste for thrills, it might have been a great
disaster.

Fortunately Washington survived not only the tornado but this editorial. That on the vital question
of the price of sugar is a restatement of the news,
winding up thus sapiently: "The public has no
means of ascertaining the facts, but it believes that
the government has such means. Senator Smoot says
he hopes that the investigation of the increase in the
price of sugar will be vigorously prosecuted by the
government and the blame placed where it belongs.
So say all of us." These are not unfairly chosen
nor uncharacteristic examples of an editorial policy
intended to arouse no antagonism, but to make much
money comfortably with a minimum of trouble, ex-
ertion, and ruffling of other people's feathers.

On questions bearing on the government of the
District the *Star* can at times become almost excited
and carry on laudable campaigns by daily articles.
Mr. Theodore Noyes is entitled to the highest praise
for his services on behalf of the public library, of
the development of fine arts, and of civic affairs generally. The coloured people trust him as they do
no one else in the District's public life. In fact the
Star is really an institution, and in its care of its
employés is beyond praise. It not only provides the
usual, or rather the unusual, sick benefit and pension

179

funds, but also maintains a dental clinic, and an Evening Star Club for its employés, and other useful associations for the advancement of its men and women workers. The management's annual banquets to its employés are attended by the President, the Cabinet members who happen to be in town, and half of the Senate and the House; yet there are no speeches and only professional entertainment, with the exception of a few jokes. It is accepted by the newspaper fraternity in Washington that a job on the *Star* is equivalent to a government pension, since nobody is ever dismissed from this daily. Idyllic as this seems, it does not add to the efficiency of the *Star*, which is reputed to carry not merely dead wood, but employés of the type who lack energy and ambition and are content merely to hold their respective jobs. This condition is intensified by the fact that there are a number of proprietors represented in the active management. Five sons of these owners have recently been introduced into the business, which fact not only discourages the other employés but necessarily gives rise to the charge of nepotism and of putting men in places of responsibility who cannot be held accountable in accordance with the ordinary rules of the game. Besides Mr. Noyes, his brother Frank B. Noyes, the President of the Associated Press, represents the Noyes family interest in the direction of the *Star*. Mr. Beal Howard speaks for his own holdings and those of several associates, and he has a son in the business. Then there are the Kauffmann interests, watched over by three members of the family. Mr. Fleming Newbold, brother-in-law of Mr. F. B. Noyes, is the able and successful business manager of the newspaper. While this large group of active proprietors and their sons gives rise to considerable office politics, it is also true that the several owners have co-operated with extraordinary good will and friendship. Mr. Theodore Noyes's editorial page, such as it is, is entirely free and is independent of the news policy of the paper. No other American newspaper of which I know has so much direct proprietary control or so much hereditary management.

That means, however, that the pressure upon the paper to earn money for them all is very great, and for years extraordinary financial results have been achieved; gossip puts the annual profit at considerably more than $1,000,000—some say $2,000,000. Indeed, it is believed to stand among the ten best newspaper money-makers in the United States. It is, however, beyond direct control by its advertisers. If news is omitted, if things are overlooked, if unpopular causes are ignored, if the aspirations of the masses outside of the local governmental field are neither understood nor interpreted, the fault lies with the limitations of the owners, their conceptions of the

181

functions of their newspaper, and their lack of intellectual courage. They are handicapped, too, by their social surroundings. Being personally popular and attractive, they are much invited into the social life of the capital, and every newspaper man knows how difficult it is to criticize or to appear to criticize those by whom one is invited and those whom one meets in the houses of one's friends or at the club billiard tables.

The pressure to make money and be up-to-date now shows itself in the appearance of the *Star*. Long one of the most beautifully printed of American newspapers, with dignified type, excellent make-up, fine paper, worthy and tasteful headlines, it has become a typographical hodge-podge, without its old beauty and distinction. Recently it added a full page of daily pictures at about the same time that Mr. Hearst's *Times* did the same thing; for years content to publish one complete edition just in time for the daily exodus from the departments, it now prints a 5:30 edition with latest news items in double column on its front page. With this it has added a complete financial news page and has improved its sporting section which is far more dignified and of a higher grade than the average.

The *Star* is still in advertising and news the cleanest of the Washington papers, as it is the most departmentalized. But for all that it lacks brains in its make-up. It will spend much money for news and features and special correspondence—it subscribes to the excellent foreign cable service of the Chicago *Daily News*—and it is giving more attention to national political happenings than ever before. But newspaper-men are careful to turn to its last page as well as its first, for the most important political news story of the day is quite likely to be buried in the back of the paper with its worth unrecognized. It has a standard which it does not itself know how to reach for lack of proper editorial guidance, which may be a good deal due to proprietary inbreeding. Unquestionably the *Star* has broadened of late, and yet it does not play any significant rôle in the eyes of the newspaper world, for it has no intellectual entity, no force, no brilliant editorial personality behind it, no cause or causes into which it can throw itself whole-heartedly and with passion, no thought of real leadership. One cannot suppress the wonder that all the national implications of Washington life have been so carefully kept out of the well-ordered, placid, and utterly conventional existence which the *Star* has shared until recently with all its Washington contemporaries. Woodrow Wilson once likened the Washington correspondents to wireless antennæ, vibrating at the seat of the government with the messages received from their home communities, which he promised to use—and then never availed himself

183

of these recording instruments. Similarly, in an atmosphere electric with messages from the whole Union, the Washington press has operated with such entirely different wave-lengths that it has known nothing of these other ethereal communications going on around it. So for years it went its naïve, rural way, incidentally giving further ground for the assertion so widely made that official Washington least of all knows what is going on in the country which lies beyond the confines of the District.

The *Star* for all its intellectual vacuity has had dignity and worth. One could hardly have said this a couple of years ago of the rest of the District press. The *Washington Post,* founded in 1877, after a long and undistinguished career has come into the hands of Edward B. McLean, son of John R. McLean, widely known as owner of the Cincinnati *Enquirer,* the most powerful Democratic daily in Ohio. The large rôle played by Edward McLean as a friend to the Harding Administration is one of the inexplicable things in connection with that recent régime. Mr. McLean, who is usually credited with a past, but not so often with a future, was appointed chairman of the committee which was to have conducted the Harding inaugural ball. The ball was soon dropped, ostensibly for reasons of economy, but there is widespread belief that the President's choice of the chairman to guide it also had much to do with the aban-

184

donment of this function.   Mr. McLean, despite his
great wealth, is not and never will be popular in
Washington, which cannot get over its wonder that
Mr. Harding lived on such terms of intimacy with
him.   Certainly it could not have been with any desire to propitiate the owner of the *Washington Post*.
The *Enquirer* was, however, far greater game.
Though a Democratic paper it was so kind to Mr.
Harding in its editorial treatment of him and its display of news of him and his speeches during the
Presidential campaign, that it practically supported
him.   Just as the *Enquirer* owes nothing to Edward
B. McLean for its long established influence and reputation as one of the most remarkable news-gathering
dailies of the country, so the *Post* has gained
nothing in moral character from its present owner.
It must be admitted, however, that a change has come
over it, that it has waked up, that it did play a
powerful rôle during the fight against the Treaty of
Versailles and the League of Nations, not merely by
its editorials, but also by the tremendous propaganda
carried on through its news columns.   It demonstrated then that a cause ably served by a daily could
make a real impression upon the District public.

Indeed, it cannot be denied, that, as already stated,
the news columns—not the editorials—of the *Washington Post* do influence the Congressional mind.
Lord Northcliffe once remarked that of all the Amer-

ican newspapers he would prefer to own the *Washington Post* because it reaches the breakfast tables of the members of the Congress. Frequently the better and more honest reports of some of the New York dailies do not offset the impressions conveyed by the first page of the *Post*. The McLean management has played upon this advantage very skilfully, placing upon its first page the signed articles of certain writers, obviously propagandists, who are, some of them, without the respect or trust of the members of their own profession. Indeed, of no other newspaper have I heard the Washington correspondents speak so unfavourably. They despise, dislike, and distrust it; to them it is not only a poison sheet—it is also a contemptible one and they question its moral integrity. To such occurrences as its sledge-hammer attacks upon the French occupation of the Ruhr they pay little attention while the public wonders whether great significance should not be attached to them owing to the McLean comradeship with President Harding. Incidentally, its recent publication of a long list of the prominent clients of a recently arrested Washington bootlegger has been severely criticized. In the crowd in which Edward McLean moves this is regarded as distinctly unclubable behaviour, quite contrary to the accepted ethics of the game, real treason to the social strata which the *Post* toadies to and upholds, and generally unsportsmanlike conduct

186

on the part of one who is usually not supposed to be inimical to the bootlegger business, although his paper fiercely attacks the Reds who defy our other laws and fail to respect our sacredly unchangeable Constitution.

At present the *Washington Post* is in full cry after the general pack of newspapers, indulging in all the current newspaper fads, such as a pink sporting supplement, "humorous" pages, comic supplements, picture pages, etc. Like all the Washington papers it specializes in society news and nowhere else is personal gossip so eagerly read because of the official character of the city and its constant entertaining. In the advertising field the *Post* finds that its chief rival is the *Evening Star* rather than its morning competitor; on Sundays, when the *Star, Post,* and *Herald* all appear, the competition is very keen. After attempting to be his own managing editor for a while, Mr. McLean has now called to this place Mr. John J. Spurgeon, the able newspaper man made free by his release from the editorship of the Philadelphia *Public Ledger.* It is too early as yet to tell what he will be able to accomplish, but if certain improvements are already noticeable it is somehow impossible to conceive of his having a free hand or being able to accomplish anything lasting under the present erratic ownership.[1] One point of interest remains. Unlike the *Star,* the *Post* has never sought to culti-

187

vate intensively the local field. Will it do so now, or will it try to increase its influence in the national sphere?

There remain in the Washington field the two Hearst newspapers, the *Herald* in the morning and the *Times* in the evening. They are typical Hearst newspapers, peas out of the same pod, typographically ugly and messy, with all the usual Hearst standardized features. The *Herald* is too new a Hearst purchase to make it possible to judge what its flair and its influence are going to be. So far neither of this pair is exerting any political power, but the *Times* has shown a steady growth without affecting the circulation of the *Star,* which in its slow but steady progress reached [2] 95,492 in March 1923 for the daily, and 98,242 for the Sunday. The *Times* has climbed to 62,555 [3] and is supposed to be showing a comfortable balance sheet. What I have already said about the Hearst papers in other cities applies to these two of the tribe. Their influence in no wise corresponds to the noise they make nor to the readers they draw.

Finally we come to the tabloid *News,* also an evening publication and one of the latest creations of the Scripps-McRae, or Scripps-Howard league as it is now called. It, too, has the characteristics of its group although it has not been able to devote itself so much to labour questions as have its sisters of the

Scripps family because of the absence in the District of any large group of factory workers. As usual, Mr. Scripps is stooping to conquer; his motto is that one must first have a paper before it can be toned up, so he stoops to the trivial and sometimes to the vulgar. The appeal of the *News* to the masses has been so successful that it now has a readership of some forty thousand. One may pick it up of an evening and find that it has given its whole front page to the marbles championship of the District, and then one may find on the inside extremely valuable and important information not to be obtained elsewhere.

Whatever the defects of the Scripps syndicate its papers are at least forward looking; they are usually on the side of the under-dog and they know what liberalism means. They are usually an oasis in a desert and for all its defects and its trivialities, for all its stooping for circulation, the *News* under the editorship of William B. Colver, Chairman of the Federal Trade Board under Woodrow Wilson, is the one hopeful note in the Washington situation. Observers feel that the *News* is already influencing the other papers in certain directions, as, for instance, when it printed its exposé of Attorney General Daugherty. Nothing on earth would have made the *Star* undertake anything like that, but it had to take notice when the *News* blazed the way. It is the only paper in Washington which has really a sincere and consistent understanding of what the whole fight in America is about, as contrasted with the momentary glimpses (so often dimmed by the owner's personal ambitions and insincerities) which mark the Hearst press. If there is to be in the near future any newspaper in Washington voicing the sentiments and desires of the masses of the American people, realizing how far we have drifted from our former American ideals and into what hands we have fallen, that can only be the *News*. Its financial success and its consequent toning up into a more serious and sober publication are devoutly to be hoped for.

Finally we come to the question whether it would ever be possible to have in Washington a really national newspaper. I am often asked whether a great daily giving a most careful survey of the government's activities as well as the news of the world would not have nation-wide influence. I cannot say that such an experiment would be successful. There is needed a weekly journal which could give to the large mass of officeholders throughout the country, postmasters, lighthouse keepers, army and navy officers, members of territorial governments, councils and ministers abroad, interesting, well-written factual accounts of the progress of the government. That weekly would necessarily have to be in the nature of a trade journal and would have to be fairly inexpensive because your distant officeholder is not a rich man. Certainly he could not usually afford to

190

pay the $12 required for a year's subscription to a first class daily newspaper.

Then to attempt to create in Washington a great daily with complete abstracts of the doings of Congress and news of the government's departments as well as the news of the District and the news of the world would require an enormous sum of money. A Rockefeller or a Ford could do it, but few if any others. There is, however, always the possibility of the appearance of a genuine newspaper personality, a man with something to say and the ability to say it that marked Godkin and Dana and the senior Samuel Bowles. Should such a man appear his personality and ability could, of course, lift his paper into the front ranks of American dailies, make it respected, admired, and feared by the politicians, and gradually extend its influence far beyond the confines of the District.

But such a newspaper ought to be in a position to make enemies. If it should have to consider local advertisers and District influences and fear the political bosses of the District who sit in a committee room on "The Hill" and in most undemocratic manner shape the development of the District, it could not fulfil its task. It must be independent and it must, above all else, have something to champion. Mr. Hearst, of course, has had the means to create a great paper at the seat of government, to confer honour and distinction upon the city and the country.

191

His vision has been blurred; the defects of his character have kept him from grasping this wonderful opportunity and have rendered him unable to obtain the right men to conduct such a fearless and, in the old-fashioned and best, though now outworn, sense, patriotic daily. The only possibility remains that the gradual breakdown of our government, which is going on under our eyes under the leadership of the Wilson and Harding types of mind, will in time produce the national emergency that will both compel and create journalistic leadership. It may well be that militant editors will then reappear in the land and not merely in Washington.

Meanwhile, a foreign visitor coming to Washington to study the institutions of our great country, may take up the capital's three evening papers, only to find the first page of one devoted exclusively to the championship in marbles, and that of another to the fact that a young widow has shot a wealthy man who jilted her. Turning to the third he may be regaled by reading the editorial announcement that the government has the means of getting at the sugar facts and that the flowers that bloom in the spring, tra, la, are happily at their task of beautifying the capital. What matters it at Washington that the world is in a turmoil and that civilization totters in Europe?

[1] This prophecy proved to be correct; Mr. Spurgeon was suddenly dropped by Mr. McLean on March 31, 1925.

[2] On March 31, 1926, the circulation of the evening *Star* was 99,442; for the Sunday it was 107,457.

[3] On March 31, 1926, the circulation for the *Times* was 54,289.

CHAPTER XI

THE CHICAGO *TRIBUNE*, "THE WORLD'S GREATEST NEWSPAPER"

"THE World's Greatest Newspaper" the Chicago
Tribune calls itself with characteristic im-
modesty and self-esteem, and not uncharacteristic im-
pudence.   It is foremost in its brazenness, it is unsurpassed in the brutality of its use of its power, and
there are few to equal it in the un-Christian spirit of
its editorial page.   Perhaps its slogan is used correctly in the commercial sense; it is beyond doubt
one of the greatest financial successes of the newspaper world—some years ago an offer of ten million
dollars for this property was refused by its owners.
It fairly reeks with prosperity and it is in the—for
it—fortunate position of offering the only opposition
to the Hearst morning daily.   If you live in Chicago
and abominate the frying-pan of Hearst and all his
works you must leap into the fire of the *Tribune*.
There is no morning alternative because Chicago will
not support more than two morning newspapers—
New York rejoices in four major dailies in English

and various minor ones. There is surprisingly little domestic advertising in Chicago, for many of its greatest industries are not advertisers, so that the press there must live largely upon department-store advertising and the highly remunerative "want" advertisements. The *Tribune* has so prospered that it has erected at least one of its great buildings, that at Dearborn and Madison Streets, entirely out of surplus earnings.

That it has survived the fierce Chicago newspaper wars, in which one property after another has gone down with heavy financial losses to the stockholders, is, of course, in itself a tribute to the excellence of the *Tribune's* business management. It came triumphantly out of a several years' struggle for survival during which all of the Chicago newspapers charged only one cent a copy and the weaker ones disappeared, the *Tribune* and the Chicago *Herald* finding themselves in a monopoly of the morning field when it was over. The *Tribune* is now in a position to snap its fingers at any advertiser if it so wishes. It is a "commercialized newspaper." To use its own words: "The Chicago *Tribune* is not a philanthropic institution. Nor is it a religious or a political institution. It is a *commerical* institution." Exalting its virtue it adds: "The *Tribune* is so prosperous that no bribe is of even passing interest. It is the weak newspaper with regular deficits that the 'interests' pick up cheap to serve as a tool"—as to the truth of which one may have one's doubts. Its management has studied its field with greatest care and adjusted the paper to it; it has harmonized editorial policy with business progress, and it has spent money freely to obtain special service from correspondents all over the world and to purchase sensations; but its sensations usually—there are exceptions—never interfere with the popularizing of its well-commercialized news columns. Like many another big daily it throws away much of the news it receives and often cuts the Associated Press news stories to snippets because of lack of space. Since it is a newspaper obviously made, above all else, to sell and not to educate or to convey information, it constantly slights National, State, and municipal matters of great importance. In its local news it is as inaccurate as most of our metropolitan dailies and does not hesitate to reveal its malice or bias in its reports of the doings of those whom it does not like—there are plenty to accuse it of falsification. Of this a conspicuous example is its long-continued abuse and ridicule of that school board which in Mayor Dunne's time comprised in its membership such liberals as Jane Addams, Louis F. Post, and Raymond Robins. It could not possibly find the way correctly to report the meetings of this board—a major reason was, of course, that the board sought to annul or revise the lease of the ground (owned by the Board of Education) upon which stands the *Tribune* building already referred to.

Yet while this colossus among dailies is savage in its attacks upon all liberals and every one with whom it disagrees, it has been shrewd enough to run a Democratic column for Democratic voters in campaign times and otherwise to bid for support from those who would naturally seek their daily reading elsewhere. Since nothing succeeds like success, its prosperity and its aggressiveness automatically attract both business and circulation to it, as a magnet draws steel filings. It has, moreover, devoted much attention to pushing its sale and influence in the territory, and, indeed, the States, surrounding Chicago. It may have been a coincidence that Mr. Hughes ran strongest in that section of the Middle West in which the *Tribune* is most powerful, but with its usual audacity the *Tribune* attributed this result to itself. In the State of Illinois its magnificent campaign to unseat Senator Lorimer won it many friends, although in Chicago its smashing attacks upon this unworthy representative of the State were cordially disliked by the financial and business powers.

Justice compels the recording not only of this case of flying in the face of its business prosperity; there are other instances in which this self-contradictory and inconsistent journal has rendered distinct public service at the risk of financial loss—in some of these cases its hurt pride and its vanity have doubtless furnished the motives. It championed the Progressives from 1909 to 1916 with skill and courage. For years it opposed the traction barons and especially Yerkes, the bribe-giver and franchise-grabber, but it opposes municipal ownership, fought Mayor Dunne and Walter L. Fisher, ex-Secretary of the Interior, when they tried to work out some solution of the street railway problem, and still has no constructive program to suggest. Similarly the *Tribune* has grown cold toward the referendum and initiative which it so warmly advocated in Roosevelt days and towards many other liberal proposals which are or were the logical result of the Roosevelt movement. It still stands, however, for a moderate tariff, and for progressive and high taxes on inheritances. Although itself the creator of great wealth and now in the hands of very rich men, it is for breaking up colossal fortunes, which it sincerely considers a menace to the Republic. Singular has been its criticism of the Federal Reserve Board, the institution which is usually credited with having saved this country from panics and disaster ever since it was created. This it has ventured to denounce as a Southern device for the express purpose of drawing money away from the North and East. Indeed, it has at times a positive hatred of the South and of

Southern political ideals and then it turns around and serves the cause of race hatred with equal facility and venom. The difficulty is that you can never be certain where it is going to stand, whether it is going to be reactionary and vicious, or whether it accidentally will be found on the side of progress and enlightenment. Thus, it bitterly opposed the seating of Senator Lorimer but it favoured Senator Newberry—because Ford was an internationalist! Howling as it does about law and order, it endorses the Ku Klux Klan. It opposes prohibition as an attack upon personal liberty, but favours a law to prohibit the use of revolvers. It constantly confuses its principles, and also its principles with personalities. Whether this is due to its double-headed control probably only the insiders know.

Its modern reputation as a great *news* daily the *Tribune* acquired under the managing editorship of James Keeley, who, for a time before the present managing owners took charge, also dictated its editorial policy. His "beats" and sensations largely increased the circulation of his paper. A glorified police reporter, he had an amazing "nose for news" and knew how to use well the unlimited sums he had to expend. He was amazingly able to foretell, to use an old saying, "where hell will break loose next and to have a man on the spot in time," and to become "interested in things a day before the public does and

to lose interest a day before the public loses it."
How closely a newsman's achievements are tied up
with the newspaper which he serves was never so
clearly illustrated as in the case of Keeley and
the *Tribune.* Leaving that paper because of some
quarrel, he took charge of the *Record-Herald,* then
backed by some rich men as an antidote to the
Tribune. Like other editors of great reputation in
similar situations, Keeley failed utterly in his new
job when the sole responsibility was his; the men who
backed his *Tribune* reputation with their money lost
it. His successor is a clean, decent, and efficient
man but one devoid of vision, and the *Tribune* has
been degenerating a good deal under the Hearst competition and example, resorting as it has lately to
prizes, lotteries, and cheap-jack devices, even to giving money away until the latter form of stimulating
circulation was stopped by request of the Postmaster
General.

A characteristic and illuminating example of the
Tribune's controversial methods is afforded by its
attacks upon Mayor Thompson. That official was undoubtedly vulnerable at various points and it was the
habit of all the Chicago dailies to pound him unmerci-
fully and to give him no credit for his good deeds or
for the, in parts, distinctly liberal and enlightened
political platform which he sponsored. But the
Tribune was so abusive, so vituperative, and so savage

in its daily assaults upon or ridicule of the Mayor as to arouse in many a quarter a feeling of sympathy for the object of its often slangy and always bitter attacks. It abandoned every rule of dignified editorial courtesy in debate to vent its feelings against Thompson, precisely as it sunk deep in its abuse of pacifists and true radicals. It observes no Marquis of Queensberry rules as to when or where to hit, but in the case of Mayor Thompson it is unfair to attribute its venom to the vexed legal question of its right to the leasehold of its older building. That fight, as already stated, goes back to an earlier administration.

Undoubtedly the *Tribune* was profoundly annoyed by the threat of the Thompson school board to condemn its building, but the *Tribune* knows, like everybody else, that the school board has no money with which to purchase this skyscraper. Long study of this exponent of the strenuous life in journalism must confirm the observer in the belief that the *Tribune* would have fought Mayor Thompson for the waste and spoils system of his administration, and what it considers his demagoguery and his lack of patriotism during the war, quite as viciously had there been no real-estate issue between them. The *Tribune* would doubtless have won the libel suits brought against it by Mayor Thompson, had they not been quashed by the courts after Mayor Thompson left office, just as it

200

won every suit in the school-board matters. The suit brought by the city of Chicago allowed it to pose as defender of the liberty of the press and the right to criticize public officials unrestrainedly, although it has itself throughout the last five years been on the side of repression or imprisonment of all dissenters. The *Tribune* desires a complete monopoly of all severe criticism of anything or anybody. One word more as to its legal battle with the school board: In every instance thus far the *Tribune* has been legally vindicated, its leases being upheld in all the courts, despite allegations that the low rentals had been obtained by the *Tribune* by unfair provisions in the lease and improper influence in its drawing. Yet the case is not quite clear and hundreds of thousands of Chicagoans still believe the *Tribune* has merely been fortified in unfair privileges by the court decisions. This is, perhaps, one reason why, despite the *Tribune's* bitter opposition, Mayor Thompson won his sweeping victories at the polls, until the tide turned on June 6, 1921, and his candidates for the city judiciary were defeated. Mr. Thompson himself denounced the Chicago *Daily News* and its owner, Mr. Victor F. Lawson, more violently than he assailed the *Tribune,* despite its breezier and more sensational warfare against him. Like Mayor Hylan in New York, Mr. Thompson seemed to fatten on the united hostility of the press. After the 1921 election

201

in New York it was remarked that "the people voted for Hylan because the business men were against him." In our largest cities there is plainly danger of the voters habitually waiting to see where the rich, powerful, and "big business" press stands and then voting directly against its advice, without further question or hesitation.

On international questions the *Tribune* lives up to its reputation for being erratic; the truth is that it is generally cynical, reactionary, militaristic, and jingo. It is enthusiastically for universal military service and would cheerfully forge for us the fetters of that peculiar bit of Prussianism, just as if the fate of Germany did not forever demonstrate exactly whither that sort of thing leads. So far as England is concerned, it does criticize the monarchy and its aristocracy and snobbery; yet in the main it would have America another England in our relations to the other nations of the earth. With regard to Japan the *Tribune* is as bad as Hearst in that it has been doing all it can to bring on the war with the Mikado's subjects which it so confidently, and apparently happily, expects. Mexico, if the *Tribune* has its way, we are to "clean up" and annex; our superior morality—as evidenced by the political conditions in Chicago and Illinois—we are to impose upon the Mexicans whether they like it or not. It is our "manifest destiny" to rule over them as we have over the Filipinos, while our capitalists are to see to it that Mexico's enormous and largely untouched resources are to be exploited as they wish. The *Tribune* would not shrink from outright annexation.

Naturally such a newspaper leaves no depths unplumbed in its efforts to discredit the present Russian Government. So base in its view are the Bolsheviks that it reprinted in 1921 a picture of rioting in Petrograd which it originally gave to its readers, November 4, 1917, representing it as a portrayal of an anti-Soviet revolt of the people of Moscow. For this, it is only fair to add, it had the decency to apologize when confronted with the facts. Along this line it is interesting to note that on August 19, 1921, the *Tribune* deliberately garbled a letter of Bernard Shaw to the editor of *The Nation* in which Mr. Shaw wrote that he would not think of taking his wife "to Texas where the Ku Klux Klan snatches white women out of hotel verandahs and tars and feathers them." For "Ku Klux Klan" the *Tribune* substituted the word "mobs." Not unnaturally this precious bit of editing was attributed to the fact that three days before the *Tribune* had carried a full-page advertisement of the Klan. An intensive study of the *Tribune* in relation to its advertising by some one familiar with newspaper methods would beyond question produce interesting but not inspiring results.

To sneer at morality in foreign relations is the

203

Tribune's stock in trade. It was, of course, a staunch defender of President Roosevelt when, contrary to morals and international law he "took"—to use his own word—Panama and argued about it with Congress and with Colombia, the victim of the theft, afterwards. That is precisely the kind of rule of might over right to appeal to the *Tribune*. Decatur's mischievous motto, "My country right or wrong," it has long carried on its editorial page as a daily appeal to that spirit of narrow, immoral nationalism which the thinking world today seeks to eradicate. It has as yet made no suggestion that we annex Canada, but the *Tribune* is quite capable of doing this very thing; nothing in its recent tradition, or its history, or its reputation for reason and stability would prevent. Before we entered the war there was much criticism of it as being too favourable to the Germans and there is no doubt that for a long time it had its eyes on the sympathies and feelings of the great German-American citizenship of Chicago. But if it was unjustly criticized at the time, that experience did not prevent its joining the one hundred percenters and those most intolerant in their persecution of all dissenters after we had entered the war. It ought, moreover, to have been sympathetic with the German cause, to say the least, so similar is its political and international faith to that held by the Kaiser and his chief advisers. If there is a more ardent journalistic advocate of the Big Stick and the Mailed Fist it would be difficult to find it in any quarter of the globe.

Who are the men who control the destiny of this tremendous engine for the manufacture of public opinion? They are two cousins, Robert R. McCormick and Joseph Medill Patterson, grandsons of Joseph R. Medill, the founder and first editor of the *Tribune*. Mr. McCormick is well educated, well read, and much travelled; physically brave, he lives up to his military teachings; he served with his militia regiment on the Mexican border and commanded another in France. Genial and democratic, he is personally popular, but his mind, like that of the *Tribune,* which he chiefly moulds, is inconsistent, shifty, generally reactionary, extremely prejudiced, arrogant, intensely nationalistic, and 100 per cent American to the full of the sinister meaning of the modern Know-Nothingism which has become synonymous with that term. One of his own employés has amusingly described him as "a cross between a Russian grand duke and Dogberry, with a liberal dose of plutocracy," but this is surely too severe if Mr. McCormick is to be credited with all the good things the *Tribune* does. Middle-aged now, Colonel McCormick has still many boyish traits and makes many quick changes and hasty decisions.

Joseph Medill Patterson is a more interesting

205

public figure. Slightly older than his cousin, he has the reputation of being even more impulsive, besides being decidedly erratic. As a mere youth he startled Chicago by openly avowing himself a Socialist, although at that time the term did not shock our privileged ones to such Berserker wrath and visions of blood as today. But for a while he had to leave the *Tribune*, his exile lasting until with growing years, or because of the influence of his wealth and associations, or because of a sincere change of mind as to the Socialistic remedy for the world's ills, he became "good," came back into the fold of the *Tribune* and of those who insist that all is well with the world, save that it needs more and not less of the old order. At any rate, he is respectable again and all but forgotten are the crude novel and the plays he wrote to denounce the present economic system, its landlords, and its plutocrats. He is, in justice be it said, still radical in certain views and still counts himself a radical. For many years he supported public ownership of utilities, but today he finds nothing wrong in being of the *Tribune's* warp and woof and in sharing the responsibility for its course with the cousin with whom he must differ at many points. Together they reconcile their differences as they do those of their staff. That staff takes its orders obediently, though, if report be true, the writers are not always sure as to which of the cousinly opinions will dominate. Mr. Patterson indubitably has ability and cleverness, fortified by much reading, but it cannot be said that he is dominated either by method or science, or the scientific spirit which takes the truth only for its lodestar. At least, he is broad and liberal in matters of individual liberty and believes in leaving social indiscretions to the power of public opinion. For moral censorships he is not to be had, and prohibition finds in him a dangerous enemy.

Under both cousins the *Tribune* is very different from what it was under their grandfather, Joseph Medill, who made it peculiarly a reflection of the ideas of the growing and then callow Middle West. Mr. Medill edited his own paper and made it strong and influential, notably through its many sided editorial page. His present-day successors have sought, without success, not only to make it the "world's greatest newspaper," but to give it the air and atmosphere of a great European daily. These two men have made their journal "live," and often interesting, by their lavish expenditures and their hiring of good news-men and correspondents. But when it comes to the *belles lettres* side they have failed. The *Tribune* is not authoritative in arts and letters. Its musical criticisms have been formally condemned by resolutions of the musical societies. Its literary criticisms approach neither those of the

New York *Times* nor the *Literary Review* of the New York *Evening Post*. Its literary style, or rather the lack of it, is laughed at by men of letters. "Fine writing" is one of its sins. Learning and knowledge do not always shine through the editorial page; this many thousands of the readers of its news columns shun like the pestilence, as is the case with the New York *Times*. By and large, despite its good qualities, the paper is distrusted and disliked by those who are making the profoundest contributions to the social, civic, educational, and moral progress of Chicago. Let the *Tribune* deny this if it can; in all intellectual and progressive circles, I repeat, the *Tribune* is hated and despised where it is not regarded with contempt. Its pretensions to being the world's greatest newspaper, the leaders of thought in Chicago know to be utterly false. They realize fully its inferiority as a *news*paper to the New York *Times*, to the London *Times*, and to the *Morning Post*, to say nothing of the *Manchester Guardian* and the great European and South American newspapers. If the good opinion of the men and women of brains and character in a given community is the truest test of a newspaper's greatness, the *Tribune* stands low in the scale.

So we have a picture of a rich and powerful daily in the hands of the third generation of the same family. Perhaps we should be thankful that it is

208

as liberal and public spirited as it is and that it is not so noxious in its editorial influence as is the New York *Times,* although lower in its tone and personally far more abusive. It is certainly far superior to its Hearst rival. Its managing owners have escaped many of the faults and weaknesses which usually accompany the heritage of great wealth. That they give it of their own time and strength shows as well as anything that they are not without civic responsibility and the desire to serve their community according to their lights—though it is a little bit hard to write that and then recall that they have within a few years foisted upon New York that lowest of dailies, the illustrated *Daily News,* darling of the office boys and shop girls. Yet the fact remains that Chicago is without either a great conservative or liberal daily, that its press does not stand in any honour with thoughtful people and that the grandsons of Joseph Medill have by no means risen to the opportunities which were theirs to make themselves the best beloved of their city among the righteous, or to guide it generously and wisely in the direction where lies its soul, or to stamp themselves as leaders of men. On the contrary they sow bitterness, hatred, and discord, and may some day reap as they sow. Should there be a competition as to which is America's worst newspaper, the Chicago *Tribune* will be a most promising entry.

CHAPTER XII

THE *KANSAS CITY STAR*, A WANING LUMINARY

A GLORIFIED organ of Main Street—thus one is tempted to describe the *Kansas City Star*, probably the most influential daily to be found west of Chicago. Upon its own townspeople its hold is copper-riveted, for it sells about 140,000 [1] copies within urban and suburban limits that hold 450,000 people. More than that, Kansas City regards it as much an institution to be proud of as the new Union Station, or the Elks Club, or the splendid boulevard system. The merchants' associations, the chambers of commerce, and the boosters' clubs are as satisfied with it as with the flag under which they all live. It is part and parcel of the municipality and he would be rash, indeed, who would attempt to say whether the *Star* made Kansas City famous or Kansas City the *Star*, or even to try to figure out just how much each has contributed to the development of the other.

It is at least clear that the *Star* owes its high estate to its founder, a vigorous, rugged, dominating

210

Westerner, William Rockhill Nelson, who indelibly stamped his dynamic personality upon Kansas City. "The *Star*," says William Allen White, "was the daily W. R. Nelson." Mr. Nelson was, Mr. White avers, an enigma to the other papers, to the politicians, and more or less to the whole town: "To be a gentleman; to be a mugwump; to refuse honest money for a peccadillo about professional ethics; to devote more space to Henry James than to Jesse [the train robber] in Jesse's home town, and still to be a big, laughing, fat, good-natured, rollicking, haw-hawing person who loved a drink, a steak, a story, and a fight—strong men shuddered and turned away from the spectacle. They couldn't be sure whether he was crazy or they were." But in the main these strong men did come to know, to like, and to admire Mr. Nelson even when they could not understand his reasons for suddenly depriving himself of $100,000 a year by cutting off all liquor advertising in his newspaper. That was truly committing the deadly sin of being idealistic and "impractical" in a community whose own ideal was to watch Kansas City grow and to make it hum. They came, however, to understand that the very idiosyncrasies of W. R. Nelson were a city asset. They passed easily over his interest in Henry James and other "highbrows," realizing that a good merchandiser often puts fine paint on the exterior of his shop and little touches within that don't bring in the dollars but create an "atmosphere," just as Bouguereau nudes were at one time considered indispensable to help the traffic in hotel bars. Then the business world of Kansas City did appreciate that there was no better booster than Mr. Nelson for city planning, for parks, boulevards, good roads, pure and efficient water, and the best possible sanitary methods. These are things that every resident of Main Street appreciates, and the advocacy of them treads upon nobody's toes, affects adversely no one's financial or economic interests.

On the other hand the Kansas City business men could not so readily understand why Mr. Nelson should assail the traction ring or the gas companies as well as the liquor interests. In his repeated fights against municipal corruption and intrenched special privilege the public gradually recognized that he played the part of a brave and unselfish man. Main Street finally came to applaud him when he stood up for the freedom of the press as when he refused to be dictated to by an advertiser who complained of the *Star's* editorial policy toward him and threatened to withdraw his advertising. "Out you go, and out you stay," Colonel Nelson replied, and his decision was never reversed. Being a pioneer by nature he was able to look into the future and so he became very rich by his fortunate investments in real estate, something that gave his enemies the opportunity to say that his championing a greater and more beautiful city was due to his desire to advance his personal fortunes —a charge as unjust as it was malicious. A short time before his death the forces of corruption and privilege tried to besmirch his reputation with a jail sentence in answer to the admirable fight he was making to reform the administration of justice in the local courts.

It was not the desire to make more money that led this restless, middle-aged contractor and bridge-builder into newspaper work, but a genuine desire to serve his community. Unlettered himself, though a user of forceful, cogent, and pointed language and a coiner of characteristic and vigorous phrases, he never wrote a line, but relied upon others to express what was teeming within him. His employés readily caught his spirit and reflected it clearly. The *Star* succeeded precisely as it embodied the qualities of its owner, including his rugged honesty, and precisely as Mr. Nelson would have succeeded in anything he went into by reason of his homely, forceful character, and the sheer weight of his personality. He typifies perfectly what a liberal minded and brave American newspaper proprietor of limited education and vision could achieve in the Middle West in the last decades of the nineteenth century.

It was in 1880 that Mr. Nelson founded the *Star,* and by 1884 he was in the full swing of the first of his two great adorations—his worship of Grover Cleveland. For Mr. Cleveland he fought, like the New York *Evening Post,* or the New York *Times,* or the *Springfield Republican,* always unselfishly and with the cleanest-cut vision that as a daily newspaper-owner he should never take office. He carried his community with him just as he did twenty-eight years later when he threw himself whole-heartedly into the Roosevelt Progressive campaign. There was an extraordinary contrast between Cleveland and Roosevelt; in many respects they were at opposite poles, and for many of the Progressive policies Mr. Cleveland felt only intense opposition. Temperamentally they were as wide apart as the Pacific and the Atlantic. Yet to both Mr. Nelson gave an almost schoolgirlish hero worship. He was not profound enough or well enough schooled to have deep abiding principles—his turning upon the liquor interests was primarily due not to a moral revulsion or to horror of their trade, but to their attempt to defeat a city charter which he was championing. Roosevelt appealed to him on many grounds; did they not both dearly love a fight? Mr. Nelson was once asked: "Now, Colonel, wouldn't you feel better if tonight you could think that in all this town you had not one enemy when you turn on your pillow to rest?" "No, no, no—by God," Nelson replied, "if I thought *that*

214

I wouldn't sleep a wink." A sound credo for any editor who would serve city and country!

But, if this virile man had his occasional periods of intense devotion to national politics, the success of his daily (or rather of both his dailies, for he bought the *Times* in 1901 to be the morning edition of the *Star*), like that of many another daily was built upon its absorption in local affairs. It used to be declared of the rich and prosperous *Brooklyn Eagle* that its staff was schooled always to remember that if a prominent Brooklynite stubbed his toe on Fulton Street that was more important for the *Eagle* than the election of a Governor. The *Kansas City Star* has covered and still covers the news of its community with most painstaking fidelity. But that community early ceased to be Kansas City, Missouri, or Kansas City, Kansas, alone. It is said of it that "Kansas, western Missouri, Oklahoma, northern Texas, Colorado, and New Mexico, have grown up on it." No one can spend a couple of hours in the waiting-room of the Kansas City Union Station without realizing that one meets in it more, and more varying, types of American citizens than in any other one place in America. Kansas City is the gateway to the Southwest, and Colonel Nelson understood this. Kansas in particular was under his wing; it is only within recent years that the Capper press has arisen

215

to challenge the *Star's* predominant editorial influence in the Free Soil State. Colonel Nelson's appeal
was always a middle-class, a bourgeois one; hence it
waked welcome echoes beyond the home town. He
was distinctly on the side of men in the fight between
property and men—and yet he had great limitations
in that fight. Toward labour he was the beneficent
autocrat. He recognized the good labour organizations have achieved, but as an unusually generous
employer he resented labour-union demands upon
himself. He wanted to have the power to treat his
employés well without any walking delegates coming to him to tell what he ought to do or must do.

In other words his social creed was distinctly that
of the middle-class liberal of his period. But, as
recorded above, he eagerly embraced the "radical"
Progressive platform of 1912 and in spots went
even further than it did. Mr. Roosevelt was later appointed a contributing editor; under the spell of his
leadership the *Star* broke away from older traditions to become a fierce exponent of a militant, "pre-
pared," armed America, without realizing how inconsistent that was with the tenets of true democracy, or
how repulsive and hostile it must be to both his
middle-class and labouring-man audience, or what a
break it represented with the soundest American
ideals.

Now how have the death of Mr. Nelson and the

liberalism-destroying World War affected the *Kansas City Star?* Where does it stand today? Having been placed in the hands of trustees under his will to be held until the death of his daughter, Mrs. Kirkwood,[2] and then to be sold to create an art foundation in Kansas City—what could be more characteristically American than Mr. Nelson's leaving his great estate for the development of *art,* something that every good, red-blooded Kansan looked down upon in 1880 as the creation of weaklings and idlers, something that was most conspicuously absent in the surroundings of his life-time?—what does the *Star* teach us about the possibilities in America of a trusteed, if not endowed, newspaper?

Well, primarily, it gives us no encouragement. The *Star* of today is but a part of what it used to be, particularly since the retirement from its staff of Mr. Dante Barton, a former leading editorial writer. Although every effort has been made conscientiously to walk in the footsteps of William R. Nelson, that original personality has not been replaced and we see once more, as in the case of the New York *World,* what happens when a vigorous editor-owner disappears and there is no direct spiritual successor. The management of the *Kansas City Star* is the same, yet it is hard to read it and to believe that this daily once had a nation-wide reputation for force and vigour of utterance. It has become more than ever the paper

217

of, by, and for Main Street. The World War has dulled its liberalism; it is kindly and has plenty of zeal for righteousness and goodwill, but it is no longer ardent and passionate, not even in its defence of the now discredited Kansas Industrial Court. It even finds it necessary, as after the November, 1922, election, to print an editorial pointing out the measures it espoused which were approved at the polls. In the spring election of 1922 the *Star's* candidate, a Republican of good reputation, was defeated by more than 13,000. The truth is that its devotion to Colonel Nelson is at once a help and a hindrance; while its knowledge that its career under its present auspices is limited to a single span of life is obviously having a deteriorating effect upon it. It is even charged that this has led the present management to place far more stress upon money-making than has heretofore been the case.

Colonel Nelson's memory has, however, fortunately prevented its lowering its high typographical standards. If there are those who wish to see how respectable American newspapers looked before the days of Pulitzer, the second James Gordon Bennett, and Hearst, before the coming of 8-column ribbon headlines or comic strips of the Mutt and Jeff type of intellectuality, they need merely buy a *Kansas City Star*. Its present managers follow Colonel Nelson's injunction never to issue a comic section or a pictorial

218

supplement. Our most prominent Eastern newspapers could take lessons from its admirable con-
densation of our usually overwritten news stories. It
is living proof that our American dailies could abandon their typographical eccentricities if they would,
and still make money. The *Star's* news is also as
good as it was in Colonel Nelson's day and it has
distinctly increased the value of its Washington service and its reports from other quarters. In its devotion to baseball it is loyally American, and it prints
some good cartoons. It is in its editorial page that
its effort to cling precisely to Colonel Nelson's policies
is a hindrance. For times have changed enormously,
and a newspaper cannot in this hour remain merely
static and retain its prestige or influence. Colonel
Nelson himself was not of that type; he could switch
easily from the relative conservatism of Cleveland's
day to the "radicalism" of Roosevelt. Today a
critical reading of the *Kansas City Star's* editorial
page inevitably produces the impression that the
paper's expression is not free and that it is not
measuring up to the opportunity of leadership which
should be its privilege, as it used to be. Whether it is
in part the dead hand of the war; whether it is in part
a lack of editorial acumen and virility, or whether it
is the effort to formulate in each case merely what
Colonel Nelson might say, the effect is there.

More than that, its news columns are warped by its

219

editorial attitudes. For instance, it is still for large armaments for preparedness—after the World War has shown their total futility to protect anybody in Europe—and so it gave about an inch of space to the visit to Kansas City of the head of the Disarmament Council, and refused to send out his message over its radio, the use of which it has since turned over to Jack Dempsey, the pugilist, with his inspiring message as to how quickest to pound a man to pulp. Its belief is that a nation's ideals are of no value except as they are backed up by armies and ships, but it is so fearful of the soundness of that doctrine that it will not give its readers a chance to read the "fallacies" of its opponents. It denounces the teaching of peace in the schools but it will give room to no replies. In other words, its present code of ethics makes it commit the grave sin of compressing or suppressing the news about people or things about which it feels keenly. (Colonel Nelson, it must be admitted, had a long taboo list of people to be ignored by his staff, just as cartoons of fat men had to be avoided because of Colonel Nelson's physique.)

The *Star* still boasts that it is independent politically and not partisan, yet its partisanship is obviously of the intensest, whatever and whomever it supports. It still claims to be liberal but its liberalism is today fossilized. True, it still has liberal impulses which make it stand against child labour

220

and for workmen's compensation and other social reforms, but it no longer advocates unpopular causes with the fervour of William R. Nelson, if it takes them up at all. During the war it was in the forefront of the heresy hunters and those who believe the absurdly un-American doctrine that the political and economic beliefs of men like Eugene V. Debs can be changed or be made less effective by locking them up in jail. It warmly supported Governor Allen in his effort to close the mouths of Kansans under the Industrial Court Act (which one of its editors is believed to have drafted)—and was promptly rebuked by its Kansas following. In 1921 it had 78,143 readers of its daily and 89,542 readers of its weekly edition in Kansas, but, as is the case with so many other American newspapers, it made the discovery that even with its large circulation its advice was once more not taken—Kansas went Democratic in the election of 1922. For lack of any other near-metropolitan paper Kansans buy it—an extraordinarily active and effective circulation department, which employs men to do nothing else but call on its outlying subscribers and ascertain their views, adds to the number of its readers—but they reserve the American right to think for themselves. Most of them seem to believe that the *Star* is as vigorous a crusader as one could expect of a rich and successful moneymaking enterprise owned by an estate.

221

In this they are wrong. Its editorials are brief—but two columns or less daily, and without distinction or charm. Rarely do they betray the hand of the expert or the knowledge with which Mr. Barton frequently illuminated and forwarded the discussion of industrial matters. The appeal to Main Street is to be found in entirely safe editorials on "October Conversation," "A Little Margin of Time Well Employed," "Education and Bigotry," "The Menacing Frock Coat," "Autumn's Court Is Open," "A Young Millionaire's Escapades." In its issue of Sunday, October 1, 1922, of its four editorials, the first dealt briefly with a remark of Senator Borah's on the need of unity in Europe. The others were entitled "The Secret of Eternal Youth," "In the Old Home Town," and "Personal Liberty and Hogs." There is extraordinarily little to suggest to the reader that American labour is desperately unhappy and that the plight of the farmer, so distressing to himself, is keeping the *Star's* editors awake at night. Not even the Ku Klux Klan's activities stir them to passion or to a moving appeal; they conclude a half-approving editorial on it in these words: "Many good citizens have been attracted by the appeal of the Klan to remedy certain specific evils. But the *Star* earnestly urges those who contemplate responding to the Ku Klux admonition for a religious test in politics to consider the disastrous effect on the national life of the general adoption of such a course"—this of an organization which has set itself to usurping some of the functions of our State governments and is generally regarded as a most dangerous menace. As for other issues of the day, it has always championed the direct primary and prohibition, as it has upheld Attorney General Daugherty's rulings against liquor on United States ships and his vicious anti-strike injunction. On the other hand, it has fought a good fight against the Fordney tariff and that whole system of corrupt log-rolling which we call tariff-making. Curiously enough for a Western paper, it has opposed the high income tax, which it would supplant with a sales tax. It waxed warm, it is true, in its attacks upon Senator Reed, without being able to prevent his re-election, but in the main the George F. Babbitts of Kansas City can retire to their sleeping porches confident that all's well with the world and without any such resentment as men carry to bed with them if their evening newspaper has been so unkind as to make them think.

As for European politics, the *Star* is opposed to the League of Nations. It writes in italics of what we should have had to do in Armenia had we taken a mandate for that territory, and it heartily rejoices because after we have done our part in producing the present unhappy conditions in Europe we have withdrawn from every effort to restore the Continent to a normal life. Indeed, one searches its

223

editorials in vain for any adequate appreciation of the gravity of the European crisis, of its daily increasing seriousness, of the steady disintegration of the Central Powers with the consequent injury to France, Italy, and England, or of any understanding that if Europe collapses the effect cannot be else than disastrous to a country which, to cite only one fact, sells six or seven out of every ten bales of cotton it raises to countries now fast approaching bankruptcy. As for Russia, every conventional American shiver as to the teachings of bolshevism passes down the *Star's* virtuous Middle-Western spine; it cannot understand how anybody could dream of turning his back upon what it calls "the co-operative (!) system on which the world outside of Russia is organized."

In other words, the *Kansas City Star* supplies most excellent Main Street fodder. It sees no deeper under the surface than its Rotary or Kiwanis Club neighbours. It knows nothing of the profounder economic issues, and by its inherited tradition it is compelled to treat the United States of today just as if the world had not been turned over and stood upon its head since 1914. To it, erstwhile apostle of Rooseveltian progressiveness, the election of 1922 with its wonderfully encouraging note of political independence, its amazing evidences of discrimina-

224

tion on the part of the voters of many States, with its swinging back of the pendulum in Montana, Arizona, Kansas, Minnesota, and many other States to sanity, independence, and the old-fashioned American ideals of liberty and free speech, was nothing but "a Hell-Raisers' Election"—the "flocking [of voters] to the men who promised to kick the table over, even though these men could not possibly bring any real help"! Obviously the *Star* will continue to grow rich and prosper. But woe to it if a prophet with a vision should come to Kansas City!

Perhaps it might be well if it were sold now to provide art treasures for the public. The prospect stirs the imagination. If it should then fall into the hands of a Hearst the evil it might do would perhaps offset even a liberal popular education in beauty and in the craftsmanship of the greatest interpreters of life through the arts and crafts. What should happen is the taking over of the *Star* by some group of public spirited men and women who might feel perhaps like suppressing its partisanship, but could agree on building a daily journal which should be a great community organ and interpreter of all the currents of life of the various human elements which go to make up an American city. Probably we cannot hope for any coming true of such a dream. The *Star* succeeds because Main Street is satisfied

225

with it. When Main Street progresses, when those
who live upon either side of it have gone stages further, then shall we have in it a lodestar and not merely
a mouthpiece of narrow and mediocre respectability.

[1] On March 31, 1926, this figure was 256,654; the circulation for
the Sunday edition was 291,611.

[2] Mrs. Kirkwood died suddenly in Baltimore, Feb. 27, 1926. On
July 13, 1926, the Kansas City *Star* and the Kansas City *Times*,
were sold to members of the staff, headed by Irwin Kirkwood, son-
in-law of the late Colonel William R. Nelson. A new company,
which will be owned exclusively by Mr. Kirkwood and his associates,
will be incorporated to take over the ownership and publication of
these papers.

CHAPTER XIII

A NEWSPAPER WITH SIX THOUSAND OWNERS

SIX thousand two hundred and fifty people own stock of the *Minnesota Daily Star* now being published in Minneapolis; these owners are even said to represent thirteen thousand others who are indirect owners by reason of their memberships in labour unions which hold stock. Six thousand two hundred and fifty men and women have cared enough about a free press in Minnesota to put their savings into this enterprise and by doing so they have made it the most interesting experiment in popular newspaper ownership in our English language press. Despairing of getting fair and unprejudiced treatment for the causes dear to their hearts from the press of the Twin Cities, they determined to have a daily organ to voice their views and aspirations. They had found themselves compelled to read commercialized newspapers among which there was no choice. The dailies have all the faults and weaknesses of the ordinary press, which means first of all that they have lost touch with the masses, even though they have large and increasing circulations. They usually print only such news as is favourable to their point of view and they do not hesitate to suppress and to misrepresent. Every thought of their having an obligation of service to the public, or any duty to record faithfully the happenings in the groups that comprise their cities, has passed out of the minds of their managers. What more natural than a revolt against them?

People still remember that the St. Paul *Pioneer Press* was one of several prominent dailies charged during the Hughes insurance investigation with printing bogus news of the inquiry at one dollar a line. The *Pioneer Press* has doubtless reformed since that time, and is virtuous so far as the honesty of its columns is concerned, but so many have been the transgressions of this group of dailies that, like so many other American newspapers, they are supported by thousands and thousands who are without confidence in them. The *Pioneer Press* and its contemporaries no more represent the views of great classes of our citizens who are struggling for economic freedom than does the New York *Times* or the Chicago *Tribune*. More than that, the Twin City dailies are at times utterly ignorant of what is going on under their own eyes. This is clearly demonstrated by the fact that one of the Minneapolis journals sent an editor to Senator Shipstead after his astounding election in the fall of 1922 with the request that he be good enough to tell them just what had happened to the State of Minnesota and why it was that he, this Farmer-Labour candidate, had been elected over the Republican and Democratic aspirants for the Senate. Another of these conservative, capitalistic dailies prophesied in a lurid front-page editorial a couple of days before the election that if Dr. Shipstead were elected the State would flow with blood! Neither the man who wrote that article nor the daily that printed it believed one word in it. They did it to threaten and to frighten, and they did it at the behest of their real masters— the masters of privilege. Beyond question that editorial made thousands of votes for Shipstead. If its author did not know what effect that editorial would have upon the intelligent voters who read it, he and his associates in the other "regular" dailies never fail to understand what goes on in business and banking circles, in the groups that control the local advertising. They need no scouting editors to tell them what the dominators of the commercial life of the Twin Cities wish to have appear in the press; they know— and they act upon their knowledge.

So the men and women who had joined the Nonpartisan League movement decided three years ago that the time had come for an effort to win a square deal from the press. That movement, now nearly deflated, was then at its bubble height and the plan was to build up the free daily through the League and to build the League around the daily. As its editor and organizer the League leaders selected a veteran journalist, Mr. Herbert E. Gaston, and largely under his guidance, spurred by the enthusiasm of many workers, stock to the amount of $750,000 was sold to farmers and workingmen, chiefly in small amounts. Associated with Mr. Gaston was Thomas Van Lear who is now the dominating force in the *Minnesota Daily Star.* For two years Socialist Mayor of Minneapolis, his administration is universally admitted to have been in most respects well above the average. Vigilant in his defence of popular rights, he persistently vetoed ordinances favouring the traction and gas companies. Being himself strongly opposed to the declaration of war, he saved the people of Minneapolis from much of the annoyance and suffering which came to most of our cities, in which the mayors at will suspended the Constitution, the Declaration of Independence, civil rights, and any laws that happened to conflict with the war hysteria of the pack. Throughout his administration the workers had the pride of feeling that at last they had a representative in the City Hall, for Mayor Van Lear began life as a workingman and came up through the unions.

Finding difficulty in getting adequate quarters, a

far too substantial and costly concrete and steel building, one hundred by one hundred feet, was constructed, the necessary presses and equipment purchased, and the enterprise launched on August 19, 1920. Since that time its growth has been so remarkable that the *Star* merits for this reason alone as careful study, by those who are hoping for the rise of a popular press, as do the New York *Call* and the Seattle *Union Record.* The *Star* grew from 35,837 readers to 53,850 in the eighteen months from October 15, 1921, to April 2, 1923, a steady gain of 1000 readers a month. This is an altogether encouraging record, for it has grown in the face of considerable hostility, especially on the part of its rivals, and without, until recently, the department store advertising which so many women read in search of the bargains which help to make both ends meet. Of this circulation a trifle over fifty per cent is in the city; the rest is in the country districts. This showing is the more creditable because, on account of the expense, the *Star* has had to abandon some 2100 patrons in St. Paul to whom the paper was being served by carriers. It has also been made in the face of the fact that the *Star* is a Minneapolis newspaper, despite its name, and is not given to carrying much news even of St. Paul, let alone the State.

But it must be frankly admitted that this growth

231

has been obtained by stooping to all the current fads, the big headlines, the comic strips, and the green night-extra sheets of the regular press. There is nothing whatever in the appearance of the *Star* to differentiate it from the ordinary daily. Its managers declare that without adopting these features they could not have built up the paper so rapidly, if at all. They insist that big headlines govern the news-stand sales, and they declare that a rival, which is much handsomer and more conservative in appearance, has steadily lost ground. Moreover, when my subscription expired I was offered my choice of a suit of overalls,—"better," it urges, "grab a pair of these while they last"!—an automobile wrench, or some cutlery if I would renew—a practice which the *Star* feels that it must adhere to because its chief rivals do the same. And that is also the reason why it imitates its competitors in its news columns and dares indulge in no originality. So it gives us fiction, sports, scandals, women's pages, and all the rest. It is feverishly endeavouring to "get itself across" and wipe out its deficit. That is its all-important objective. Plainly, the *Star* has not endeavoured to tone up the rest of the press by a return to old-fashioned journalism.

When it comes to the advertising side, the *Star* has succeeded in getting enough to enable it to reduce its monthly operating deficit at this writing

(May, 1923) to a small sum. It has obtained a considerable volume of announcements and has hit upon the expedient of getting merchants in certain sections of Minneapolis to do what is practically neighbourhood advertising. It has just succeeded in inducing all the large department stores to use its columns, and it has lately been taken up by some of the large banks. Whether that is to the advantage of the *Star* or not remains to be seen. It is precisely in advertising of this kind that the pitfalls lie. For there is a subconscious as well as a conscious pressure upon business managers who are in the unfortunate position of having deficits and bond interest to meet to soft-pedal when it comes to dealing not only with the existing advertisers but with potential ones. There are those who think that the *Star* is already beginning to weaken. At least they are wondering if it will now attack mistaken banking policies such as the efforts of the Twin City banking-ring to control the rural banks and to close those whose owners dare to be politically independent. Time will show this. For the rest, the *Star's* advertising is clean and its extent is a tribute to the skill of the selling force. It has in its business manager, Mr. John Thompson, an able executive with Eastern newspaper experience to whom belongs much of the credit for the progress made.

The forceful personality of the *Star* is, however,

233

Mr. Van Lear. Because of his knowledge of the *Star's* field, his personal friendships running into thousands, the faith of Labour in him, his intimate understanding of the political situation, and his dogged will power, he has, since the retirement of Mr. Gaston, become the controlling power—there are those who think that his leadership runs to dictatorship. But in judging the *Star* so far as it has gone, it must be recalled that the experiment is still in a formative stage; that it is not yet three years old. It must be remembered, too, that it was never organized on a truly democratic basis or as a co-operative enterprise. It is a pity that it was not, for if it could have succeeded as a wholly democratic institution the value of the experiment would be far greater than it will be if it merely succeeds in making money for its stockholders without demonstrating that there can be democracy among the workers as well as among large groups of owners. The stockholders' meetings usually draw together from one hundred and fifty to two hundred owners and there is free discussion and free criticism, as there should be. But I have a feeling that the paper loses because it is without a workers' council as well, to meet frequently and to discuss freely the peculiar problems and difficulties of this precious experiment. I have the faith to believe that such a council would create loyalty and *esprit de corps,* stiffen the backbone of all

234

concerned, and pay for itself many times over, besides being in direct accord with the principles of the co-operative movement which the *Star* so earnestly champions in its editorial columns.

The *Star* started off with a vigorous and virile editorial policy, but it no longer makes a deep impression with its editorial page. It lacks distinction and vital force. It is without that passion for its causes which one expects from an organ dedicated in advance to certain specific battles. Its editorials are not only short comments, but usually lack both information and power. In this respect the *Star* has indubitably lost ground since the departure from its staff of Mr. Herbert E. Gaston because of a clash of personalities and Mr. Gaston's refusal to recede from his view of what are the rights and privileges of an editor. His departure is still lamented by many of the *Star's* staunchest friends.

Under his guidance it was finding its way into the middle-class homes which must be won for Labour if its cause is to succeed in the long run. It still, of course, stands for liberalism and tolerance; it still records on its editorial page much news of the progress of the labour movement the world over, and it is not recalcitrant to the political Farmer-Labour movement which has made such remarkable headway in Minnesota, since the Nonpartisan League has faded away. But it does not give the educational guidance

235

it should; its managers seem to have the conventional fear of the long editorial, and while the editorials it prints may at times burn with righteous indignation, such are few and far between. Yet here, it seems to me, is the crux of the whole experiment. Why should one wish to carry on another daily unless as a flaming evangel of some cause or causes? Is not the surest way to success to make the *Star* so distinctive editorially and so valuable that it will not only preserve its present excellent standing in its home community but will be turned to by editors throughout the Northwest for its information and for its editorial leadership?

As for its policies, the *Star* advocates state-owned grain elevators, government ownership of railroads and mines, the use of our government-owned ships to compete with the shipping combine, a full-crew train bill, co-operative marketing and co-operative buying and the rest of the Farmer-Labour program which simply means the abolition of all special privilege— not such a terribly radical platform for a daily which is continually denounced as bolshevik! Of course, it is against the tariff robbery and ship subsidies, as well as the proposed restoration of capital punishment by hanging, and against bond issues for public expenses—"Let's Pay As We Go" is its motto. Naturally it opposes the Fascisti movement here and abroad. Its sense of righteousness compels it to

236

oppose the Ruhr infamy and to demand justice for the Russian people. In other words it stands, more or less firmly, for what in England would be considered very mild Labour policies, national and international. It has surely taken the right side on most public questions.

It has been the experience of the liberal weeklies that among their readers are many editors who do not share their views but who read to get another point of view and the many vital facts not found elsewhere. It is also true that many thousands of people read the Hearst dailies because of their desire to see "what the other fellow is saying," and because of admiration for the style of certain of the Hearst editors. The *Star* should profit by these and other examples; at present it seems to think that an unimpressive editorial page is all that the situation calls for. This may be due to fear of repelling possible advertisers by achieving a reputation for dangerous radicalism or to a policy of lying low until a paying readership is built up. But when the circulation of the *Star* reaches about 60,000 or 70,000 it will probably be near the limit of the number obtainable in Minneapolis by means of big headlines and green night-extras. Then will come the test of the paper's ability to widen its field by sheer, intrinsic merit. There can be no better way to accomplish this than to make it intellectually distinguished and famed for its editorial courage and plain speaking. Again, it is surely a mistake to think that the average intelligent American workingman or farmer wants his newspapers written down to please him. There must be multitudes who wish their daily to be instructive and informative. Minneapolis contains many able men who are sympathetic with the *Star's* causes; in local university circles there must be many willing to contribute to the editorial page for slight, if any, recompense. It is, moreover, astounding that in such a city the *Star* is without a book page and never serves as a guide to good reading. A good book page would speedily attract an advertising clientele—it never fails to—as witness the success of the literary page added to the Chicago *Daily News*, whose large popular following long made its managers doubt the wisdom of the experiment which is now paying so well.

Plainly the *Star* ought to have something of the flavour of a university extension movement. I am well aware of course that the paper is compelled by its limited means to condense and to hold down its size to twelve or fourteen pages when the other dailies are printing more than thirty. Yet I believe that careful editing could always steal a couple of columns from other departments, such as the sporting page, which could be used to good advantage, if space for a literary feature could not be gained on the editorial page itself. Nor must it be thought that a development of the paper along this line would mean running it into great expense. Far from it; a good exchange reader it does call for and intelligent editing and the willingness to reprint from other journals and, as suggested, to call in expert outside help. At present the difficulty seems to lie with the business department and its disheartening belief that any "high-brow" policy would not help but hinder—disheartening because it would seem to bear out the theory of the yellow journalists that one must stoop low to win the necessary readership to make both ends meet. Most of them usually console themselves with the promise that when the red figures disappear from their balance sheets they will improve their papers and make them more like what they know they ought to be. It is surprising how many such promises have helped to pave the journalistic road to the Inferno! After examining the plant and going over the situation in Minneapolis, I can but feel that far less money should have gone into mortar, bricks, and cement, and more cash should have been saved to underwrite the deficits and to buy more editorial brains to pull the leadership up to it, rather than that the paper should stoop. A grave responsibility rests upon the *Star's* managers, and not only to the Farmer-Labour movement in Minnesota and the whole country. Between it and its backers, both readers and stockholders, there is a solemn social contract. Any violation of that tacit contract to supply the promised kind of independent daily would hearten the enemies of progress throughout the Republic.

One must not, however, underestimate the *Star's* achievements to date or fail to realize the enormous difficulty of the undertaking. Really to succeed in the best sense, Mr. Van Lear must expect to make the *Star* unpopular, especially in those circles which control the great volume of advertising. If I am right in believing that the paper is burdened with an undue capital investment which should not have been incurred until it was much farther along—many a successful newspaper has started in wretched quarters with second-hand machinery—that can be overcome, as well as the loss of the support of the Nonpartisan League, if the paper can but maintain a reputation for grappling courageously with local abuses as well as with State and national economic problems. Dealing easily with existing evils does very well for a time, but in the long run the *Star* will live or die as its leadership is fearless, outspoken and constructive and as it can convince the community which it serves of its absolute and unswerving rectitude and honesty of purpose. The slightest justified suspicion that it is yielding to advertising pressure or that it could be called off from any crusade for the benefit of the public, would damage it irretrievably, for then there would be but slight reason why anybody should prefer it to the conventional dailies. Indeed, I am heretic enough to believe that in the long run it will succeed best as it ceases to ape the follies of the ordinary press and will prosper directly as it differs from the class dailies with which it has to compete. The necessity, for instance, for its green extra-pages does not seem so convincing when one notices that 20,000 copies of the *Star* are delivered to homes while only from 6000 to 7000 are daily sold on the stands. That is a small percentage of the whole 53,000 or 54,000 to cater to by such meaningless sensationalism. But the proof of the pudding is the eating ; if the *Star* succeeds its managers will be able to claim their justification. As to that we shall see what we shall see.

To date the greatest of the *Star's* many services is that it has printed much news which would otherwise not have seen the light of day in Minnesota and it has had a considerable effect in compelling its rivals to carry news which they would otherwise have ignored. Thus, the existence of the *Star* makes the other editors watch to see what it is going to say and, if it carries on a crusade, the other papers are after a while compelled to take public cognizance, even if they originally did not intend to do so. If this is a somewhat negative influence it is none the less extremely important. One cannot overestimate, too, how much the *Star* has done to hearten and to bind together the groups for which it is pleading. It played a large part in carrying Minnesota for Shipstead and it can be counted on to give much publicity to what is being done and what must be done to safeguard this victory and to win new ones. Its influence ought to spread throughout the whole Northwest if it but lives up to its opportunity.

Finally, the success of the *Star* is of enormous moment to the cause of good journalism everywhere. None of the popularly-owned and group-created dailies of similar type is on a firm financial foundation. Whoever first achieves success with a newspaper which has thousands of owners will have rendered a service to journalism and to the country much more worthy of a distinguished service cross than many of the recipients of these freely-bestowed tokens of a grateful Republic. If it can find a way out of its difficulties, if it can win success without serious compromise and then gradually lift its readership to higher standards of journalism by adopting them itself; if it can steer between the Scylla of violent radicalism and the Charybdis of timid silence for the sake of advertising; if it can make money but save its soul, the *Star* with its 6250 owners will be worth acclaiming throughout the Union. For if it

242

wins its battle it will incalculably advance the democratic movement in America by demonstrating that
one road to the recapture of the press lies open for
other groups to take.

This interesting experiment came to an end when the paper passed
through bankruptcy and was sold to a new company on June 2,
1924. This chapter is retained here as an historical record and
because the cause of failure—bad business management—in no
wise proves that such an experiment in cooperative ownership is
impractical.

O. G. V.

CHAPTER XIV

FREMONT OLDER, A PACIFIC COAST CRUSADER

FROM William Allen White to Fremont Older; from Emporia, Kansas, to San Francisco. It is a long jump, yet he needs must take it who seeks an interesting and vital newspaper editor in the West. That, in itself, is evidence enough of the way modern newspaper conditions have eliminated forceful personalities from the profession. There is no Middle Western editor of national prominence between the Mississippi and "the Coast" except Mr. White. He has been shrewd enough to see that his residence in Emporia is a capital asset of great value; he has preferred to be a big frog in a small puddle. Fremont Older has put in his life in the journalism of San Francisco, and made his mark first as a reporter and then as editor of the *Bulletin*. Now he is the editor of the *Call and Post,* and is one of the two first-rate journalists of the Pacific slope, the other being Chester Rowell, formerly of Fresno.

The distance between Emporia and San Francisco is no greater than that between the poles of thought

244

in San Francisco as to Older. To the well-to-do,
contented, and privileged, Older is anathema. They
not only hate, fear, and distrust him, they honour
him by their disbelief in his sincerity and honesty.
To them "the friend of crooks" is as good as a crook
himself. They lay endless labour agitation and
social unrest at his door, and they cannot forgive
him for his never-ending battling in the Mooney case,
to say nothing of those of Calhoun and Ruef. They
would cheerfully see him drowned in the waters of
San Francisco Bay, and they would gladly pay one
thousand times over for the regalia of any Ku Klux
Klan that would administer correction to him after
the manner of Mer Rouge. But his friends see in
Fremont Older a journalistic knight-errant of superb
power, who can never be made to know that he is
beaten when it comes to a straight-out fight like the
Mooney case. They realize that there is today much
of a Tolstoian Christian in him, that his power of
sympathy and understanding for those who have
erred is almost beyond description. They thank
heaven daily for his courage and determination; they
are ready to go through an earthly purgatory for him
—and they sometimes do—for they know what sacrifices he has made for principle. They admit freely
that at times he has done inexcusable and cruel deeds,
and used indefensible means to his ends. But they
remember, also, that his errors came through sudden,

245

passionate acting on impulses, usually good, which took possession of him and carried him off his feet. They never forget, these loyal friends, that he has done fine things every day of his life, has always fought some good fight or opposed some evil, albeit often in moods like sudden spring gales that blow grains of dirt into eyes never meant to be hurt.

To an outsider, Older fits in well to the social and political life of the California of his time. If he has been ungoverned in assault, it is also true that he has lived among the ungoverned. If he has struck unsparingly it is because his nature had to cry out with bitterness, yes, for years to call for personal vengeance and to seek to inflict it, whenever a single case of individual wrong and suffering cut him to the core. Older is of those who can endure with some philosophy great wrongs of groups; the crime or the pain of one person, or a single bit of human injustice has often—perhaps usually—been the match to explode the whole tremendous magazine of his pent-up idealism, his craving for justice, his amazing sense of outrage at the injury a ruthless human society can do to a single, hapless individual. When the spark reached Older, so his associates say, he worked "like a whirlwind," he was absorbed and obsessed. His terrific power of concentration was never so exemplified. He lived and breathed only for the purpose in hand. In his hunt for his quarry

246

he was remorseless to himself and as untiring as a tiger; in his sheer power he was like a mad elephant charging upon a helpless human.

This man is no great writer, and no *littérateur*, although he has "played up" on his first pages, just like a murder or a prize fight, exquisite bits from Tolstoi, or Shaw, or Chesterton, or Galsworthy. Though in earlier years he loved to write, and though he has read deeply and well, and speaks admirably, he usually writes without distinction of style or literary touch. His autobiography, "My Own Story," gives the measure of this editor as such volumes of self-revelation rarely do. For it is a plain and unvarnished, almost disjointed, collection of human incidents, lengthy anecdotes strung together, which reflect vividly the strength of the man, but prove that in this case again he made no effort for real literary form. It gives us his vigour and power in action, his direct, frank statement, his truthful portraiture, his vivid remembrance of the many extraordinarily interesting and dramatic happenings in which he played his journalistic part, and what is more important, a human part. There is in it no theorizing, no political philosophy, no constructive suggestion for the lasting betterment of human society, whose seamy side he knows so well, no single reflection on the increasing breakdown of government. It all spells action, action, the pursuit of the

247

criminal, the rescue of the debauched, the exposure of the hypocrite, the jailing of the evil-doer and of the political scoundrel. It is always the individual who concerns him, and has called forth the exercise of his indomitable powers.

Self-made, a graduate of the school of hard work, with very little book training, Older's profound reading in the best of literature comes from no outside impulse planted within him. His father having died as a result of Civil War service, he fled at fourteen from the home of a stern, puritanical aunt and emigrated to California at seventeen. Like William Lloyd Garrison he began early his career as a printer's devil, and like him, too, Older received a complete mechanical training—he was foreman of a printing shop at eighteen. In his reporting he showed the same qualities which found full play when he became not only a managing editor, but the kind of managing editor all directing editors try to be and few succeed in being—a director of his newspaper, free from detail and routine drudgery, free to come and go, to give orders like a generalissimo in accordance with the tactics and strategy laid down by himself. Then when the battle was joined the editorializing went on as before under his direction by the pens of others, while he himself plunged into the fray. For he was never a general to stay safely in his headquarters far behind the lines. In addition this editor had a marvelous trick of finding talent where no other editor would think of looking for it. Never was there a more stimulating atmosphere in any newspaper office.

Place this man in any setting and he would be heard from. Placed in San Francisco, the exact background he needed was provided by fate. Political and social rottenness without end, intertwined with big business depravity, and the resulting political upheavals; the control of the State by corrupt corporations, notably the railroads; and then the mighty convulsion of nature and the fire that so nearly wiped out all of the good and the bad alike—surely all of this needed to be matched and more or less moulded by an elemental force in newspaperdom. A hurly-burly, indeed, in which the heaviest blows were given and taken! Probably the pen of a Godkin would have availed little under such circumstances; probably a rough-hewn sledge-hammer and not a rapier of Toledo was needed. At any rate, it was a sledge-hammer which Older used, sometimes inflicting wounds upon the innocent as well as the guilty. So Older's own story is one of incessant battling, often against the heaviest odds. And often he fought in changing moods, for he can alternate swiftly and surprisingly from unbounded optimism to the blackest despair, and even fundamentally alter his whole viewpoint.

How, it may be asked, could such a runner-amuck obtain a newspaper medium with which to fight? Why, in these days of control by advertisers, and of soft-pedaling owners in search of dividends, was he allowed to have a vehicle for his views, for his vicious assaults on things as they are? It was a fortuitous circumstance that he went to the *Bulletin*, which was then in the hands of a trustee, R. A. Crothers, the uncle, and for years the trustee, of a callow young owner who had inherited the paper from his father. No two men could have been more dissimilar than Mr. Crothers and the man who was for so long his editor. But Older had the great merit of being a remarkable circulation-getter and built the *Bulletin's* circulation up to 110,000, keeping it above 100,000 for some years. Nothing succeeds in journalism like circulation success. Mr. Crothers utterly failed to comprehend much of what Older was really driving at; he raged at many things that Older did and said; he winced under the criticism of the business and club world he went about in, but for twenty-four years he did not dare to let Older go. "In adapting Hearst methods to the *Bulletin* Older put a wholehearted sincerity into his work," writes a California journalist who has watched him for years at close range, "so that at the worst it lacked that banal, vulgar, sophisticated, calculated quality of Hearst's stuff. Behind it was always a passionate

250

interest in the stuff of life burning hotter than the biggest headline. If Older could have been a writer instead of an editor, and had developed a critical faculty, he would have been a great literary artist like one of the Russians. He has a passion for life that makes me think of Jean Christophe."

Doubtless Mr. Crothers could not analyze or define Older's power, nor could he possibly have understood why Older could not compromise, why he had to go after people hammer and tongs. But Mr. Crothers could see that Older gave to the *Bulletin* in fullest measure what the newpapers call the "human interest" story. Certainly no man who was so possessed of a sincere passionate interest in humans could fail to put it into his papcr. To talk with Mr. Crothers in his office was only to feel pity for this man who was doomed to be harnessed for years to a whirlwind he could neither understand nor control. When Older sent a man to Honduras to live among all the American beachcombers and fugitives from justice who made that country their home, Mr. Crothers approved because the resulting "stuff," throbbing as it was with amazing stories of errant human beings, was obviously just the matter to sell the paper. But when Older suddenly had a vision of what the present social struggle is all about, became convinced that the theory of the punishment of the individual as a curative was all wrong, and

251

reacted passionately toward the I. W. W. and other stormy petrels of our industrial and social life, Mr. Crothers must have winced, indeed.

Probably he shared the opinion of a critic who wrote in *Collier's Weekly* for November 15, 1913: "Fremont Older has suddenly gone soft—insane, some people call it, being a trifle careless of their lexicology. He was the Nemesis of the crooks. He has become their best friend. . . . " So it was. He who had put Ruef, the corruptionist, into jail after the bitterest and most sensational of prosecutions, turned around within six months and did his utmost to get him out. His man hunts had ended. His was thenceforth the duty to bind up the wounds of the victims of the social fray. The personal bitterness, yes, the flaming hatreds he had felt toward those with whom he had fought, entirely disappeared. "Older is so changed that his friends wonder and his enemies cavil."

No sooner, however, did he begin to speak his enemies fair than there happened the bitterest of all his experiences. The Preparedness Day bomb outrage in San Francisco blew up the *Bulletin*, metaphorically speaking, and nearly finished Older, too, besides inflicting mutilation and death upon those who stood near by. San Francisco went wild, and when Mooney sent to Older a copy of the telegram which he had sent from a near-by resort to the authorities, asserting his innocence and stating that he was returning to San Francisco, the public was in full cry after the editor in an instant. Of course, they said, this is all Older's work. Has he not been taking the I. W. W. and all sorts of wild radicals and wild labour men to his bosom? Has he not printed the most provocative interviews with Bill Haywood, Clarence Darrow, and many other radicals? Is he not pacifistically inclined? Obviously he was the real malefactor, and a storm burst over Older's head, the like of which few journalists have ever had to endure and still fewer could survive. Men fell away from him to right and to left; old friends were mum. Labour helped him little, if any; he had already learned that gratitude is not to be expected from labour sources, and that the labour leaders would not stand by him in a pinch—when he first made this discovery he was as hurt as a child, with a passionate child's surprise and resentment. Well, Older survived the hurricane that swept down upon him, but shaken to the core, though capable yet of great campaigns like those to free Mooney, which he still carries on.

Then came the World War which Older saw through and despised. None of the catchwords which the gullible swallowed availed with him. The useless slaughter left him hopeless for humanity. I met him about that time to find him despairing; he had

253

no fundamental philosophy or faith to fall back upon; no confidence left in the divinity of man. He had, finally, to leave the *Bulletin* and to go to Hearst's *Call and Post,* to the service of a man he must despise, whom he for years opposed. He is pretty free within his field of activity—there were also limits on the *Bulletin* under Crothers—and there are flashes of the old talent. The editorials which he suggests and inspires are wise and philosophical, at times earnest, but wholly without the passion of yesteryear, which, however great the lengths to which it carried him, was the real strength of this editor. It is the Older of a different phase, mellowed, not embittered, but no longer flaming, no longer given to Berserker rage, no longer in search of victims for his passionate sense of outrage.

The change that has come over this man is as extraordinary as anything in his career. A spirit of benign tolerance has taken possession of him and is the key to the Older of today. No longer breathing fire and flame, he preaches tolerance, understanding, good-will, gentleness, forbearance—as if in expectation that the final trump is not far off. What a transformation! This is not the spirit of the great spiritual martyrs, of the men who have ploughed the lonely furrow, paid the price of their dissents, and accepted defeat in the struggle for humanity, conscious that in defeat alone is there victory for the greatest

254

of causes.   We are not yet men on a raft in mid-ocean with but a few hours of life left and nothing to do but to make peace with one another and to face the inevitable.   The fight is not yet lost, the flag not yet hauled down, the battle not yet over.   Perhaps, a friend suggests, any radical, particularly one who came to his radicalism after forty, is entitled to a few years of quiet philosophizing, even if it is the philosophy of defeat.   But for a man who, like Older, was for years the inspiration of young idealists desirous of bettering human conditions, who even through the war stuck to his belief that war and the Christian way of doing things are incompatible (John D. Barry wrote almost pure pacifism in his daily articles for the *Bulletin* throughout the war to the honour of both men), the nobler part, if temperament permits, is surely to go down with ardour unquenched, hope undimmed, and faith unbroken.

It is well, of course, for those of us who can to see with years the sins of our youth and to discard them; but pure unadulterated benevolence and good-will lead nowhere save to a comfortable old age.   For the editor who would achieve something more than circulation the fighting edge must not be dulled, the lash must still crack and sting.   Fremont Older's contribution to journalism has been the proof that a powerful, honest, truthful personality, free to speak out, can, even in these times, achieve great good,

255

though he produce a paper patterned in its externals after the worst. No one can commend the *Bulletin* or the *Call* under Older for dignity or sobriety of type, or excellence of make-up, or modesty of statement, or even adequate presentation of all the world's news. It has been his sincerity, his earnestness, his romantic belief in the traditions of San Francisco and in the future of the city of the Golden Argosy, his unselfishness, his willingness to court and take punishment, which have won for him the description of "a great editor" and carried him forward, despite all his mistakes of temper and method and the crudity of much of the journalism which won him more than 100,000 readers.

So I see in Fremont Older a typical figure of the Far West, a product of his surroundings, who probably could not have flowered similarly in any other portion of the United States. Had he been transplanted to New York he must have been affected by the atmosphere of that city. He would still have been a violent, elemental force; he would still have unhorsed politicians, jailed boodlers, and run grafters out of town; he would still have been the helpful, understanding friend of ex-convicts and of courtesans. But somehow he belongs in that setting of the Golden Gate. There is the tallness and the strength of the Sequoias in him; there is, or was, the suddenness of the California rains; there was in him something of

256

the brutality of that still backward and often crude civilization which rides roughshod to its materialistic ends, and there is also in him the softness and appealingness, the insight and intuition of a woman. To the challenge of the essential goodness in him has leaped the goodness of thief and murderer, of the sin-stained woman and the hopeless opium fiend. In a period when personality and even personal force are disappearing from journalism one turns with joy to such a character, difficult as it is to analyze, great as are its contradictions. For, at least, Fremont Older has done and dared.

CHAPTER XV

HENRY WATTERSON AND HIS *COURIER-JOURNAL*

FOR Henry Watterson geographical location did
much. To be the leader of the press for a section of the country is to speak with much authority
and influence and after the death of Henry W. Grady
of the Atlanta *Constitution*, there was no one to challenge Mr. Watterson's pre-eminence in the South.
His death, indeed, left the old Confederacy without a single editor whose pen has made itself known
outside the confines of his State. Whether Col.
Watterson would have been as large a frog in the
Northern puddle is open to much question; he, at
least, was clear in his mind that he belonged to Louisville. There Col. Watterson typified the opinion of
the Border States, if not of the entire South, in the
minds of most Northern editors. It was his opinion
which was sought and quoted as the representative
one of his part of the country.

That he held this position because of unusual gifts
is beyond question. He had a rich, picturesque, and

powerful, though usually verbose and often bombastic
style, a style so characteristic that everybody recognized in it the man, with all his rich and human
qualities, and understood that the picturesqueness
was as potent in the editor himself as in his expression
of his thoughts.   He wrote at great length as was the
habit of his teachers and predecessors and many of
his generation, like Carl Schurz, of whom Watterson
once said: "His is immeasurably the best intellect
which has appeared in this country since Calhoun."
Indeed, Watterson never yielded to the modern demand for "brief, pungent paragraphs" and to the end
did not hesitate not only to write two- and three-col-
umn editorials, but nine-column, spread over three
successive editorial pages, often signed, often ini-
tialed, just as if it were necessary to label what could
never be concealed or by any chance attributed to
any one else.   The older he grew the richer, of course,
became the vein of his reminiscence and his historical background.   If his historical interpretations
were by no means always sound, he could at least
fortify them with a wealth of detail; *quorum pars fui*
was a phrase he could justly quote as to himself in
connection with many an episode of national political importance in which he played a part behind the
scenes—notably the ill-starred Greeley campaign.
Undoubtedly he was the last survivor of his *genus*
and this he sensed himself for he wrote in his "Marse
259

Henry" [1] of the newspaper of today: "Neither its individuality, nor its self-exploitation, scarcely its grandiose pretension, remains. . . . There continues to be printed in large type an amount of shallow stuff that would not be missed if it were omitted altogether. But, except as a bulletin of yesterday's doings, limited, the daily newspaper counts for little, the single advantage of the editor—in case there is an editor—that is, one clothed with supervising authority who 'edits'—being that he reaches the public with his lucubrations first, the sanctity that once hedged the editorial 'we' long since departed."

But it is not only that the public is wearied of long editorial fulminations. It is no longer interested in the same degree in political events and political machinations. Once of absorbing interest to the newspaper public, they no longer arouse the enthusiasms, the bitter antagonisms or the intense loyalties of the seventies, eighties, and nineties. The emphasis in national life is shifting to matters industrial and economic which Col. Watterson barely sensed and perhaps never plumbed. True, he was an ardent and enthusiastic tariff reformer, a never failing champion of tariffs for revenue only. Yet his main interests were in the political game. There, he was shrewd enough to see, an editor can only wield

[1] "Marse Henry," an Autobiography by Henry Watterson. George H. Doran, New York, 1919.

great influence if he himself refrains from political office—he put it: "Disinterestedness being the soul of successful journalism, unselfish devotion to every noble purpose in public and private life, he should say to preferment, as to bribers, 'get behind me, Satan' . . ." His reminiscences clearly show his appreciation of the weakening effect of the political career of Whitelaw Reid. Indeed, Col. Watterson himself often ventured too deep into practical politics, as the episode of his clash with Woodrow Wilson shows; the safest course for the editor is after all to let the politicians come to him and to sit as an independent judge upon them and their actions.

But wherever the Colonel went he took deep feeling and intense emotions with him. Sooner or later he quarrelled with almost every President. Of Grover Cleveland he once declared at a Kentucky Democratic Convention, that if he should be a candidate in 1892: "I will not vote for his nomination, if his be the only name presented, because I firmly believe that his nomination will mean the marching through a slaughter house to an open grave and I refuse to be a party to such a folly." Of Theodore Roosevelt he wrote that he was "as sweet a gentleman as ever scuttled a ship or cut a throat," and much of the same character which, however, did not prevent their dining together after Theodore Roosevelt had returned to a dissatisfied and restless private life.

Watterson found in Grant an easy target for his diatribes, and it is certain that if Horace Greeley, whom he profoundly admired and ardently supported, had been elected their friendly relationship would not have lasted long.

But these and other eccentricities and his offences against taste, like his long list of unfulfilled prophecies, were readily forgiven by the audience which hung upon his words. For them he was a licensed editorial libertine; his lapses were laughed aside as just one of "Marse Henry's" pleasant idiosyncrasies. What other editor could so have abused a President as popular as Roosevelt and escaped unscathed? The truth is that the South took a pride in him as in any other noted Southern institution and the Haldeman family, with him the owners of the *Courier-Journal,* were wise enough to agree to complete editorial autonomy as his share in the publication and were shrewd enough to realize that he was their greatest asset and a national one. They soon found that educated Kentuckians who moved to other parts of the United States usually subscribed to the *Courier-Journal* to read what the Colonel was saying. He lifted the *Courier-Journal* out of the position of a purely local or sectional paper. Together owners and editor produced a daily which in its ability, its cleanness, and its dignity, its excellent display of news and its varied and informing correspondence was a credit to the country—it still ranks high in some respects. His unique position Col. Watterson fully realized; it is only natural that he should have played up to his part. How could he help knowing that whenever he appeared on a Southern platform men and women beheld the "Lost Cause" and identified him with the romance with which the South has sanctified and glossed over its memory of the abortive effort to break up the Union? Yet Southerner that he was he could swim counter to the stream of public opinion. It is related of a poor white in Col. Watterson's section that in defending his wayward son after atrocious misbehaviour he sought to palliate the boy's offence by assuring an eye-witness that, whatever else might be said of his scion, his son had "never cussed his ma at the table." Col. Watterson never cussed his Southern motherland in a way to offend the prejudices of his friends and neighbours. But he was not a hide-bound partisan, as his advocacy of the Greeley Liberal Republican ticket showed; he was politically truly independent.

He was not, therefore, to be classed politically with the "professional Southerners"; there were distinct streaks of liberalism in him. Booker T. Washington wrote of him: "If there is anywhere a man who has broader or more liberal ideas concerning the Negro, or any undeveloped, I have not met him" and the great coloured orator gratefully recalled Col.

Watterson's going on short telegraphic notice to speak in New York on behalf of Tuskegee, although the death of one of his children had led him to forswear all public appearances. Watterson came to speak extremely well of the Abolitionists, and could write in 1910 with considerable detachment and much discernment of the puzzling character of John Brown. It is a fact that the Colonel drifted almost accidentally, largely because of social ties, into the Confederacy and entered its service without enthusiasm. Hence he never shared the bitterness of many and was early without rancour in the field for the restoration of the old feeling of good-will between the sections. The very fact, however, that he was a conventional Southerner in aspect and bearing and often in mode of thought, made it easy for him to say things and to take positions which would in others have aroused fierce antagonisms. He could advocate changes which, when they came from the pen of a Northerner, gave rise to coarse abuse and anger. Indeed, Col. Watterson must have appreciated the unique character of his position; he could differ with almost every Administration without being called a fault-finding, carping critic, or a pessimistic or un-American one; or one never satisfied, or a holier-than-thou person, or any other of the epithets applied, for instance, to Carl Schurz, George William Curtis, Samuel Bowles, and other editors of the Mugwump school, as the early independents were called. In another man in another place this going scatheless might have been set down as proof of the fact that he could be safely ignored. No one could suggest that in Col. Watterson's case.

Yet when the measure of the man is taken it cannot be said that, for all his extraordinary knowledge and range of writing, he left a profound impress upon his time. Undoubtedly he suffered from the lack of a more complete intellectual and cultural training in his youth, and was, perhaps, not wholly beyond a familiar fault of the successful orator or editorial preacher of being himself the victim of his alliterations and his swelling periods. He once wrote thus pessimistically of his tribe: "The editor dies even as the actor, and leaves no copy. Editorial reputations have been as ephemeral as the publications which gave them contemporary importance." It will always be difficult to assay Watterson, the editor, apart from Watterson, the darling of his Southern gods. Yet his limitations as editor were marked. No one need quarrel with him because he was a sharp critic and, therefore, ever disappointed in the politicians he helped to make and unmake. By that critical faculty he served well. But at bottom his professional philosophy was faulty. The editor he thought "should keep to the middle of the road, and well *in rear* of the moving columns; loving his art—for such it is—for art's sake; getting his sufficiency, along with its independence, in the public approval and patronage, seeking never anything for himself." Naturally with this code it is not surprising that, for all his liberalism, for all his anti-imperialism and anti-militarism, there was little love lost between him and men of the type of Samuel Bowles, Edwin L. Godkin, and Horace White.

Curiously enough he never even mentions Mr. Godkin in his memoirs and finds in Mr. Godkin's newspaper antithesis, Charles A. Dana of the New York *Sun*, his editorial ideal—which is perhaps one reason why in the indices to the New York *Nation* from 1870 to 1900 there is only one reference to the Kentucky Colonel. Dana, "Marse Henry" declared, was "the most scholarly and accomplished of American journalists, he made the *Sun* shine for all. . . . I never knew a more efficient journalist, what he did not know about a newspaper was scarcely worth knowing"—a correct estimate in some respects but one which leaves out all moral valuation and touches not at all upon the moot question of Mr. Dana's cynicism and the character of his contributions to American political and cultural life and its advancement. Dana, however, surely did not believe in keeping "well *in rear* of the moving columns." Perhaps it is due to that principle as well as to some human weaknesses and the lack of a closer political reason-

266

ing that Col. Watterson failed to leave as rich a heritage as his talents would have warranted. Towards the end of his life he, like all of his generation, was more and more apart from the deep underlying economic currents of our national life; he wrote some of the bitterest, sharpest, and most prejudiced editorials of his career when the war came on. There are still many younger who fail to realize how completely the national stage setting has changed, how different the language of the actors is destined to be.

Probably Henry Watterson will be best remembered in the years to come by what he did to bring North and South together when to be a liberal Republican and politically independent took courage and character; by his efforts for true reconstruction, by his realization that even after Emancipation it is true that this nation cannot exist half slave and half free. With real individualities all but gone from the American press, it is a melancholy reflection that there is no editor remaining South of Mason and Dixon's line—indeed, anywhere—whose written or spoken word can deeply influence so many people, or voice the aspirations of a group, or any editor who can be so freely a law unto himself.

Even before Henry Watterson's retirement from active editorial service a great change had come over the *Courier-Journal*. A conflict—over prohibition, it is said—between the members of the Haldeman family paved the way to a sale in 1918 of this historic daily and its evening edition, the Louisville *Times*, to a "rank outsider," Judge Robert Worth Bingham, who, by his marriage, acquired great wealth and now figures as "the editor" of both newspapers. His editorial writers are hired to do the job as he outlines it and under him the *Courier-Journal* now has the aim and vision and the weaknesses of a metropolitan daily. Whether there is a gain here to compensate for the disappearance of so vivid a personality, for the loss by the community of the sense of proprietorship it had in "Marse Henry's paper," of the local loyalty and somewhat provincial devotion of its earlier readership, it is too early to tell, but it seems utterly improbable.

Changes of policy there already are. Col. Watterson resigned after a year as editor emeritus because Judge Bingham swung his paper to the support of the League of Nations. Where the famous editor was bitterly anti-German and anti-British, the *Courier-Journal* of today is neither. Where Col. Watterson never accepted Wilson personally, the *Courier-Journal* now upholds and rejects him by turns. "Watterson loved the Irish, the South, the Negro, the valiant, the oppressed, and the unequal" writes a prominent citizen of Louisville; "today the *Courier-Journal* has no loves." Where Col. Watterson opposed prohibition, the *Courier-Journal* today hesitantly accepts it.

The paper also accepts the woman suffrage Col. Watterson so vehemently opposed, but balks at its logical consequences. The paper is truly no longer the vehicle of a personality, but has become, like the New York *Tribune* and *Sun* and others which were once distinguished by powerful editors, a business institution. It is conservative in policy, and "practical" in aim; yet it is still a paper of distinction. Its owners have sensed in considerable degree the desire of the public for unbiased news and the opportunity to do its own thinking and the readers of the *Courier-Journal* are today probably making up their own minds more often than in the days when they allowed Col. Watterson to do that for them. The editorial page of their favourite daily is certainly no longer challenging, vibrant, or so informative. It is almost without distinction. It can now be safely ignored. If this fact at one time raised the interesting question as to whether the *Courier-Journal* would be able to hold its clientele—about half of its purchasers are urban and the other half residents of rural sections not particularly interested in Louisville happenings—the circulation figures show that it is not only holding the following of Col. Watterson, but is steadily growing. Thus it had only 25,000 readers in 1917. The war had carried it up to 41,361 when Col. Watterson's retirement took place. Today it has 51,484, while the sale of its Sunday issue has

269

gone to 73,000 copies.[2] Yet its political influence is today almost nil.

When all is said and done, the fact remains that the *Courier-Journal* is now the property of a very rich man, new to the business, whose interests in the coming struggle over economic issues must necessarily be on the side of privilege and property. Already it is accused of unfairness and lack of truth-telling in its reporting of the activities of unpopular minority groups. Already it is said that in the personnel of the present *Courier-Journal* there is no longer left a single link between it and the paper of Watterson. In writing of the retirement from the *Courier-Journal* of Mr. Arthur B. Krock, long its able Washington correspondent and managing editor, the Louisville *Herald,* a morning rival, declared that no one was left on the *Courier-Journal* with similar journalistic knowledge and experience. It then made the following extremely pertinent and interesting comment upon the problem presented by the *Courier-Journal* of Judge Bingham:

It is the singular fate of newspapers which become the property of men of large wealth, which are bought to satisfy and to subserve an ambition, that they have a tendency to become separated from the newspaper world as such and to plane in an orbit of their own. It does not matter whether the new owners are bitten by political ambitions or not. It does not signify whether their purposes

270

are of a lofty beneficence or inspired by some generous ideal. The story is the same. Its progress follows a regular course. The newcomers are convinced that money will buy anything, a fallacy which in the newspaper world has been proved time and time again. They are convinced that all they have to do is to open wide the purse, to distribute largesse broadcast, and victory will perch on their banners and the blessings of a grateful people reward their efforts. But we do not recall a case where that desired result has been achieved. And we have in mind a great many where an ancient prestige has been lost, a solid reputation imperiled, a great influence squandered and nothing has been left but a plant and a staff.

With the Louisville *Herald's* further dictum that "newspapers demand and require a personality" it is no longer possible to agree. That was true forty or fifty years ago. It is not so today, as witness the New York *Times,* the Detroit *News,* the Cleveland *Plain Dealer,* and many others whose material prosperity is enormous. It is true, as the *Herald* says, that "without the guidance and the driving-power of the individual whose heart and soul, whose gifts and whose knowledge are dedicated to the labour with an unremitting zeal, there will be not a newspaper in the high acceptation of the word, but a collector of news expensively produced and voicing no opinions any one cares to heed, shaping no policies constructive, independent, and worthwhile." But that is what the vast majority of the American press is today under the

271

pressure of undue commercialism and materialism and there is little chance of any paper like the *Courier-Journal* being anything else.

As stated, it is becoming more and more opposed to change and to constructive criticism; it is nearly if not quite the conventionalized rich man's daily—it is now quite conventional in its make-up and features. Leaving aside any question as to how that rich man acquired his money, the fact is that what is good in his papers is being handed to the community somewhat in the manner of favours from the fortunate to the less fortunate and that is an attitude likely to be resented by the readers even though their numbers may grow. Beyond question, Louisville owes some considerable meed of thanks to Judge Bingham for keeping the *Courier-Journal* as clean and as high-toned; but it is not in the ownership of our dailies by rich men without the journalistic *flair,* and without ideals warmly cherished and warmly held, that the salvation of our press is to be found—or the solution of its so menacing problems.

² On March 31, 1926, these figures were 71,921 for the daily, and 112,850 for the Sunday issue.

CHAPTER XVI

THE JAMES GORDON BENNETTS AND THEIR NEWSPAPER

IT would be easy to moralize about the late James Gordon Bennett—he died in 1918—and to dwell upon his frailties, for the lesson of his career is obvious. As a young man there came to him a wonderful opportunity to serve his country through a great newspaper then near the zenith of its prosperity and power. The end of his life of self-imposed exile and absentee ownership found his newspaper but a shadow of its former self, with so little to distinguish it that newspaper-men frequently forgot to glance at it on their way to work—overlooked the New York *Herald* with its international reputation of yesteryear unsurpassed by any journal in the world, the New York *Herald* with more great "beats" to its credit than any other newspaper! There were years and years when no rival journalists dared to go to bed before seeing a copy of the early edition of the *Herald*, which they picked up in fear and trembling lest they find in it one of those record-breaking "stories" which made its name as famous as that of "The Thunderer" in every capital of the globe. Who can forget the thrills that ran through the world when the *Herald's* "special commissioner," Henry M. Stanley, reported the discovery and rescue of Livingstone in darkest Africa, when out of the forlorn Lena Delta came the story of the stark tragedy of the *Jeannette* sent to the Arctic by the *Herald?* No one who experienced them.

The truth is that, if the Bennetts, father and son, were short of some of the ordinary moralities, they were the most remarkable news men this country has ever produced. The father revolutionized the whole science of news-getting, and the son outdid him by creating exclusive news. He would invest thousands of dollars in a news story, knowing that it might be two years before he could get any return. There must have been many thousands spent without any result, but the younger Bennett had learned in his father's school that nothing pays like news. The father began his career as a rank sensationalist, a muck-raker, a purveyor of scandal. People read his sheet—as so many thousands read Hearst's today— "to see what the demagogue is saying," and lamented that so great a scourge could come to harry staid and respectable New York. From having to write the whole sheet himself, the father was soon able to hire many to write for him—it was his boast that he

THE NEW YORK HERALD.

WHOLE NO. 8184.　　　　　　MORNING EDITION—MONDAY, JANUARY 31, 1859.　　　　　　PRICE TWO CENTS.

The "Sensational" First Page of the *Herald* in 1859 under
the Management of the Elder James Gordon Bennett

sent sixty-three special correspondents into the field during the Civil War, to some of whom he guaranteed and gave complete freedom of utterance unchecked by any blue pencil. Gradually what we should today call the "yellowness" of the early *Herald* began to fade away. It has always had a penchant for personalities and gossip, but it became a remarkably accurate news sheet. Take up its files for 1858 and 1859—printed on a splendid rag paper which is white and strong to this hour—and you will find it mild, indeed, compared to the conservative dailies of 1918, and what is more interesting, you will find that it reported local news with an accuracy nowhere equalled today. Any one who has had occasion to test those files of the *Herald* knows that they are remarkable historical material, whereas no historian would care to rely upon the daily journalistic records of today—woe to future generations if they should trust the contemporary press accounts for the true story of the great war of the nations!

Not that the morals of the *Herald* of 1850-1860 were what they should have been. The first James Gordon Bennett was pro-slavery, pro-Tammany, and pro-everything which we should say today "made against good government." "Intercourse with him indeed quickly revealed his cold, hard, utterly selfish nature and incapacity to appreciate high and noble aims," wrote one of his war correspondents.

When the Civil War broke out, he was in much the same plight as his modern imitator, Hearst, in 1917; people denounced him as disloyal and unpatriotic and threats of a mob compelled a radical change of front. At once he became a loyalist of the loyalists; he gave a yacht to the Government, his son became a volunteer officer in the navy, and he saved the day by redoubling his news efforts. Politicians still had to reckon with the *Herald's* influence. Count Gurowski wrote in his diary in August, 1861, that it was generally believed that Lincoln read only the *Herald*. John Bright at the same time blamed the "reckless tone of your New York *Herald*," which, according to Rhodes, "spoke for a potent public sentiment outside of New England." The best news from the front was in either the *Herald* or the *Tribune*. For decades the special foreign service of the former was unsurpassed; even though it carried trivialities and scandal, one had to read it if one would be posted as to events and political personalities in Europe.

To this service the younger Bennett gave his personal attention when events took him to Paris to live. There is no doubt of his ability, and no doubt that he had it in him also to play a great part in his country's history had he desired to live another life than he chose. To have guided the destinies of his newspapers—he founded both the *Telegram* and the Paris

276

Herald—by cable is evidence in itself of his power, for he was always in closest touch with the smallest details and constantly upsetting this or that for some freakish reason as his eccentricities grew upon him. There was much of the pioneer in him. As his father speedily recognized the news possibilities in the cable, the son became one of the owners of the Commercial Cables in order that the *Herald* might profit thereby. When the automobile appeared, it was Mr. Bennett who saw the news and business value of being first in this field, and the same was true of the aëroplane, as it had been of the bicycle. He liked the novel and the bizarre and he did not mind if people ridiculed him and the *Herald;* what he dreaded was their not talking about his papers. Until late in life he kept the faculty of looking far ahead; it was not by accident that a correspondent of the *Herald* stood beside Dewey on that memorable morning in Manila Bay when he said to Gridley: "You may fire when you are ready."

Again, the second Bennett had the great good sense to make himself supreme in several fields, realizing the value to a daily of specialties. Thus, the *Herald* was for generations the great shipping medium because it spent thousands in special dispatches from all over the world reporting ship arrivals and departures. In the theatrical field, as in that of sports, it was long without a rival. Every naval officer, yachtsman, and lover of horses read it, as did every sporting man, the latter tempted for years by a class of immoral advertisements to which the Department of Justice, in the person of one Henry L. Stimson, put an end, the famous proprietor himself being fined $25,000—a remarkable public achievement as to which the press of New York was silent—to its shame. Moreover, the *Herald* succeeded without a strong editorial page. Outside of Mr. Bennett's own name, there is hardly that of a virile journalist to be recalled in connection with his properties. This may have been because many men may not have wished to be associated with one whose whims were so apt to terminate careers without warning. In his last years Mr. Bennett apparently lost all faith in the uses of an editorial page, and the *Herald's* influence, unlike that of the *Tribune* and the *Times*, rested exclusively upon its presentation of the news. Gradually, as Mr. Bennett grew older, his grip relaxed, his visits to this side became fewer and fewer, and the *Herald's* star began to wane. Its circulation rapidly fell off until he was compelled to drop the price to one cent in order to achieve 100,000 readers where once there had been 500,000. On April 1, 1918, it swore to 128,814; in 1916 to only 92,853; years previously its finances had compelled the dropping of its costly special dispatches from every quarter of the globe.

Whereas for years the *Herald* had met the deficits of the *Telegram,* that pink drab of lowest journalism kept its elder sister afloat during the last years of the Bennett ownership, despite the fact that during the war it was the soul of mendacity, killing off in a few months of the war more Germans than were ever in the Kaiser's empire and preaching the worst kind of bitterness and hate. Incidentally, the *Telegram* knew itself how it feels to be killed because, in one of his unaccounted for moods, Mr. Bennett, on November 21, 1897, thus took the public into his confidence and notified his advertisers by the following editorial in the *Herald* that he had been deceiving them:

The *Evening Telegram* ceases to appear from yesterday for the time being, in accordance with Abraham Lincoln's wise saying that "you can fool all the people some of the time and some of the people all the time, but you can't fool all the people all the time."

And he was right. The public also can fool publishers all the time and advertisers can fool publishers some of the time and they seem to be continuing to fool them all the time. But the *Evening Telegram* doesn't propose to be fooled all the time.

An up-to-date evening newspaper at one cent doesn't pay. Therefore those who are publishing evening newspapers at one cent are either fooling the public or fooling themselves.

As the *Evening Telegram* doesn't intend either to fool itself or fool the public it has ceased publication until the time becomes ripe when it can stop being fooled and stops fooling.

This was on a Sunday and the entire newspaper world was agog the next day to see if Mr. Bennett would really slay his journalistic child. Whether on sober thought he came to it himself, or whether he was persuaded by cablegrams from New York, the *Telegram* was granted a stay of its execution by the following announcement in the *Herald:*

> In view of its many outstanding advertising contracts and large circulation and for other considerations, the several editions of the *Evening Telegram* will continue to appear as usual every day, with all the latest news and the numerous bright features that have made the *Telegram* the favourite evening paper of Greater New York.

The death of Mr. Bennett on May 14, 1918, revealed the fact that his fortune had been rapidly shrinking and that there were not available the means to carry on the newspapers. For years the faithful men of long service, who had kept the Bennett properties alive, had been assured by their employer that these properties would be left to them to conduct as a co-operative experiment. These pledges were broken in the will and the executors directed to continue to publish the papers. This being impossible for several reasons, they passed in January of 1920 into the hands of Mr. Munsey, whereby there ended one of the most brilliant chapters in American journalism and the *Herald* became a hybrid, part *Sun* and part *Herald*, without the great characteristics of either.

CHAPTER XVII

EDWIN L. GODKIN, MASTER OF COMMENT AND OF STYLE

TO the senior Samuel Bowles, of the *Springfield Republican*, George Harvey has awarded the distinction of being the greatest of American editors. If by that Col. Harvey means that he was the greatest of our editorial writers, he errs; that palm belongs rightfully to Edwin Lawrence Godkin, founder of *The Nation* and its editor until its merger, in 1881, with the New York *Evening Post*. Of this newspaper he, after two years of rule by a triumvirate consisting of Horace White, Carl Schurz and himself, became the directing head, with complete editorial power and freedom. Few men in American journalism have had so untrammelled an opportunity when not owners of the newspapers they directed, and none others have so nobly used it. To his adopted country Mr. Godkin, like many another foreign-born citizen, brought an enthusiastic loyalty and devotion, a veritable idealization of its traditions and its possibilities rarely found in native-born Americans, who take their birthright as a matter of course and have no European experience by which to measure the richness of their heritage. But he brought far more than that; a determination to do everything in his power to serve America, to better her, to uplift her standards, and to keep her true to the ideals of the Founders who made their country in their time such a beacon light to all the world.

This he did easily because he was a master of prose style. His English was clear and straightforward, wonderfully powerful, free from all unnecessary verbiage. No one else, no Bowles, or Watterson, or Raymond, has approached that style in our press except occasionally. For one thing, it was the writing of a completely educated man polished by travel and the society of intellectual leaders everywhere, who wrote only with profound conviction, who till the last of his long career burned over injustice with the ardour of youth. To this he added a power of irony and sarcasm never equalled by any one, almost too great at times.[1] Woe to him who laid himself open to that trenchant attack! But not even those familiar with his style by contact with its daily expression can run over his editorials now without a sense of amazement at their clarity and logic, at

[1] A writer in the *Atlantic Monthly* for January, 1897, declared of Mr. Godkin's style that "for lucidity and directness it is unequalled among contemporary writers in this country or in England."

their ability to interest at all times, at the way in which he dissected the statement he proposed to attack with the skill of a great surgeon in laying bare the seat of a disease before actually beginning to operate. That dissecting, or restating in Mr. Godkin's words, of the position taken was often in itself enough to refute the fallacies or shams he set out to expose. But to it knowledge, logic, and power added fact after fact and argument after argument, until the column editorial was complete. "Never write without conveying information or expressing an opinion with reasons," was his injunction to a youthful writer. That rule was always followed by the office. Indeed, his ordinary style could be imitated—one of his subordinates used to flatter himself that his writings were often mistaken for his chief's. But that mordant humour and that biting irony of Mr. Godkin's at his best no one could imitate. Not even Horace White, indubitably for three decades the ablest writer in journalism on questions of currency, finance, and economics, could so clearly analyze and set forth the essentials of an issue, could so strip the clothes from the puppet held up to deceive the public and lay bare its hidden stuffing.

And behind it all lay great cheerfulness, joy of life, and the keenest appreciation of the humour of every situation. It was the custom to picture the most brilliant editor of the *Evening Post* as sour and crabbed, as a continual scold and fault-finder, because he was incessant in his attacks upon evil, unyielding in his return again and again to a subject—no editor has ever more clearly understood the editorial power of constant iteration. Just as it was actually asserted by some that Mr. Godkin opened his editorial council every morning with the singing of "God Save the Queen" and the distribution of gold received in the morning's mail from the Cobden Club in London, so it was believed that his council was marked only by pessimism and gloom—exactly as in England today Dean Inge for his setting forth truly the darkness and dangers of a given situation or policy has earned the sobriquet of the "gloomy Dean." Instead, the editorial council sparkled with wit and good humour and cheer; rounds of laughter were its usual accompaniment. No matter what his political defeats, Mr. Godkin's faith and good cheer never waned save that at the close of his career, when ill health had come upon him, the American plunge into the needless and, therefore, wicked war with Spain profoundly depressed him. His prophetic eye visioned then our subsequent overseas conquests in the Caribbean and elsewhere, our big navy mania, and all the other symptoms of that imperialism which in the long run has wrecked more than one rich and powerful nation.

Mr. Godkin was like most reformers gifted with

285

unusual political imagination and the ability to look into the future and to foresee the results of a given procedure. Like all men whose lives are steeped in principle and fortified by beliefs held with profoundest conviction, he could not be content to sail with the wind or to go with the popular passion. Hence he was nearly always engaged in stemming the tide with the result that the superficial newspaper reader—and there are few others in America—wrote him down for a scold. Was he not perpetually criticizing? For opposition editors this was, of course, the most natural opening. They played upon his "un-Americanism"—his English birth was naturally constantly brought out and the kindly invitation to go back where he came from, which one type of American thinks the fitting answer to any one born abroad who dares to criticize anything American, was frequently given to him, always to Mr. Godkin's amusement. Where men thought their arrows would penetrate they fell harmlessly from his armour of humour. No one who has not gone over the files of the New York and Chicago newspapers for the summer of 1884, the Cleveland-Blaine campaign, can have any idea of the lengths to which personal abuse went in those days.

The respectables of that day, only nineteen years after Appomattox, were horrified at the decision of Mr. Godkin and the *Evening Post* to support a Demo-

First Page of the New York *Evening Post* in the Closing
Days of the Exciting Blaine-Cleveland Election, 1884,
under the Editorship of Edwin L. Godkin

crat for the Presidency. Were that newspaper today to declare for Lenin and Communism its editors would be subjected to no greater abuse or more emphatic social pressure. This campaign of 1884 gave Mr. Godkin precisely the opening he was looking for and established his reputation as a first-class "fightin' man" and a superb political campaigner. But for Godkin, George William Curtis, and Carl Schurz, Grover Cleveland must have been defeated. As it was, the press associations insisted that Blaine was elected—it all turned on a matter of a few thousand votes in New York State where the efforts of the *Evening Post* were, of course, most felt. Every other newspaper except the *Evening Post* conceded Mr. Blaine's success, but, thanks to the excellent work of the *Evening Post* in getting special dispatches of its own from up-State, the tide was turned and perhaps even the danger of another stolen Presidency ended. For Mr. Godkin it was not merely a question of fighting against a candidate who was obviously unfit; for him there was a straight-out moral issue at stake and it was his ability to see moral issues more clearly and more often in the complexities of personal politics and the confusion of issues, and his readiness to stand for the ethics of politics, quite as much as his style, which made him the greatest of our daily editorial writers. As Viscount Bryce put it: "It is not for his intellectual gifts that Mr. Godkin was most admired, but for the moral qualities that directed the exercise of those gifts."

For the student the significance of the "Mugwump" movement of 1884, with Mr. Godkin as its chief exponent and protagonist, lies in the fact that it marked the beginning of political free thinking in our modern America. Voters had, of course, changed parties before that, notably on the Free-Soil and Slavery issues; but this was the first time that the principle of independence in politics had been avowed by a large body of voters who announced their determination, thereafter, to vote according to convictions and not according to inherited partisan allegiances and party ties. The hidebound Chicago *Tribune* and the New York *Tribune* were justified from their point of view in pouring out their vials of wrath upon Mr. Godkin's head and in waving the "bloody shirt" anew and insisting that the Democrats were still the party of treason and disunion, for the custom of "bolting" thus begun has persisted to this day. In every election since then party ties have sat looser and looser until the Harding election gave the full measure of the way the voter has arrogated to himself that right to switch from one party to another which in 1884 filled his father with horror as a species of infidelity to the two-party system and to the country. So with the press; from the day that Blaine was nominated down to the present hour there have always been independent political journals in place of the practically absolute partisans before that time. Of these independent journals the two greatest were unquestionably the *Springfield Republican* under Mr. Bowles and the *Evening Post* under Godkin.

From 1884 to 1900 marks the final period of the wielding of great power by the editorial page of the dailies; certainly it is a commonplace that no single daily editor today ranks with Bowles or Greeley or Raymond or Godkin. Had the last-named done nothing else than sponsor the bolt from Blaine his fame would still be secure; the establishment of party independence and the assuring of an able, independent press, if only for a brief period, were achievements enough, great and constructive as they were. Few, of course, estimated them at their true worth or even recognized their constructive value. Like every other severe critic he was constantly accused of being *de*structive instead of *con*structive.

The reforming editor has no more tiresome or banal critic to meet than he who is for ever crying out that the editor who sees many evils to attack is destructive—unless it is the platitudinous and dull person who says to the editor parrot-like, "I read your paper but I don't always agree with your views"— as if the aim of a true editor were to obtain unanimity of belief and agreement instead of stimulating independent thinking and formulating of views. Mr.

Godkin's constructive services were enormous at all times, but for these he never got credit, nor will any critical editor who aspires to follow in his footsteps. It is the highest constructive service to unveil evils, to castigate the wrong-doers, and to insist upon the fundamental moralities in the conduct of public life and the policies of a nation. This Mr. Godkin never ceased to render. But far more than that, he championed every constructive reform that came into being. Civil Service reform, honest and humane treatment of Negro and Indian, the establishment of a respectable consular and diplomatic service, sound money—but why go on? Almost every one of the reforms in government of our day Mr. Godkin championed and always by going to the root of the thing, by seeking the underlying principle and setting it forth.* The now familiar signs against spitting that one sees everywhere should have his name upon them. When he began his campaign for this great cultural and sanitary reform every one laughed and said: "Godkin's crankiness again." But with his leadership the crusade was taken up by the health authorities, whence it spread all over the country as the knowledge grew of what spitting meant for the

* The anonymous writer in the January, 1897, *Atlantic* says that "there is not a distinctive principle underlying the independent movement of his period for which he [Godkin] has not found its best and most forcible expression, and not an impulse to action that has not received impetus, and in many cases life, from him."

propagation of deadly disease. At last the disgraceful spittoon was banished from private house and public place. But did anybody credit Mr. Godkin with leading in the press this great constructive achievement? Oh, dear no. It was merely his crankiness again.

Never one of his critics had a hundredth part of the constructive record to disclose that lay to Mr. Godkin's credit. But that made no difference. Were he to live his life over again now the shallow pates would once more be lamenting Mr. Godkin's total lack of any constructive suggestion. Indeed, his views on war and peace—he went through the Crimean and witnessed our own Civil War—would have subjected him to endless abuse if not prosecution had he lived through the World War. Certainly he would not have been permitted to print again in the *Evening Post* his bold prophecy, as yet entirely unfulfilled, that some day the soldier would find himself properly ranked next after the hangman. In fact, the whole trend of daily journalism is entirely away from the Godkin type—and if there are men of his stamp available they will not take service with owners who run great business institutions and give to no editor the complete and unhampered control of a great daily which Mr. and Mrs. Henry Villard bestowed upon Edwin L. Godkin; such as he cannot under modern conditions give vent to their construc-

291

tive ideas. It was, of course, constructive service of highest moment to tear off the mask from Tammany Hall and to be the first editor to reveal clearly that Tammany was itself but a mask for great and crooked corporations and those malefactors of wealth who profited by them. In this field Mr. Godkin's service was enormous. His ridicule of the leaders of Tammany was as scorching as it was eminently useful. For all the discouragements, New York and our American cities have since progressed enormously in the science of government—everybody would recognize that if we were to have re-established overnight the New York and Philadelphia of 1881. We should, for once, face a revolution if we were to go back to the dirty, ill-paved, unlighted, foul smelling, "wide open" towns with all the open, coarse immoralities which that term signifies. No civic worker in this field but owes a debt to the unconstructive Mr. Godkin. No city but has profited by his labours.

To the masses he was unknown—the *Evening Post's* net circulation under him never reached 25,-000; it was to leaders of thought that he appealed. To a secretary Gov. David B. Hill once remarked during the Maynard campaign (in which the reformers, Mr. Godkin again leading in the press, waged a successful, though at first apparently hopeless, fight against the efforts of Hill's machine to elect a totally unfit man to high judicial office): "I don't care anything about the handful of Mugwumps who read it [the *Evening Post*] in New York. The trouble with the damned sheet is that every editor in New York State reads it."

So did every public man. For Grover Cleveland it was a daily Bible until Mr. Godkin broke with him over the still utterly inexplicable bringing of the United States to the verge of war with Great Britain over the insignificant Venezuelan boundary issue; then Mr. Cleveland, with the politician's characteristic gratitude, went out of his way to sneer at the *Evening Post* by saying publicly that he daily read one portion of its editorial page—the newspaper jokes in the lower righthand corner. The politicians who felt Mr. Godkin's lash were naturally the ones to echo that brilliant but shallow woman who declared that Mr. Godkin made virtue odious. What he did was to make the *Evening Post* an extremely unpalatable daily diet for those who wanted things left as they were, or were fattening because of their ownership of certain public privileges; for those who, being dulled or tainted of conscience, were resentful of being made to think, or to feel their own guilt, or were merely disturbed in taking their ease on the fat of the land. Within the journalistic profession Mr. Godkin never stood well, he was far too aloof. If he ever went to gatherings of journalists it was in his earlier years. He was unknown personally to the

293

bulk of the profession, which neither liked nor appreciated him and was only too happy to join in the
hue and cry against him. For one thing there was a
not unnatural touch of intellectual snobbery about
him. In training, antecedents, in his friendship for
the great minds of his day who were devoted readers
of him in *The Nation* and the *Evening Post*, men like
the two Jameses, Charles Eliot Norton, Charles W.
Eliot, Ruskin, Morley, Bryce, in brief the intellectual
élite of two worlds, Mr. Godkin found his *metier* and
his happiness. Few if any other American daily
journalists entered that sphere.

Then, Mr. Godkin was, quite beyond question,
never a great editor, but a noble and unsurpassed editorial writer. He was no Bennett to build a great
daily and to guide its news editors and reporters.
He was no directing head of a great news-gathering
institution—had he been the *Evening Post's* story
would be quite different. True he supervised the
style of its writings, laid down the principles upon
which it should be conducted and often suggested
notable articles and striking and far-reaching campaigns in the news columns. There was much truth
in his laughing statement that he had one editorial
rule: "I see no one before one and at one I go
home." He not only, as his biographer, Mr. Ogden,
writes, "more and more threw off the drudgery of an
editor's work," but in his later years thought his

294

work done just as soon as his leader was written and all the editorial proofs read. The financial and business progress of the newspaper interested him scarcely at all, although he was himself, by the bravery and independence of his pen and his fiery championship of unpopular causes, the chief reason for the failure of the *Evening Post* to have else than occasional years of great prosperity. That in the main was as it should be and the owners welcomed this price of his service. Yet the often sorely tried business manager did feel much upset, and the owners a little disgruntled, when the magnificent assault upon the hundred dollar tariff exemption for travellers abroad and the barbarous customs methods on our wharves was so marked by bitter personal attacks upon New York merchants as to result in 1897 in a boycott of the *Evening Post* from which it never wholly recovered during the Villard ownership. This cost it hundreds of thousands of dollars and for years made dividends impossible; another method of attack would have avoided this yet been as effective. In his subordinates Mr. Godkin was little interested; many of them he did not know by name—the reporters often not by sight. Such a thing as getting the whole staff together for a meal never occurred to him. Yet he did inspire the staff and set the standards. Hard as he was upon the shortcomings of his subordinates, the writer of these lines is one of those who records with unending gratitude that for a brief time he sat at this master's feet—even though that master at times thought too much of himself and too little of the others whose daily toil or whose large financial sacrifices made possible the great medium in which he for twenty-one years enjoyed complete freedom of utterance without a financial care or responsibility.

Why was it then that a man and a journal, the one so brilliant and incisive, the other so free and untrammelled, failed after twenty-one years of this editorship and thirty-seven years of this ownership to achieve a permanent place in journalism? The conjunction seems so ideal, so precisely what the public today cries for in our daily press, that an analysis of the failure is certain to be of value. Indeed, this deduction of the moral of this unique episode in American journalism, if there is any, in order to see what lesson it has for the student of modern journalistic problems must be the excuse for putting into a volume chiefly composed of contemporary journalistic figures this analysis of one who is merely a memory or a tradition even to the teachers in our schools of journalism, which seem unitedly to ignore the great moral leaders in our journalism of the past. As to that ownership, the assaying of its shortcomings must be left to other hands since the writer was so long a party to it. As to the editorship of Mr. Godkin and

that of Mr. Ogden which succeeded it, after a brief
control by Horace White, one of the purest and most
lovable of characters, there can be no question that
its failure to make a wide appeal is not merely to
be explained on the ground of its high intellectual
quality and the severity of a journalism which clung
to lofty standards, eschewed cheap cartoons and every
appeal to the groundlings, and followed the best English models of propriety, taste and style. The truth
is that in addition to these things, Mr. Godkin, for all
his constructive achievements, was not a thorough-
going democrat. He fought magnificently for the
higher education of women, but he failed utterly to see
that the day they turned the leaves of the text-books
of even the high schools made inevitable the victory
of the movement for their admission to the suffrage.
He felt deeply sympathetic for the plight of the coloured people and steadily opposed every discrim-
ination against them, but the working-class movement
he did not understand and the evils of labour unions
with him far outweighed the good they accomplished.
Mr. Godkin was obviously a devoted adherent of the
Manchester School; the lofty idealism of Cobden and
Bright had made him its own. But their *laissez-
faire* theory went steadily into eclipse during Mr.
Godkin's life-time. When the first factory-inspection
acts were passed in England the entering wedge for
government supervision of industry and business was

297

driven. The simple fact is that theoretically ideal as the Manchester theory is human nature cannot live up to it. The exploitation of the worker under our intense modern industrial competition was such that one restrictive legislative step followed another, one organization of workingmen arose after another until we have today unions of intellectuals for mutual defence and advancement. The follower of Manchester could not look upon this steady advance toward State control (and State Socialism) without dismay.

Even so Mr. Godkin, though he fought for political ideals and sound economic theories like Free Trade which would benefit the workingman most of all, never had that deep personal sympathy for and understanding of the toiler, that infinite and loving pity for all who struggle, which must have given a much wider appeal to the *Evening Post*. Thoroughly convinced theoretical democrat that he was, and staunch believer in the republican theory, he yet had an instinctive shrinking from men without intellectual power or achievement. Theoretically he was with Lincoln in trusting the common sense of the people; he honestly believed that the cure for a stumbling democracy was more democracy. Yet when it came down to the concrete he was an aristocrat in taste and concept. His fault-finding with our shirt-sleeve diplomatic service was less that the men were intellectually out of place than that they were without polish and social

298

manner. The commonness, not to say vulgarity, of the Tammany crowd irked him as much as their venality. From the English bourgeoisie he did bring with him one trying inheritance—prejudice against the small tradesman. In his attack on the personal baggage restriction he gave his greatest offence because he ridiculed the merchants association responsible for the $100 exemption limit as little tailors of Tooley Street, as haberdashers, "miserable shirtmakers," and bootmakers.

Again, the fundamental economic background of many issues wholly escaped him. A profound anti-imperialist, utterly opposed to our overseas conquests as destructive of the character and the idealism of our American democracy, he yet did not realize the connection between the exportation of capital and political conquest. How profoundly economic forces have moulded national policies and national destiny escaped him. He was like James Bryce in that it was the political phases of life and our political institutions which interested him, as to which he became expert. Under him and his successors the real significance of the Roosevelt cult and following was overlooked; they saw with justice just how shallow the man was, how lacking in true statesmanship, how barbaric and Prussian in his views as to armaments, how untrustworthy even to his friends and adorers— as witness his deliberate hamstringing of the Progres-

299

sive Party when it had served his own personal purposes. But the *Evening Post's* editors failed to realize and to interpret the great surge for more democracy of which Mr. Roosevelt took advantage and upon
which he rode into office in 1904 and became the
idol of great masses who excused every bit of wrongdoing because they thought he was *their* Teddy.

Above all the editors of the *Evening Post* had too
few social contacts beyond their own circles. They
had little or no real understanding of the sufferings
of the poor, of that labouring class who are without
any margin between a bare existence and starvation.
Perhaps they lacked heart somewhat, perhaps social
imagination. The fact remains that they never
brought the *Evening Post* to the position occupied by
the *Manchester Guardian* in its city and that whatever
the cause Mr. Godkin could make his paper respected
and admired the world over but not beloved by many.
It never seemed the champion of the plain people
that it really was—yes, infinitely more so than many
another which mulcted the people of their pennies by
posing—for profit only—as the protagonist of the
multitude. The *World*, in the latter years of Mr.
Pulitzer's régime, much more nearly approximated
the ideal of a great public defender than the *Evening
Post*, but without its ability and brilliancy on the editorial page. Of course, there will be many to say,
like the land reformers, that it is because Mr. Godkin

did not espouse their particular pet reform that he
failed to become the great popular leader and force
his talents should have led him to be. Perhaps
it was because some fundamental economic truths
escaped him; perhaps the hard function of critic, of
censor of public morals, is not to be combined with
leadership. To be absolutely independent and de-
tached as an editor, to spare not even one's friends
when they merit castigation, is to serve the State well
but usually not to raise up multitudes to call one
blessed. Yet one can but wonder if at some time
in Mr. Godkin's life there had been hard places, if he
could have lived in the Middle West and come to see
for himself the pure, sound gold that lies underneath
the commonness of exterior, the commonplaceness of
much of the thinking of our rural and small-town multitudes, there might have come that fuller understanding and appreciation of American democracy
which even this noble defender of it lacked.

Whatever his faults what would we not give today
for such another? In all the field of American daily
journalism there is not one today to measure up to
him as critic, writer, or scientific student of politics—
nor one pen so brilliant, so brave, so free and so
unrestricted.

CHAPTER XVIII

WILLIAM LLOYD GARRISON, EDITOR; "THE GOOD OLD DAYS"

A FIVE thousand dollar reward for him, "dead or alive," offered by the Legislature of a sovereign American State after a single year of editorial activity—this would seem to be a striking enough achievement for an American journalist in what history and civilized opinion everywhere have since proclaimed to be a holy cause, the freeing of the slave. It certainly entitles William Lloyd Garrison to a position as an editor as well as a reformer, for I do not know of any other to whom quite such a handsome tribute has been paid as that reward constitutes. This and other protests from the South induced the Mayor of Boston to send around some of his minions to investigate the fire-brand whose weekly journal was being publicly burned, barred from Southern post-offices, denounced wherever it penetrated—precisely as if it were what is called a "red," or bolshevik, journal of today—and was generally throwing a half of the United States of that day into spasms of rage and fear. What Mayor Otis's agents found James Russell Lowell has described as follows:

> In a small chamber, friendless and unseen,
> Toiled o'er his types one poor, unlearned young man;
> The place was dark, unfurnitured, and mean;
> Yet there the freedom of a race began.

There is no poet's license in this description of Mr. Garrison's beginning. He had not a single dollar to his name nor a single subscriber secured in advance. The first paper he used was obtained on credit. On the floor of the attic he and his partner, Isaac Knapp, slept, eating what they could get from a nearby bakery, and in that attic they set and distributed every bit of type, made up the forms, put them on their little press, printed from them, and wrapped, addressed and mailed the copies. Theirs was a workshop, office, and home in one. For a year and a half Mr. Garrison lived thus in what Mayor Otis's men declared to be "an obscure hole, his only visible auxiliary a negro boy, and his supporters a few insignificant persons of all colours." This editor had had to go to work as soon as his common schooling ended; his passion for justice, his love of humanity were his high school and his university. Of friends he had but a few, of influence none. How preposterous that he should attack an evil so firmly entrenched in American life, customs, and laws!

303

How absurd that the State of Georgia should think his
dead body worth $5000 or that the Vigilance Asso-
ciation of Columbia, South Carolina, composed of
"gentlemen of the first respectability," should offer a
reward of $1500 for the "apprehension and prosecu-
tion to conviction" of any white person caught dis-
tributing or circulating the *Liberator*. Why should
church and State tremble before the attack of a youth
so utterly ridiculous?

It was, of course, because he had "a faith so absolute in the sacredness and power of moral principles,
a trust in God so firm and immovable," and because
the hideous institution he attacked was rotten to its
core and bound to tremble before the blasts of any
honest and fearless man. But, aside from any spiritual or moral reasons, Mr. Garrison was to be dreaded
because the press was free to all men. It was not
the enormously costly, commercialized undertaking
of today, and it took no large circulation for a newspaper to make itself felt. There was, moreover, time
in the newspaper offices of that day for the editor
to read his exchanges, in consequence of which editors knew well the characteristics of their rivals, their
power and their weakness. Mr. Garrison was not
unknown in the profession—he had worked on several
other papers before starting his own and there were
a few cordial greetings from Northern associates
when he began. It was soon seen that he could not

be ignored. To attack him was a regular duty; at best one deprecated his "harshness of language," the "bitterness of his tone" and was shocked at his refusal to spare the Northern respectables who coined so many dollars out of the bodies of the slaves.

The point is, that he had a self-created weapon and that none could wrest it from him. Whereas it takes hundreds of thousands of dollars to carry on a little political weekly today he produced his with a few hundred. Whereas one must build circulation today in order to succeed, he cared little whether subscribers came or not. In his Valedictory when he voluntarily, in December, 1865, ended the life of the paper that had been his life, he wrote: "I have never consulted either the subscription list of the paper or public sentiment in printing or omitting to print any article touching any matter whatever. Personally, I have never asked any one to become a subscriber nor any one to contribute to its support, nor presented its claims for a better circulation in any lecture or speech or at any one of the multitudinous anti-slavery gatherings in the land. Had I done so no doubt its subscription list might have been much enlarged."

A hopeless editor, indeed; but the freest and happiest of all the profession! Indifferent to subscribers and advertisers and unfavourable public opinion; bent only upon giving forth the deepest and best he felt—how many such are there today? Two, or three, or half-a-dozen? Surely his was the golden age of American journalism, for in it any man of similar or lesser parts and similar industry, who burned with similar fire could also have the rare privilege of complete and fearless self-expression. Many another such an anti-slavery paper found its way to the hearts of men, able, keen, often inspired; the smallest community might have its *"Clarion"* or its *"Standard,"* which likewise were content with a few hundred dollars of revenue.

That was the joy of those days, that was one explanation of the thoroughness with which public opinion was educated up to supporting Lincoln when the day of emancipation came. It was a time of teeming intellectual life, enormously stimulated by the fact that the Stowes, Whittiers, Lowells and Emersons had behind them a small but virile and out-spoken press to give them aid, comfort, support, and the avenue of expression. Fortunate the country which finds itself and its press in such a situation!

It was a day of small things in journalism, if you please, in comparison with our huge dailies and monster circulations of today, and things then were cheap—notably the pay of wage-earners who stood at the fonts or composed more or less laboriously in the sanctums of the editorial quarters. Mr. Garrison's pay was probably never much over $1000.

The subscription price was but $2 a year. In the first year he found five hundred adherents and readers. Only a similarly embattled editor can possibly know what it meant when, after the start, one subscriber in Philadelphia sent $54 for 27 subscriptions; what a vision of vast success that check must have aroused! By the third year this editor had won a thousand to his banner and by the fourth fourteen hundred when he, or some one for him, begged for six hundred more. Of his $2, fifty cents, he reported, had to go for postage, agents' fees, free copies, and distribution costs. The other $1.50 per copy had to pay all wages, including the editor's, who in time had a wife and five children to support, but for years the deficit ranged from only $700 to $1700 a year—the day of low costs and self-denying. Efficient management did not begin in this century! Never did the circulation go far beyond 3000 copies; yet they counted in the political life of the country as if they were a full 300,000. It seems, too, as if every copy must have been preserved, for New England attics still give up their treasures of scattering copies which make possible the putting together now and then of fairly complete files.

As for advertising in the *Liberator*, hardly ever did it run over three columns, and usually two columns sufficed to contain it. It seems as if a wide-awake advertising manager could have overcome the deficit, but such a one there was not. Then the sad truth must be told that much of the advertising was of patent medicines, for which the editor himself had a weakness. Frequently the editor endorsed an advertiser, as in the case of a dentist who illustrated his announcement with a cut of himself applying a huge instrument to a resigned patient's mouth, while setting forth that the rates were reasonable—twenty-five cents for pulling a tooth, $1 for a filling and $2 for a false molar. Surely this dentist was as modest in his charges as the editor who endorsed him. The very last issue carried a patent medicine card urging the merits of Ayer's Ague Cure, which was quite fitting and as it should be, but not as touching as a little inch announcement that all the furniture and type of the *Liberator* were now for sale— it had had its own printing office and press for all the thirty-five years during which this comet took its fiery way through the constellation of journalism. A "Free Labour Dry Goods Store" in Philadelphia was one of the most faithful advertisers; no article in that store, it boasted, was the product of slaves, and nothing, we venture to say, that Mr. Garrison ever said or did—no lengths to which he went—could ever make that particular advertiser take his announcement out in indignation. "Stop-my-paper" subscribers even this most fortunate of editors must

have had; but surely no advertiser ever complained
that the rates were too high, or the returns unsatisfactory, or asked for rebates, or begged for a free
reading notice to go with his advertisement. The
menace and the tribulation of advertising were here
reduced to a minimum; unsolicited all the advertising must have been, like one notice from a distracted
mother of colour asking for the return of her little
boy who had run off once more and—wayward, indeed—was likely again to impose upon Abolitionists
by representing himself as a fugitive slave! Not
much resemblance in all this to the *Saturday Evening
Post* with its rate of $7000 and more a page!
Which will live longest in history, one wonders;
which bulk largest in the history of American ethics
and reform?

Well, though the editor boasted that he never so-
licited subscriptions his friends did it for him. Frequently one finds notices from a friendly committee
that four or five hundred subscribers are in default,
coupled with a stern demand that they pay up
promptly. Frequently there were cash or other gifts
to the paper. The anti-slavery fairs took notice of
its needs and there were plenty to see that neither it
nor its editor perished from starvation. No journal
ever had warmer friends, or more devoted contributors, and when the editor stated at the death of the
Liberator that he ended it "without a farthing as the

309

pecuniary result of the patronage extended to it during thirty-five years of unremitted labour" the fact was not forgotten. A national subscription resulted in a small fund which kept him free to use his pen as he saw fit for the rest of his life. The more he was, as one of his staunch adherents said, "taunted, ridiculed, caricatured, misrepresented and denounced by the vulgar and treated with contemptuous scorn by the rich and great," the more his friends rallied to him.

For one thing, Mr. Garrison was of those rare editors who never failed to let his readers see the worst that was said about him. The more atrocious the calumny of himself, the more ready he to print it. Some of the unending threats to assassinate him he cheerfully reproduced in his columns, which were not too pure for those beginning: "You damned rascal." That was part of his original conception of what a journal ought to be and that conception varied very little during the thirty-five years of the *Liberator's* existence—there is but little difference between the first and last numbers in editorial policy and execution. The editor always maintained a department of poetry—in which, among others, John G. Whittier's poems first saw the light of day—and there was plenty of verse in the final issue. Like many modern editors he believed in departments and "stock" heads. The back page, like the back page

of many a daily of today, was meant to be of feuille-
ton quality, and Mr. Garrison anticipated the editors of today with their bed-time stories by a department entitled "Juvenile" by which the children were
surely edified and enlightened but hardly amused
or entertained, as the effort was to bend the twig that
the tree might incline. Besides "Poetry" and "Literary" and "Miscellany" one finds "Philanthropy,"
columns or half-columns devoted to foreign news,
"Non-Resistance" (to which, like woman suffrage,
the editor was ever devoted), and "Moral," and curious above all there were for years a "Refuge of
Oppression" and a "Slavery Record," in which latter
not only appeared some of the most telling blows at
slavery, but many a horrifying or enlightening item
culled from the enemy's own Southern press. What
is today the most convincing argument against American slavery and the clearest proof that it was not the
kindly beneficent institution which our Thomas Nelson Pages and other latter-day romancers portray it
is a solid pamphlet entitled "American Slavery As
It Is; Testimony of a Thousand Witnesses." This
contains hundreds of extracts from the Southern
press telling of lynchings, beheadings, brandings,
flogging to death, and all the minor tortures of the
system—the inevitable outrages which happen in
every clime in which white men, be they Germans,
English, Spaniards, French, or Americans, have pos-

session of the bodies and souls of men and women of another race. Many of these thousand testimonies were clipped in the *Liberator* office and appeared originally in its columns. Indeed, the editor was a master of the shears; his "Refuge of Oppression" never lacked material to stir the slaveholders to mighty wrath.

Undoubtedly from our modern standpoint the *Liberator* could have been much improved journalistically. We certainly should hardly expect a journalist of today to do what Mr. Garrison once did—supply his readers with one whole page and a column of texts from the Bible with which to confound the upholders of slavery. The sameness of its headlines and of its make-up would pall today. The dispute whether its editor should have abandoned it when he did, just when the freedmen were so profoundly in need of help and support and safeguarding, will doubtless go on indefinitely, exactly like the controversy as to whether Mr. Garrison's vigour of language was or was not justifiable and whether effective reform is or is not furthered by such violence of assault upon the other side. The dispute as to whether one reforms best by the uncompromising spirit or by compromise goes back to the ancients and will continue as long as there are reforms to be achieved. But the fact remains that for all its

312

heavy moral calibre, its Biblical language, its ponderousness and what seems today its stiltedness and flowery writing, the *Liberator* achieved its purpose with the middle class, bourgeois Americans at whom it was directed and in whose keeping there rested the conscience of the United States. Crude as the weapon seems to us of today it accomplished its aim of a moral regeneration of America anent the question of freedom. To this Lincoln attested when he received its editor in the White House.

To not many editors has it been or will it be given to achieve in the space of forty years so much. But that others shall have a similar opportunity to do their jobs as well as or better than Mr. Garrison is the great need of our journalism of today. American journalism of the first half of the Nineteenth Century was crude, narrow and perhaps entirely too self-centred, but its freedom was boundless, its open avenues vistas of patriotic usefulness which no republic ought to be without. The cry of today that the period of the great editors is gone is directly connected with the commercialization of the press and its domination by the owners for whom the editors are but hired men. Greeley, Garrison, Bowen, Godkin, Bowles, and others, the journalists who have profoundly stirred the conscience of America, either owned their own journals or were given a complete

313

freedom of expression. That they were also profoundly engrossed in moral causes helps to explain their power.

The need of such moral leadership in the press was never greater than today and that the public is ripe for it appears from the eagerness with which it a few years ago welcomed and supported *Collier's Weekly* in its Norman Hapgood days and the muckraking magazines which had so brief an hour. That Mr. Bryan and Senator La Follette have been able to maintain for so long their weeklies is further proof that there are plain masses seeking a journalistic Moses to clarify their minds, to give them a program of reconstruction, a moral issue through which to rebuild a broken-down society.[1] The difficulty is that even to carry on a liberal weekly, as already said, is to call for hundreds of thousands of dollars. No legislature has lately been kind enough to advertise a beginner by offering a reward of $5000—the modern method is to suppress or to imprison as Mr. Garrison, the pacifist, would have been imprisoned had he lived and written during the last few years. Probably it is not only the money which is lacking; there is as yet no large enough prophet, no editor to burn with sufficient Garrisonian vigour, or so able to lash with scorpions the idle, the privileged,

[1] Since these lines were written Mr. Bryan's *Commoner* has suspended publication.

314

the money-changers who pollute the temple of our American democracy. Should such a man arise the question will still prove profoundly difficult, perhaps insurmountable. Not today can one, however trenchant one's pen, be in a garret and expect to reach the conscience of a public by seventy millions larger than the America of Garrison and Lincoln and by at least two hundred years remote from them in its failure to comprehend and apply the fundamental, basic principles of American liberty. Yet somehow the prophet of the future will make his message heard, if not by a daily, then by a weekly; if not by a weekly, then by pamphleteering in the manner of Alexander Hamilton; if not by pamphleteering then by speech in the market-place. However it shall be, the truth must out.

APPENDIX

FOREIGN LANGUAGE DAILIES OF THE TWELVE
LARGEST CITIES. PROGRESS OF THE GROUP
OWNERSHIP DEVELOPMENT. CITIES OF MORE
THAN 100,000 POPULATION HAVING BUT ONE
MORNING DAILY.

FOREIGN LANGUAGE DAILIES IN THE TWELVE
LARGEST CITIES OF THE UNITED STATES

NEW YORK

Syrian Eagle (*Arabic*)
Al-Hoda (*Arabic*)
Ash-Shaab (*Arabic*)
Den (*Slovak*)
Dennik (*Slovak*)
Slovak v Amerike (*Slovak*)
Listy (*Bohemian*)
Courrier des Etats Unis
(*French*)
Herold (*German*)
Staats-Zeitung (*German*)
Volkszeitung (*German*)
Atlantis (*Greek*)
National Herald (*Greek*)
Amerikai Magyar Nepszava
(*Hungarian*)
Uj Elöre (*Hungarian*)
Il Popolo-Il Bollettino della Sera
(*Italian*)
Corriere d'America (*Italian*)

Progresso Italo-Americano
(*Italian*)
Glas Naroda (*Slovenian*)
Jugoslovenski Svijet (*Croatian*)
Srpski Dnevnik (*Serbian*)
Laisve (*Lithuanian*)
Nowy Swiat-Telegram Codzienny
(*Polish*)
Novoye Russkoye Slovo
(*Russian*)
Russky Golos (*Russian*)
La Prensa (*Spanish*)
The Day (*Yiddish*)
Freiheit (*Yiddish*)
Jewish Daily Forward (*Yiddish*)
Jewish Daily News (*Yiddish*)
Jewish Morning Journal
(*Yiddish*)
New Warheit (*Yiddish*)
Rassviet (*Russian*)

CHICAGO

Ludovy Dennik (*Slovak*)
Slovensko-Americky Dennik
(*Slovak*)
Denni Hlasatel (*Bohemian*)
Narod (*Bohemian*)
Spravedlnost (*Bohemian*)
Dziennik Ziednoczenia (*Polish*)
Zgoda (*Polish*)
Prosveta (*Slovenian*)
Draugas (*Lithuanian*)
Jewish Courier (*Yiddish*)
Svornost (*Bohemian*)

Abendpost (*German*)
Naujienos (*Lithuanian*)
Skandinaven (*Norwegian*)
Dziennik Chicagoski (*Polish*)
Dziennik Ludowy (*Polish*)
Jewish Daily Call (*Yiddish*)
Jewish Daily Forward
(*Yiddish*)
Jewish Press (*Yiddish*)
Amerikanski Slovenec (*Slov.*)
Russian Daily Herald (*Russian*)

319

APPENDIX

PHILADELPHIA

Gazette-Democrat (*German*)
Tageblatt (*German*)
Opinione (*Italian*)

Jewish Daily Forward
(*Yiddish*)
Jewish Morning Journal
(*Yiddish*)
Jewish World (*Yiddish*)

DETROIT

Abend Post (*German*)
Dziennik Ludowy (*Polish*)

Dziennik Polski (*Polish*)
Rekord Codzienny (*Polish*)

CLEVELAND

American (*Bohemian*)
Monitor (*Polish*)
Svet (*Bohemian*)
Wachter und Anzeiger
(*German*)
Szabadsag (*Hungarian*)

Voce del Popolo Italiano
(*Italian*)
Enakopravnost (*Slovenian*)
Wiadomosci Codzienne (*Polish*)
America (*Roumanian*)
Jewish World (*Yiddish*)

ST. LOUIS

Westliche Post (*German*)

BOSTON

Dielli (*Albanian*)
Hairenik (*Armenian*)

Notizia (*Italian*)
Kuryer Codzienny (*Polish*)

BALTIMORE

Jewish Daily Forward
(*Yiddish*)

PITTSBURGH

Volksblatt und Freiheits-Freund
(*German*)

Amerikan Srbobran (*Serbian*)
Pittsburczanin (*Polish*)

LOS ANGELES

Japanese Daily News
(*Japanese*)

Heraldo de Mexico (*Spanish*)

320

APPENDIX

BUFFALO

Volksfreund (*German*)
Dziennik Dla Wszystkich
(*Polish*)

Telegram (*Polish*)

SAN FRANCISCO

Chinese Republic Journal
(*Chinese*)
Chinese World (*Chinese*)
Chung Sai Yat Po (*Chinese*)
Young China (*Chinese*)
Chinese Times (*Chinese*)
Echo de l'Ouest (*French*)

Franco Californien (*French*)
Telegraph (*Greek*)
Italia (*Italian*)
Voce del Popolo (*Italian*)
Japanese American News
(*Japanese*)
New World (*Japanese*)

THE PROGRESS OF GROUP OWNERSHIP

WILLIAM RANDOLPH HEARST NEWSPAPERS

MORNING

Chicago Herald and Examiner	383,936
New York American	225,081
San Francisco Examiner	167,025
Los Angeles Examiner	171,606
Boston Advertiser (Tabloid)	137,226
Seattle Post-Intelligencer	84,368
Washington Herald	54,029
Baltimore American	56,764
New York Daily Mirror	310,333
Total	1,590,368

EVENING

Albany Times-Union	39,689
New York Evening Journal	696,447
Chicago Evening Journal	488,492
Boston American	243,721
Detroit Times	241,481
Washington Times	54,289
Wisconsin News	94,308
Atlanta Georgian	58,070
Oakland Post-Enquirer	47,507
* Syracuse Journal	65,326
Rochester Journal	43,188
Baltimore News	115,647
San Francisco Call	101,098
Los Angeles Herald	182,313
San Antonio Light	34,454
Total	2,506,030

* Syracuse Journal and Telegram consolidated Nov. 4, 1925.

SUNDAY

New York American	1,083,911
Chicago Herald and Examiner	1,151,978
Boston Sunday Advertiser	502,565
San Francisco Examiner	346,510

Los Angeles Examiner	393,168
Detroit Times	304,779
Washington Herald	121,978
Seattle Post-Intelligencer	148,841
Milwaukee Sunday Sentinel	172,206
Atlanta American	131,606
Syracuse Sunday American	78,873
Rochester Sunday American	67,581
Baltimore American	154,945
San Antonio Light	55,671
Total	4,714,612

APPENDIX

SCRIPPS-HOWARD NEWSPAPERS

	CIRCULATION
Birmingham Post	48,536
San Francisco Daily News	68,120
San Diego Sun	20,534
Denver Express	14,865
Washington Daily News	65,008
Evansville Press	21,790
Indianapolis Times	54,676
Terre Haute Post	16,812
Baltimore Post	102,438
Akron Times-Press	44,031
(Cincinnati Post)	
(Kentucky Post)	192,323
Cleveland Press	222,637
Columbus Citizen	84,510
Toledo News-Bee	92,854
Youngstown Telegram	33,790
Oklahoma City News	41,552
Knoxville News	16,432
Memphis Press	44,982
El Paso Post	12,015
Fort Worth Press	21,846
Pittsburgh Press	183,440
(Sunday . . . . . 243,673)	
New Mexico State Tribune	10,608
Houston Press	33,287
Total	1,447,086

APPENDIX

EMPIRE STATE GROUP

	CIRCULATION
Rochester Times-Union	72,000
Utica Observer-Dispatch	39,000
" " " (Sunday)	24,000
Elmira Star-Gazette	33,500
Elmira Advertiser	8,150
Elmira Sunday Telegram	25,350
Ithaca Journal-News	7,500
Newburgh News	12,150
Total	221,650

THE BOOTH PUBLISHING COMPANY NEWSPAPERS

	CIRCULATION	
	Daily	Sunday
Grand Rapids Press	88,054	No Sunday
Flint Daily Journal	37,818	33,135
Saginaw News Courier	25,520	25,168
Kalamazoo Gazette	27,062	26,751
Jackson Citizen Patriot	28,934	27,570
Bay City Times Tribune	18,639	17,275
Muskegon Chronicle	17,316	No Sunday
Ann Arbor Times News	9,893	No Sunday
Total	253,236	129,899

CITIES OF MORE THAN 100,000 POPULATION HAVING BUT ONE MORNING NEWSPAPER

Detroit
St. Louis
Milwaukee
Newark
Minneapolis
Seattle
* Jersey City
Portland, Oregon
Denver
Toledo
Providence
Columbus
St. Paul
* Oakland
* Akron
Worcester
Birmingham
Syracuse
Richmond
New Haven
Memphis
San Antonio
Dallas

* None.

Dayton
Bridgeport
Houston
Hartford
Scranton
Grand Rapids
* Youngstown
Des Moines
New Bedford
* Fall River
Lowell
* Cambridge
Trenton
* Camden
Nashville
Salt Lake City
Norfolk
Albany
Wilmington
Reading
Fort Worth
Spokane
* Kansas City, Kansas
* Yonkers

INDEX

327

INDEX

330

DATE DUE